Seventeenth and Eighteenth Century French Porcelain

By the same author

Eighteenth Century German Porcelain
Eighteenth Century English Porcelain
The Art and Antique Restorer's Handbook
The Antique Collector's Handbook

I. Vase and cover in the form of a ship (*vaisseau à mât*) decorated with *gros bleu* and apple-green grounds and rich gilding, the painting of birds in reserves by Ledoux. The Banner of France has the *fleur-de-lys* emblem. Vincennes. c. 1755. (Wallace Colln.)

George Savage

Seventeenth and Eighteenth Century French Porcelain

Spring Books

London·New York·Sydney·Toronto

Originally published 1960 by
Barrie and Rockliff (Barrie Books Ltd)

This edition published 1969 by
The Hamlyn Publishing Group Limited
London · New York · Sydney · Toronto
Hamlyn House, Feltham, Middlesex, England

Printed in Great Britain by Fletcher & Son Limited,
Norwich, and bound by Richard Clay (The Chaucer Press) Limited,
Bungay, Suffolk

SBN 600 03649 9

Contents

List of Illustrations

COLOUR PLATES

BLACK AND WHITE PLATES

ACKNOWLEDGEMENT

The illustrations are reproduced by courtesy of the Museums and Collections listed below. The following abbreviations have been used throughout:

Ashmolean-Andrade Colln.	The Ashmolean Museum of Fine Art, Oxford. Cyril Andrade Collection.
Bedford	The Trustees of the Cecil Higgins Collection, Bedford Museum.
Boston	The Boston Museum of Fine Art, Boston, Mass.
BM	The Trustees of the British Museum, London.
Christie's	Messrs. Christie, Manson & Woods Ltd.
Fitzwilliam	The Syndics of the Fitzwilliam Museum, Cambridge.
Hastings	The Hastings Museum and Art Gallery.
Metropolitan	The Metropolitan Museum, New York.
V&AM	The Victoria and Albert Museum, London.
Wallace Colln.	The Wallace Collection, Hertford House, London.

Preface

The porcelain of France occupies a unique position in the history of the ceramic art. In its earlier manifestations the wares are, for the most part, a reflection of the difficulties experienced in handling the artificial porcelain body used. At mid-century it blossoms forth as a plaything of the Court, and the finest talent of the time was lavished on it. Thenceforward, its development was, to a great extent, governed by the various prohibitory edicts designed to protect the peculiar position of the Royal factory.

The products of Vincennes-Sèvres are largely a reflection of life at the Court, and for this reason I have included a brief sketch of the principal events of the period covered by this book. Something of the kind is essential to an understanding of the wares themselves. Porcelain is not only an art, it is also a social document, and it cannot truly be understood apart from a parallel understanding of the time in which it was made.

The history of French porcelain is like that of England. Apart from Vincennes-Sèvres, where documentation is much more precise and less lacunary, its history has to be reconstructed from the wares themselves, and from brief and often isolated references from contemporary sources. The wares can safely be left to speak for themselves, and the photographs illustrating this work testify to the particular artistic genius and innate good taste of the French, as obvious in porcelain of the period as in most other things. The skill with which they steered a certain course between the Scylla of vulgarity and mere tawdriness on the one hand, and the Charybdis of ostentatious tedium on the other, has surely seldom been equalled.

I am indebted to the museums elsewhere listed for the assistance which has made it possible to illustrate this book with so many fine examples of the period, and, in particular, to the Department of Ceramics of the Victoria and Albert Museum, who were kind enough to have a large number of important early examples specially photographed. I am grateful, too, to Mr. Cyril Andrade and the Ashmolean Museum for several rare and unusual plates. Many examples are also illustrated from the superb collection of Sèvres of the best period to be seen at Hertford House. The Wallace Collection is justly celebrated for its richness and variety.

I am indebted to Mrs. Diana Imber for much assistance with research into French sources, and to the authors listed in the Bibliography, whose works have frequently been consulted. I am especially grateful to the shade of Dr. Martin Lister, whose journals have been frequently quoted. The temptation to digress, and to include some of the more amusing passages which did not bear directly on the matter in hand, has been resisted, but I hope that some day this book will be reprinted for wider circulation.

G.S.

Guestling
  Sussex
March 1960

SEVENTEENTH AND EIGHTEENTH CENTURY FRENCH PORCELAIN

Introduction

I

THE history of porcelain in France until the end of the eighteenth century spans part of the reign of Louis Quatorze, and that of Louis Quinze and Louis Seize, as well as the period of the Revolution and the early years of Napoleon. It is intimately connected with the fortunes of the Bourbons, many of the factories being owned or patronized by members of the reigning house. Porcelain, too, is connected with the life of the Courts, and the most fashionable artists of the time contributed to its development as an art form.

The study of French porcelain, therefore, cannot be isolated from the time in which it was made, and for this reason an examination of the principal events of the period is necessary properly to understand its history.

The importance of porcelain ought not to be underestimated in any study of the art of the eighteenth century. Too often in the past this has happened, and writers of popular treatises in particular have limited themselves to a consideration of painting, sculpture, and architecture, with the principal emphasis on the first.

If there were no other reason, porcelain would require attention because it was largely responsible for the influence exerted on European fashions by Chinese art. The principal variety of Chinese art known in Europe at the time was porcelain, and European porcelain was, in the first place, the result of attempts to copy the Far Eastern product.

The first Chinese porcelain arrived in Europe during the fourteenth and fifteenth centuries, although it did not become widely known until the sixteenth century. At this time possession of specimens was limited to kings, a few members of the nobility, and to high ecclesiastical dignitaries. It was treasured for its sensuous qualities, not the least being its translucency, which excited both wonderment and admiration.

The first examples of the kind to reach Europe came through the traditional trading centres of the Near East, probably those through which Chinese silk had reached the Roman Empire, and most such specimens belong to the Ming dynasty. They were, therefore, the characteristic porcelain of this period, covered with a brilliant feldspathic glaze,* and decorated either with cobalt blue pigment under the glaze, or in enamel colours over it. The earlier wares of the Sung dynasty did not then exist in Europe, although a small piece of *ying ch'ing* ware had reputedly been brought to Venice by Marco Polo, who visited the Court of Kublai Khan during the thirteenth century.

In the twelfth century Sālāh-ed-dīn (the Saladin of the Crusades) who was Sultan of Egypt, sent forty pieces of Chinese ware with a celadon glaze to Nūr-ed-dīn, Sultan of Damascus, and a few specimens of this ware also filtered through to Europe from time to time, but it remained a great rarity until the opening of trade with the Far East at a later date.

The fifteenth century saw the rise of Portugal as a mari-

*Porcelain without a glaze was occasionally used by the Chinese, but was much more popular in France. The Sèvres factory, in particular, used it for modelling figures and groups. Without a glaze it is termed *biscuit* porcelain

time power, and Vasco da Gama reached India in 1497. Three years later, King Manoel took the high-sounding title of 'Lord of the Conquest, Navigation, and Commerce of India, Ethiopia, Arabia, and Persia'. By 1517 Portuguese ships had reached China, and trading relations were established. Their arrival took place during the reign of the Ming Emperor, Chêng-tê—a period of distinction in the manufacture of porcelain. By 1543 Portuguese navigators had reached Japan, although for many years European trading with the Japanese was on a very small scale.

During the sixteenth century Lisbon was the great European centre for the Oriental trade. Towards the end of the century this began to decline, principally because of the persecution of the Jewish community by the Inquisition, much of the trade having been due to their commercial enterprise. Portugal eventually became a satellite of Spain.

At the end of the sixteenth century a new maritime power appeared—the Dutch. Their ships attacked Portuguese merchantmen *en route* from the Far East, and their rich cargoes were brought as prizes to Holland.

This was by no means simple piracy, but part of the struggle of the Netherlands against Spain. They had been united to Spain at the end of the fifteenth century, and the ensuing fight for freedom was long and bitter. The people rose against the horrors of the Inquisition, and the Union of Utrecht in 1579 brought together the northern provinces in the fight against Spanish tyranny. This fight was continued by sea and land, and successful sorties against the Spanish Navy were followed by raids on merchant shipping whereby the Dutch renewed the sinews of war. This struggle culminated in the Treaty of Munster in 1648, by which the Netherlands gained independence, and the skill of their seamen preserved them subsequently from assaults by England and France. Hostilities with England came to an end with the marriage of William of Orange to Mary of York, and their accession to the English throne. The struggles with France are mentioned later.

In 1602 the *San Jago* was brought into a Dutch port with much porcelain among its cargo, and vast quantities were captured in 1604. These prizes were dispersed to eager buyers, among them Henri IV of France and James I of England. The Dutch East India Company started to trade with China in 1600, and they reached Japan ten years later, establishing a trading station at Hirado. In 1641 they were granted a trading monopoly with Japan.

II

As soon as interest in Chinese porcelain became widespread, demand inevitably outran supply, and, equally inevitably, European potters sought a way of copying it. The state of chemical knowledge was not sufficiently advanced for a synthesis to be made from analyses of the Chinese material. Almost all industrial processes at the time were empirical, and proceeded by trial and error. The very principles on which a logical investigation could be made were not understood.

The potters of the time, therefore, had to proceed by analogy. They knew that Chinese porcelain was the product of operations similar to those used in the manufacture of *maiolica*—that is, formation on a wheel of a plastic body and subsequent firing in a kiln. Therefore, any substitute necessarily had to be susceptible to manufacture in the same way.

Chinese porcelain was translucent when held to the light, and no ceramic body known in Europe possessed the same property. European potters, of course, used a kind of glass to glaze their own pottery, and opacified it by adding oxide of tin. Glass opacified with tin oxide and used by itself (i.e.

not as a pottery glaze) was white and translucent, and to this extent had some resemblance to porcelain. Porcelain substitutes, such as the German *milch-glas*, were sometimes made in this way.

Nevertheless, there is a great difference between the methods of formation used in the manufacture of glass and of porcelain. The ingredients of glass—sand, soda, lime, and so forth—are melted into a syrupy liquid, and then 'blown', and harden on cooling. Working temperatures, too, are comparatively low. Porcelain, on the other hand, is like other ceramic bodies. It is formed in a plastic state, and then fired in a kiln at a high temperature.

The difference in the methods used to form articles of glass and of porcelain is easily apparent on inspection, and it must have been obvious at once that glass could never be more than a poor and ineffective substitute. Nevertheless, nothing else presented itself, and glass remained the only manufactured product known to be either transparent or translucent.

Eventually, a mixture of clay and ground glass was tried, the clay providing the necessary plasticity, and the glass, which remelted into a homogeneous substance in the kiln, supplying the vitrifiable part. Clay is a refractory substance. It will, in fact, only melt under the most intense heat, and this is certainly above the melting point of glass. For this reason, most objects made of the clay and glass mixture held together fairly well in the kiln, although, because of the uneven distribution of heat, a proportion collapsed into shapeless lumps, whilst others became cracked and distorted. Such defective pieces are termed 'wasters'.

This method of making a porcelain substitute required a very careful balance to be held between the plastic ingredients (usually clay, although Sèvres used a proportion of soft soap) and the vitrifiable part, represented by the powdered glass. If too much clay was used, the object held together well during firing, but vitrification was poor and translucency negligible or non-existent. If, on the other hand, the plastic materials were too small in quantity, formation was difficult, and kiln wastage high. Such porcelain was usually exceptionally translucent, and sumptuous in appearance. For this reason a high kiln wastage was sometimes accepted as an inevitable accompaniment of fine quality, more particularly in cases where the factory was subsidized and not expected to make a profit.

In principle the method of making this artificial (or soft)* porcelain was the same as that of the Chinese; the differences were rather in the substances used. The Chinese added to the clay a feldspathic rock, termed *petuntse*, which vitrified under heat into a natural glass. But the degree of heat required, about 1400 degrees Centigrade, was beyond the capacity of European kilns of the period, and, indeed, this aspect gave by far the greatest trouble to the eventual discoverer of the Chinese secret, Ehrenfried Walther von Tschirnhaus of Dresden.

The first European country to experiment with artificial porcelain was Italy, during the sixteenth century. This was natural, since Italy was the most important centre for the manufacture of pottery at the time, the making of *maiolica*, or tin-glazed pottery, being the principal manifestation of the ceramic art during the Renaissance.

The first porcelain of which specimens survive was made at Florence, and these Florentine wares are usually referred

*Although, in this work, I have consistently referred in later pages to 'soft' porcelain when writing of the substitute, and to 'hard' porcelain when that made after the Chinese formula is meant, I have done so because these terms have been sanctioned by long usage, and, for this reason, seemed likely to be clearer to most readers. The terms 'artificial' and 'true' porcelain respectively are, of course, exact.

to as 'Medici' porcelain because the manufacture was patronized by the Duke Francesco I de Medici. It is by no means certain that this represented the first Italian attempt to discover the process. Nor is it certain that the original inspiration was Italian. Contemporary records mention the assistance of a Levantine potter. The term 'Levant', which is now more or less restricted to the littoral of Anatolia and Syria, probably had a much wider significance at the time, being used as a general term for what we should now call the Near East, and Italy had many trading connections with both the Near and the Middle East.

Probably connected with Florentine porcelain manufacture are some specimens of a kind of Persian pottery which are referable to the sixteenth and seventeenth centuries. These are often translucent in places, and it appears to be due to a permeation of the body by the glaze material which, of course, was a type of glass. It is difficult to see how this could have arisen accidentally, and Persian potters were at least as interested in imitating Chinese porcelain as those of Europe. They had, in fact, been making copies of it since the tenth century, and seventeenth-century Persian copies of Chinese blue and white wares are particularly close.

It seems probable, therefore, that these represent a Persian attempt to make a translucent ceramic body, and that some account of these experiments was available in Italy during the sixteenth century. Obviously, as reference to surviving Persian specimens will show, the problems were far from solved, and the Florentines no doubt carried them to a more successful conclusion. The eastern origin is to some extent confirmed by the obvious Oriental influences to be seen in the decoration of some Medici porcelain, although the forms owe their primary inspiration to the work of the Italian *maiolicanti*.

Florentine porcelain was short-lived, and only about

sixty pieces survive, most of which are in the important public and private collections. The next venture in the field appears to have been an application by Claude Révérend in 1664 for a monopoly of porcelain manufacture. Révérend was a Paris merchant who imported *faïence* from Holland, but he later had a *faïence* factory of his own in or near St. Cloud at which porcelain may have been made. This point is considered in a later chapter.

A privilege was granted to Louis Poterat of Rouen, *faïence* manufacturer, in 1673 for the making of porcelain without reference to that given to Révérend, and these records are sufficient to show that, by the middle of the seventeenth century, interest in the making of porcelain had shifted to France, and artificial porcelain in the Florentine tradition remained a French monopoly until the middle of the eighteenth century.

III

Some discussion of the historical background against which the manufacture of artificial porcelain grew and flourished is here desirable.

The years which followed the death of Louis XIII were, in some ways, among the most difficult of Europe's long and troubled history, and without some kind of patronage it would have been impossible for so exotic an art as the manufacture of porcelain to have survived at all.

When Louis XIII died, the Dauphin* was little more than four years of age, and a Regency was established with

---

*The title, *Dauphin*, given to the King's eldest son means *dolphin*. Originally the Comte de Vienne Dauphiné presented the title and some property to the grandson of Philip VI. Dauphiné was one of the old Provinces of France, between Provence and Savoy. The dolphin is frequently used in French ornament as an allegory of the Dauphin.

Anne of Austria at the head. She took for her chief minister an Italian, Giulio Mazzarino, better known as the Cardinal Mazarin, and suggestions that he also shared her bed have not been wanting.*

Mazarin was a protégé of the autocratic minister of Louis XIII, Cardinal Richelieu, the 'Grey Eminence' whose policy of concentrating power at the top was continued, first by Mazarin, later by Louis XIV when he reached his majority, and then by his successors.

Richelieu died within a few months of his nominal master, Louis XIII, and, within a short time of his appointment, Mazarin experienced a stroke of singularly good fortune. Inspired by the changes in government, the Spaniards attacked, and were heavily defeated at Rocroi by a hastily-gathered army under the Duc d'Enghien. After this, Mazarin's dominance was hardly in doubt.

This early success led to other military adventures which culminated in a decisive victory for French arms at Lens, and the Peace of Westphalia followed in 1648. Nevertheless, Mazarin had neither the strength nor the breadth of vision possessed by Richelieu, and troubles multiplied at home. The people were oppressed by a corrupt and vicious system of taxation, whereby taxation districts were sold to tax-farmers who proceeded to squeeze from the unfortunate

---

*Dr. Martin Lister (*A Journey to Paris,* 1698) writes amusingly of the collection of the Duc of Mazarin:

> 'The Low Gallery (in the Palais Mazarin) is furnisht with a great Collection of Ancient Greek and Roman Statues. . . . They were most brought from Rome by the Cardinal. Those which are *Togatae* and Cloathed are as they were found; but such as were made *Nudae*, are miserably disguised by the fond Humour of the Duke de Mazarin, who in a hot Fit of Devotion caused them to be castrated and mangled, and then frocked them by a sad Hand with I know not what Plaister of Paris, which makes them very ridiculous.'

people whatever they could, the least powerful paying proportionately the most.

In 1648 hatred of Mazarin and his policies which, in contrast to those of Richelieu, had become 'meaner, pettier, and more timid', resulted in the outbreak of the Civil War of the Fronde. The immediate cause was the arrest of several members of the *Parlement* of Paris. This, despite the similarity in name, had little in common with the English Parliament, being primarily concerned with points of law, but it had possessed the power to delay action under Royal edicts from the reign of Louis XI in the fifteenth century.

For a time affairs became so threatening that both Anne of Austria and Mazarin were compelled to leave Paris, accompanied by the young King, and doubtless this flight was remembered by Louis when he later took the government into his own hands. In 1653 matters had improved sufficiently for the Court to return to Paris, although the struggle continued in a desultory fashion until 1659. In its later stages it degenerated into a struggle between the Court and the Prince de Condé.*

Condé, one of the most successful military commanders of the time, made his peace with Louis in 1660, and his *château* at Chantilly, which had been confiscated, was returned to him.

In foreign affairs Mazarin had been somewhat more successful. The war with Spain dragged on, and in 1657 an alliance with Cromwell led to the landing of an English force in France. The alliance was, in Cromwell's judgement, a declaration of war on the Papists, since the influence of the Pope in French affairs was negligible, whereas it was predominant in those of Spain.

The combined force attacked Dunkirk in 1658, and

*Roland modelled a portrait of the Prince de Condé in biscuit porcelain for Sèvres in 1785.

routed the Spaniards at the Battle of the Dunes. In quick succession the victories of Gravelines and Oudenarde followed, and the French were at the gates of Brussels. The fighting concluded with the Peace of the Pyrenees in 1659, and a marriage was arranged between Louis and the Infanta, Maria Theresa, of Spain. Although Maria Theresa renounced her right to the Spanish succession, this marriage was later used as a pretext by Louis to place his grandson, Philip, on the throne of Spain.

When Mazarin died in 1661, Louis was twenty-two years of age, and had occupied the throne of France for eighteen years.* Throughout this period the Cardinal had guided the affairs and destinies of France. There had been political difficulties at home, and almost continual strife abroad. France had emerged with increased power and prestige in Europe, but internal conditions were more or less unchanged, and discontent of massive proportions simmered under the surface.

Mazarin was much maligned at the time, and his character was undoubtedly marred by greed. As a diplomat he probably had no equal, but his handling of home affairs caused his death to be a matter of little regret. A courtier, writing at the time, said, 'The King seems to be the only person touched by the death of the Cardinal.'

The death of Mazarin left Louis without a chief minister, and he announced his intention of occupying this position himself. Saint-Simon refers to his always majestic gallantry, and his inspiring presence at State functions. The same writer, whose sentiments were hardly friendly, remarks on the silence, and even fear, which his mere presence inspired.

Declaring 'L'état c'est moi', Louis proceeded to rule with absolute authority, and with a splendour which earned him

*A comet appeared in the sky whilst Mazarin was dying. When told of this he said: 'A comet? That does me too much honour.'

the *soubriquet* of *Le roi soleil*—the Sun King. The risks of concentrating so much power into the hands of a hereditary monarchy are obvious. No man in such a position can be sure that his son will be a worthy successor, and Louis XV (his great-grandson), who succeeded him, made the Revolution inevitable, despite the efforts of Louis XVI and his ministers to avert disaster by some much-needed reforms which, by then, were too little and too late.

The place of Mazarin was not filled, but the King was assisted by three ministers, of which the Finance Minister, Fouquet, was undoubtedly the most brilliant. Dishonest manipulation of the country's finances, however, proved his undoing, and his place was taken by Jean-Baptiste Colbert who held an increasingly influential position for many years.

The career of Colbert is one of the greatest adornments of the reign. Originally a protégé of Mazarin,* his first task was to reorganize the country's finances. He performed the almost impossible feat of both reducing taxes and increasing the money available to the Treasury. One of the ways in which he did this was to decimate the ranks of bureaucracy —a method which has much to commend it.

From this beginning Colbert proceeded to encourage trade and manufactures of all kinds, improving roads, rivers, and canals to enable travellers and commodities to move freely throughout France. As Minister of Marine he did much to build up the French Navy, and colonization was encouraged. His major fault lay in the imposition of protective tariffs which inevitably aroused resentment abroad, and which, when Louis later decided on military adventures, undoubtedly had the effect of increasing France's enemies.

*Shortly before his death, Mazarin said to Louis, 'Sir, to you I owe everything, but I believe I pay part of the debt in leaving you Colbert.'

In the field of the arts we find Colbert as active as elsewhere. He reorganised the Academy of Architecture, and was responsible for the work on the Louvre by Charles Perrault.

The palace, now the greatest of the French museums, had its origin in the times of the Merovingian kings. The name is probably derived from its function as a *Louveterie*, or lodge for wolf-hunters. It was constructed as fortress by Charles V towards the end of the fourteenth century, and demolished and rebuilt by François I. Subsequently various additions were made, and, in 1665, Bernini was invited to Paris and asked to submit designs for further additions to the east side. He found it difficult to agree to the conditions imposed, and Perrault's design was accepted instead. As a picture gallery the Louvre owes much to Colbert, who increased the royal collection of Louis XIII amounting to about two hundred pictures to no less than two thousand five hundred.

Nevertheless, the King did not like the Louvre as a residence. At Versailles Louis XIII had built himself a hunting lodge, the architect being Lemercier. It was to Versailles that the Court had fled during the rising of the Fronde, and it was to Versailles that Louis XIV returned, probably intending it, at first, as a secluded place in which to continue his *amour* with his mistress, Louise de la Vallière. The gardens were reconstructed in the grand manner, and as his absorption with it grew, money was poured out on the project. Colbert wrote protesting that money which should have been spent on the Louvre was being diverted to Versailles. Ultimately Colbert himself appears to have been converted to the project, and under the architect, Le Vau, the original *château* was extended by new building on three sides. In 1678 further extensions were undertaken under Jules Hardouin-Mansard, a relative of François Mansard who has given his name to the mansard roof.

Under Mansard as many as thirty-six thousand men were employed on the work at one time. Mortality was high, from malaria and other diseases, and Mme de Sévigné wrote of cartloads of corpses being carried away each night.

The decoration of the interior was under the supervision of Charles Le Brun, who personally designed many of the statues and murals, particularly those for the 'Galerie des Glaces'. The gilded *stucco* frames and surrounds of the pictures were also designed by him.

Le Brun requires especial mention for his influence on the arts of the period. Colbert founded an association of artists under the name of the Royal Academy of Painting and Sculpture, and appointed Le Brun as Director and as his adviser in artistic matters. Colbert was also the prime mover in the establishment of the Manufacture royale des Meubles de la Couronne on the site of a house belonging to the Gobelins family. This supplied furniture, tapestries, jewellery, paintings, and other such things to the Court. It, too, was directed by Le Brun, and sent vast quantities of works of art of all kinds to the Palace of Versailles. Le Brun was an admirer both of Poussin and Raphaël, and the latter's influence can be seen in the use of Raphaël cartoons for the design of Gobelins tapestries from the Manufacture royale.

Versailles, even before it was completed, was the scene of *fêtes*, and theatrical performances by Molière's company were mounted with the utmost elaboration, and with complete disregard for cost. The lakes and fountains, the latter operated with great ingenuity by immense water-wheels driven by the Seine, were used for water spectacles.* When

---

*For an impression of the splendours of Versailles we may profitably turn once more to Martin Lister (1698):

'As to the Palace of Versailles (which is yet some miles further within the mountainous Country, not unlike Black-Heath or Tunbridge) 'tis without dispute the most magnificent

Plate 1. Ewer painted with *lambrequins* in blue. Mark:
AP in blue. Attributed to Rouen. 1680–1695. See
page 83. (Metropolitan.)

Plate 2 (a). Teapot decorated with *lambrequins* in underglaze blue. St. Cloud. c. 1700. (V&AM.)

(b). Vase decorated with *lambrequins* in blue underglaze. Attributed to Rouen. 1680–1695. A similar vase in the Chavagnac sale of 1909 was attributed to St. Cloud (B.M.).

Plate 3. Covered jar decorated with *lambrequins* in underglaze blue. St. Cloud. c. 1700. (V&AM.)

Plate 4 (a). Spice-box with three compartments and a single cover decorated with *lambrequins* in underglaze blue. St. Cloud. c. 1710. (V&AM.)

(b). Candlestick and snuffer decorated with *lambrequins* in underglaze blue. St. Cloud. c. 1700. (V&AM.)

Plate 5 (a). Cream-jug decorated with prunus sprigs in relief. St. Cloud. c. 1725. (Bedford-Cecil Higgins Colln.)

(b). Jug of imbricated or scale pattern with contemporary silver-mounts. c. 1725. St. Cloud. (V&AM.)

(c). *Pot-pourri* vase with applied flowers. St. Cloud. c. 1725. (V&AM.)

Plate 6. Tureen and cover of silver-pattern moulded with a fantastic bird amid flowers and foliage in the Oriental manner. St. Cloud. c. 1720. (V&AM.)

Plate 7 (a). *Cachepot* based on a silver-pattern painted with Oriental figures in polychrome. St. Cloud. c. 1730. (Metropolitan.)

(*b*). Tureen and cover painted in polychrome with subjects taken from Chinese and Japanese sources. St. Cloud. c. 1730. (V&AM.)

Plate 8 (a). Mustard-pot painted in polychrome with an Oriental pattern. Contemporary silver mounts. St. Cloud. c. 1735. (V&AM.)

(b). Covered oval basket decorated with applied flowers—the flowers naturally coloured, the leaves green and the basket edged with yellow-ish-brown. St. Cloud. c. 1735. (V&AM.)

Plate 9. Vase in the form of a rabbit, mustard yellow pot, green washed base, remainder white. Contemporary mounts. St. Cloud. c. 1735. (V&AM.)

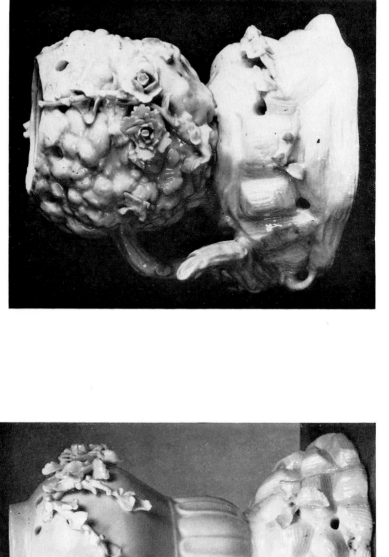

(b). *Pot-pourri* vase with applied flowers. St. Cloud. c. 1755. (V&AM.)

Plate 10 (a). Pot-pourri jar decorated with modelled flowers. Ivory-white paste. St. Cloud. c. 1755. (V&AM.)

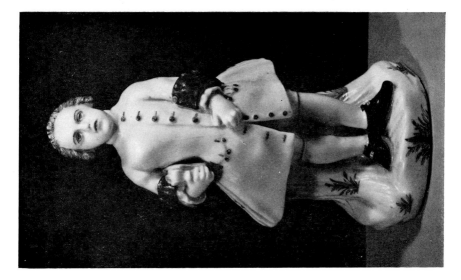

Plate 11 (a). Figure of a Chinese. St. Cloud. c. 1730. (V&AM.)

(b). *Le garçon,* after Chardin. St. Cloud. c. 1740. (Christie's.)

Plate 12. Goat attacked by a dog. Mark of the crossed arrows in blue, probably that of François Hébert of the Rue de la Roquette. c. 1740. A similar group was in the Chavagnac sale in 1909. (Ashmolean-Andrade Colln.)

Plate 13. Cachepot with a yellow ground and flowers in the style of
Kakiemon in the reserved panel. Chantilly. c. 1735. (V&AM.)

Plate 14 (a). Vase of baluster shape and vertical flutings painted in the Chinese style. Chantilly. Mark: hunting horn in red. c. 1735. (Metropolitan.)

(b). *Cachepot* decorated with flowers in the style of Kakiemon. Chantilly. c. 1735. (V&AM.)

Plate 15. Lobed jar decorated with a Kakiemon pattern.
Chantilly. c. 1735. (V&AM.)

Plate 16 (a). Lobed bowl painted in the Kakiemon style. Chantilly. c. 1735. (Bedford-Cecil Higgins Colln.)

(b). Octagonal bowl in the Kakiemon style. Chantilly. c. 1735. (V&AM.)

Louise de la Vallière was replaced as the principal mistress of
the King by Mme de Montespan in 1667, a *fête* of fantastic
proportions was given. For a time Louise de la Vallière and
Mme de Montespan both resided at Versailles; the new
mistress gradually gained ascendancy until she, in turn, was

---

of any in Europe. Yet what of it was first built and much
admired 30 years ago, is now no longer relisht. However this
King intends to rebuild it, where it is faulty.

'There are Books writ to describe this famous Palace in
every part, to which I refer the Reader. The Way to it is new
and in some places the Mountains are cut down 40 foot, so
that now you enjoy a mile in prospect before you come to
it. . . . The Gilded Tiles and Roof have a marvellous effect
in prospect. The Splanade towards the Gardens and Parterres
are the noblest things that can be seen, vastly great, with a
large Basin of Water in the middle, walled round with white
Marble, on which are placed a great number of incomparable
Brazen Vasa, and large Brass figures *couchant* of the best Masters
in Sculpture; it were endless to tell all the Furniture of these
Gardens of Marble Statues, and Vasa of Brass and Marble,
the multitude of Fountains, and those wide Canals like Seas
running in a streight line from the bottom of the Gardens as
far as the Eye can reach.

'The Orangery, or Winter Conservatory for Tubs of
Winter Greens is what corresponds to the greatness of the
rest. 'Tis a stupendous half square of underground vaults, like
the Naves of so many Churches put together, of exquisite
Workmanship in hewn Stone, well lighted and open to the
South Sun. It contains 3000 cases of Greens, whereof near
2000 are Orange Trees, and many hundreds of them are as big
as generally they grow in the Earth. . . In the Pottagerie
there are 700 cases of Figs, besides Wall Fruit of all other
kinds.

'I observed in small Fiance [*Faïence*] or Painted Pots a vast
number of the narrow leaved *Laurus Alexandrina*. . . . These
are not yet Ornaments in our Gardens that I know of.'

Of Marli, which he saw soon afterwards, he says:

'In one of the Ground Rooms was a Semicircular Gilt Bar
or Rail. . . . Within the Bar was disposed several Rows of
Porcellain or fine China on Gilt Shelves.'

eventually replaced by Françoise d'Aubigné, Marquise de Maintenon.

By 1684 Louis had transferred his entire Court of about sixteen thousand persons to Versailles.

Much had happened in the meantime. Following the death of Philip IV of Spain in 1665, Louis laid claim to the Spanish throne, and fighting broke out in 1667. This began a period during which war was frequent, and peace short and uneasy. Life for the common people had always been 'nasty, brutish, and short', and now for a century and a half there was to be no alleviation.*

Louis seized Franche-Comté and invaded the Netherlands, but was temporarily halted by an alliance of England, Holland, and Sweden. In 1672 war broke out afresh, and this time England and Sweden stood aloof. France gained some temporary success against the Dutch in consequence, but Louis also succeeded in raising most of Europe against him. He was saved only by the skill of his commanders, the Prince de Condé and Henri, Vicomte de Turenne. The latter fell at Sasbach in 1675, and by this mischance Louis lost one of his most loyal and skilful generals who had supported the Crown against Condé during the war of the Fronde. Condé died in 1686.

The war concluded in 1678 with the Peace of Nimegen, which gave Franche-Comté to the King but weakened his position elsewhere. No one expected the peace to last. Colbert's influence was declining with the rise to favour of Louvois, the Minister of War, and the Treasury had been drained to keep the armies in the field. Colbert died in 1683, harassed to the last by Louis, who continually pressed him to raise more money. As he was dying he was heard to say,

*An official report, later presented to the King, records that 'many women and children have been found dead in fields and on the roads with their mouths full of grass'.

'Had I served God as I have served the King, I should have been saved ten times over; now I cannot tell what will happen to me.'

By now Mme de Maintenon was indisputably the King's favourite. The Queen died in 1683, and, in 1684, Louis married his mistress secretly in the chapel of Versailles. Both she and the King turned their thoughts to religion. Undoubtedly she was much influenced by the Jesuits, although her part in causing Louis subsequently to persecute the Huguenots has probably been exaggerated. The King had already stated his position clearly and unequivocally in 1682 when it was set forth that 'kings and princes are not by the law of God subject to any ecclesiastical power' in temporal government—an action censured by the Pope. It made the Church entirely dependent on the goodwill of Louis, and his subsequent actions were probably as much due to political motives in his quest for absolute power as to any influence exerted by the clergy.

Whatever the reason, in 1685 he revoked the Edict of Nantes. This had been promulgated in 1598 by Henri IV, and gave the Huguenots freedom of worship. The revocation was followed by religious riots. Huguenot ministers were ordered to leave France on pain of being sent to the galleys, churches were torn down, and children were required to be baptized by a Catholic priest.* About a quarter of a million Huguenots streamed across the frontiers and fled to England, Holland, Prussia, and the other Protestant states. Many of them were craftsmen, and they enriched the arts of the countries to which they fled.

In 1700 Louis made his greatest mistake which led to the

*Huguenot families had dragoons billeted in their houses who had been ordered to make themselves generally unpleasant. They were called 'missionaries in cavalry boots', and many Huguenots became Catholics in order to get rid of their tormentors.

War of the Spanish Succession. A Treaty of Partition in 1699 had shared the Spanish succession between Philip of Anjou, grandson of Louis, and the second son of the Holy Roman Emperor, Leopold I. The latter had already been involved in two wars with Louis, and the treaty was designed to prevent a third. Immediately before his death in 1700, however, Charles II of Spain altered his will, leaving everything to Philip. Wisdom and discretion counselled adherence to the original treaty, but Louis, after two weeks' deliberation, accepted the crown of Spain on behalf of Philip.

Louis, in the course of his military adventures, had made too many enemies. By recognizing the 'Old Pretender' as James III of England in defiance of promises to the contrary, he brought William III against him, and by 1702 a Grand Alliance between England, the Emperor, Holland, and Prussia, led to the declaration of war. The neglect of the French navy made certain that no serious opposition could be offered at sea. An English Admiral, Rooke, captured Gibraltar in 1704, and the fleets went on to occupy Sardinia and Minorca. Louis had, in fact, succeeded in accomplishing an almost complete encirclement of France by her enemies, forcing on her that worst of all strategic positions—the reliance on interior lines of communication.

On land he faced two brilliant commanders, John Churchill, Duke of Marlborough, and François Eugène, Prince de Savoie. Eugène had left France after being refused a commission by Louis, and had then taken service with Leopold. A brilliant tactician, he distinguished himself in a number of wars, becoming a Field-Marshal in 1693. He was associated with Marlborough in several important battles.

Marlborough moved into Germany in 1703 with the object of 'teaching the Germans how to beat the French,' to use his own words. He joined the Austrians under Eugène in Bavaria, and the combined armies inflicted a serious defeat on the French, who were assisted by Bavarian troops, at the village of Blenheim, near Hochstadt. French losses totalled more than thirty thousand, those of Marlborough and Eugène little more than twelve thousand.

In 1706 Marlborough again defeated French armies at Ramillies, in Brabant, which virtually gave him control of the Netherlands. He was temporarily delayed by an invasion of Germany by Charles XII of Sweden who advanced on Augustus the Strong of Saxony, but Charles turned towards Russia, and Marlborough proceeded to crush the French armies at Oudenarde in 1708. But the tide was turning, and although he defeated a French army under the Duc de Villars at Malplaquet in 1709, he paid heavily for the victory. 'If God gives us another defeat like this', wrote de Villars to Louis, 'your Majesty's enemies will be destroyed.' Malplaquet proved to be the turning point of the war by which Louis was saved from ultimate disaster.

In England the political climate was changing. The Tory party, which opposed continuance of the war, came to power, and the Duchess of Marlborough was dismissed from her post at Court by Queen Anne who could no longer suffer her arrogance. Marlborough was relieved of his command and offices in 1711, and remained for some years in the wilderness, returning to favour with the accession of George I as a reward for his support of the House of Hanover.

The pendulum had reversed its swing in earnest. By an astute manoeuvre the Duc de Villars, who was at the head of the last of the French armies, won a decisive victory over Eugène at Denain in 1712. The Treaty of Utrecht a year later gave the throne of Spain to Philip, but France lay exhausted and ruined.

In quick succession two personal disasters had befallen Louis: the death of the Dauphin in 1711, and that of his grandson soon afterwards. This narrowed the succession to the throne of France to his great-grandson, the Duke of Anjou, who succeeded eventually as Louis XV.

Louis died on September 1st, 1715. His reign had lasted seventy-two years, and he was within a few days of his seventy-seventh birthday. Towards the last, he spoke of his grandson: 'He is only five. He will need your zeal and your fidelity. I ask for him the same sentiments as those you have shown to me. I advise him to avoid war. I have made too many, and I have laid grievous burdens on my people because of them. This I regret profoundly, and ask God's pardon.'

The reign of Louis is fittingly summed up in his own words. The first years were troubled. Under Colbert the country enjoyed a period of prosperity, but the King's military adventures brought it to virtual bankruptcy. The population had decreased alarmingly as a result of war casualties and starvation. Cultivation of large areas had ceased, and riots were common. Taxes had been heavily increased, and every conceivable financial trick had been used to get money. In 1709 Louis sent much of his silver to the Mint for coinage, and forced his nobles to do the same. This helped the porcelain and *faïence* industries, since they supplied replacements for silver vessels and dishes, but it is an indication of the seriousness of the financial predicament.

The passing of Louis was little regretted. The passage of the funeral cortège through Paris was attended with rejoicing, and Louis XV* reigned in his place.

IV

When he succeeded to the throne the new king was five years of age, and the country was administered by Philip,

*A *biscuit* porcelain statuette of Louis XV in armour was made by J.-B. Lemoyne for Sèvres in 1760.

Duc d'Orléans, as Regent. The part played by Orléans in the affairs of France has been the subject of controversy. Irreligious and dissolute, his *affaires* were a common scandal throughout Europe, and he has even been accused of incestuous relations with one of his daughters. On the credit side, his friends found in him many good qualities, and he seems to have been much attached to the young king whose health was far from good. Accusations that he desired to usurp the throne for himself seem to have little foundation. He worked hard, and did what he could with a situation which would have been beyond the powers of a far more skilful statesman. He disliked the rising *bourgeois* class, which was acquiring both money and influence, and endeavoured to restore the aristocracy to the position from which they had been thrust by Louis XIV. He also permitted a greater measure of freedom for the ordinary citizen.

An attempt was made to alleviate the financial position by the issue of bank-notes. This scheme, in which the State Bank participated, was hatched in the fertile brain of a Scotsman, John Law, and soon led to an inflationary situation, the government, in a manner familiar today, trying to shed the load of debt to its citizens by debasing the currency. Numbers of speculative companies were started, including the Compagnie des Indes. Many were more or less dubious, and all promised high profits. Like the no less notorious 'South Sea Bubble' in England, the final result was a spectacular crash, in which large numbers of people lost money, and only the Compagnie des Indes survived.

The Regent quarrelled with the *Parlement*, who were against the inflationary methods adopted, and for a time it seemed that civil war was inevitable. In 1723, however, the Regency came to an end with the majority of the King, and the Duc d'Orléans, his reputation, such as it was, tarnished and diminished, died in the same year.

v

The death of Orléans left the country without a Chief
Minister. The vacancy was filled by the Duc de Bourbon, with
the King's tutor (later to be succeeded by Cardinal Fleury)
acting as adviser. The Duc de Villars, whose generalship
had saved France during the closing phases of the War of
Succession, was associated with them.

When Louis XV was fifteen years of age, the question of
marriage was discussed. For one reason or another most of
the princesses of Europe were regarded as unsuitable, and
the choice fell eventually on Maria Leczinska daughter of
Stanislas Leczinski, the elected King of Poland who had
been deposed by Augustus the Strong of Saxony, then
living in retirement in the Rhineland.

Stanislas Leczinski was in low water financially, and the
match was much to his taste, particularly as it was accompanied by a pension and a house at Wissembourg. The
bride was not a beauty, but she had many virtues to commend her—cheerfulness, a kindly disposition, tact, and
intelligence—all of which she was to need in the coming
years. Her comparatively humble origin—Stanislas was
elected and not hereditary—at first excited some opposition
at Court, but her personal character won her many friends,
and the opposition was short-lived.

Louis, too, was not displeased with the match, although
he later found her dull and unable to provide him with the
kind of lively company he craved. From 1727 onwards she
had ten children in quick succession, two of which were
boys. One boy and a girl died in infancy.

The Duc de Bourbon and Fleury clashed, and the King
dismissed the former in 1726, leaving Fleury, at the age of
seventy-three, in an unassailable position. His power
equalled that of either Mazarin or Richelieu, but his disposi-

tion was entirely different. His tastes were few and simple, and his ambitions modest. He tried to give France a much needed breathing space, and to some extent he succeeded.

The King certainly did not resemble his great-grandfather. Reserved, indolent, and with small taste for the business of government, he spent his days in such pursuits as hunting. He needed encouragement to overcome shyness, and to take part in his public duties as king. The work of government was delegated to Fleury because Louis was not interested in it, and on the occasions when he was called upon to undertake the burden, he showed a marked incapacity for it.

The Cardinal's tragedy was that he failed to recognize when he had outlived his powers. He clung to office, and the King was unwilling to dismiss an old friend. Ultimately, an attempt was made to promote him to the Papacy to leave the way open for a younger man, but nothing came of it. A strong party was in favour of his continuance in office because of the mildness of his rule, and there is little doubt that, despite his advanced age, he did his utmost to keep France from becoming involved in the War of the Austrian Succession in 1740.

Fleury had already kept France from participating in a major war with Russia in 1733 when the death of Augustus the Strong temporarily left vacant the throne of Poland. Stanislas again laid claim to it, and was elected. Russia once more intervened, this time on behalf of Augustus III, and Warsaw was ordered to elect him. Louis XV provided a little money and fewer troops to enforce his father-in-law's claim, and the troops were withdrawn with the advance of Russian armies. Stanislas returned to France, and was rewarded with the Duchy of Lorraine. He held Court at Lunéville, and was much esteemed by the more enlightened people of his day, Voltaire being a frequent and honoured guest.

By 1740 Fleury was deaf and partially blind, and the

misery of the peasantry was unabated. D'Argenson in his *Memoirs* says that more Frenchmen died of poverty in the years 1738–40 than perished in all the wars of Louis XIV, which was probably an exaggeration, but is, nevertheless, a sufficient indication of conditions at the time.

In 1740, too, occurred the death of Charles VI of Austria and Frederick William of Prussia. Their successors were Maria Theresa and Frederick II, later to be called 'the Great'. The temptation of an Austria ruled by a woman who was thought to be vulnerable was too great for her neighbours. Frederick invaded Silesia, and others were not wanting to claim a share of the Empire.*

This hardly concerned France immediately, but a strong war party headed by Marshal Belle-Isle, the grandson of Fouquet, opposed the efforts of Fleury to prevent the country from participating. The traditional enmity of the Bourbons for the Hapsburgs was the primary cause, and the final result was that almost the whole of Western Europe aligned itself on one side or the other, England supporting Maria Theresa.

Fleury died in 1743 at the age of ninety, using his influence for peace until the last. Louis viewed his passing with mixed feelings. He had regarded Fleury in some ways as almost taking the place of his parents, but he had outgrown his willingness to be guided and lectured by the Cardinal. The King made small effort to take matters into his own hands, and the government was carried on by a Council of about forty, presided over by the King, or, more often, the Chancellor.

*Maria Theresa was left the Crown indisputably in her father's will, but Frederick characteristically remarked that it would have been better had her father left her 'fewer papers and more soldiers'. An equestrian portrait of Frederick was later done by Boizot at Sèvres to the order of the Comte d'Artois and presented to Louis XVI.

Abroad, France was at first successful in her military campaigns, and her armies, under Marshal Belle-Isle, gained important successes in Germany in support of the Elector of Bavaria. Maria Theresa was forced to take refuge in Hungary, but the tide turned with the intervention of Russia, Holland, and England on her behalf. The French executed a mid-winter retreat from Prague leaving thousands of corpses and abandoned equipment to mark the road they had taken. George II of England defeated a French army at Dettingen, and forced them back into Alsace, and Maria Theresa was free to return to Austria.

French armies had been more successful in the Netherlands, but their defeats elsewhere prevented them from exploiting the victories. In 1744 the French conceived the plan of landing the 'Young Pretender' in Scotland, which led to the Rebellion of 1745, but nothing came of it except to stiffen English determination. The 'Young Pretender' was crushed at Culloden, and Maria Theresa made peace with Frederick. The naval war had gone badly for France in India and elsewhere, and hostilities closed finally with the Peace of Aix-la-Chapelle in 1748, leaving France weakened and discredited.

The picture now began to change. 'To the government of an old priest succeeded that of a young mistress', wrote Michelet. Louis had taken mistresses before his meeting with Madame de Pompadour, but none had exercised influence on the government of France. This was now to be changed by the daughter of a swindling Army contractor.

Since Antoinette Poisson, Marquise de Pompadour, will appear frequently in the later discussion of the work of Vincennes-Sèvres, she deserves especial attention here.

Her father, the son of a peasant, had made a fortune by supplying provisions to the Army, but his peculations were so blatant at a time when honest contractors were almost non-existent that he was sentenced to be hanged. He fled, and later managed by bribery to get himself reinstated, with a title for his 'services'. Her mother was the daughter of a butcher who had managed to make the acquaintance of a certain M. de Tournhem. When her husband fled, she turned to him for protection.

It would seem that, from the first, Madame Poisson and her daughter schemed to attract the attention of the King. The daughter was educated in accomplishments which would be useful at Court, and this may have been inspired by a fortune-teller who predicted that she would be 'not a Queen, but almost a Queen'. Later, after she had married M. Le Normant d'Etiolles, nephew of M. de Tournhem, she rejected suitors by saying that she would be unfaithful with no one but the King. The marriage took place in 1741, principally because d'Etiolles was rich, and could introduce her to wealthy and influential circles. He was, therefore, an invaluable step on the way to the highest pinnacle.

Apparently she was brought to the King's notice by his valet, Binet, who sometimes acted as the King's procurer, and soon she had access to the private apartments at Versailles.

In 1745 she was established at Versailles, and shortly afterwards the King bought for her the estate and title of Pompadour. Soon she became the leader of a brilliant literary and artistic circle, and turned her attention to learning and the arts, as well as to influencing matters of State policy and the appointment and dismissal of high officials of State.

The Peace of Aix-la-Chapelle settled very little. It left behind a legacy of bitterness and hatred. Maria Theresa had yielded to *force majeure* in the matter of Silesia, but she waited an opportunity to wrest it from Frederick. England had an acquisitive eye on French possessions in India,

Canada, and Louisiana. French American possessions, in particular, threatened the English colonies on the Atlantic seaboard, and, in 1754, England attacked French ships without warning, whilst the forces of the East India Company under Clive struck at French forces under Dupleix.

In Europe Maria Theresa discussed the question of an alliance with France. Madame de Pompadour detested the Protestant Frederick, and used her influence in favour of a Catholic alliance. England, in turn, supported Frederick, and the Seven Years' War started in 1756.

The influence of Madame de Pompadour ultimately proved disastrous because it involved France in a land campaign fought, once more, on interior lines of communication. The English, under Clive, won the Battle of Plassey which laid the foundation for the eventual subjugation of India. Wolfe captured Quebec in 1759 and English armies overran the whole of the Province of Canada in the following year. Large elements of the French fleet were destroyed by Boscawen, and a serious naval defeat was suffered at the hands of Hawke.

On land Frederick suffered continual reverses at first, despite generalship of the first order, because he had to meet superior forces. By 1762 his position was extremely serious, and it seemed impossible for him to continue. He was saved by the death of the Czarina, Elizabeth, and the subsequent withdrawal of Russia from the war. Hostilities concluded in 1763 with the Peace of Paris, by which the French relinquished Canada, and ceded some of their Indian possessions. By a separate peace Frederick retained Silesia.

In 1758 the King gained a new Minister of Foreign Affairs, Etienne François, Duc de Choiseul, who was a protégé of Madame de Pompadour. The new Minister had made a successful career as a soldier during the War of the

Austrian Succession, and in 1757 had been Ambassador at Vienna. As Foreign Minister he controlled French policy during most of the Seven Years' War. His skill and energy were too late to save the situation, and his efforts to avoid ceding possessions in Canada and India by an alliance with Spain, were also doomed to failure.

He achieved his final ruin by assisting Madame de Pompadour to expel the Jesuits, and after her death was dismissed from office. The suppression of the Society of Jesus was almost universal in Europe at the time, the movement against it starting in Portugal in 1759. Choiseul, persuaded by Madame de Pompadour, requested the *Parlement* of Paris to decree its abolition in France, and this was confirmed by Louis in 1764. For many years the Jesuits had been attempting to gain influence in secular affairs, and opposition to this intervention in things outside the province of the Church was so strong that the Pope was compelled to decree the abolition of the Society in 1773.

In 1763, at the end of the Seven Years' War, Louis still had eleven years to reign. By now the Court had reached a state of corruption almost unequalled in European history. The King remained at Versailles, leaving almost everything in the hands of Madame de Pompadour. She, in person, carried on the tradition of autocratic government laid down by Richelieu. The nobility, which occupied itself almost entirely with pleasure and debaucheries, no longer influenced the conduct of affairs. The clergy were privileged landowners who paid few taxes. The rising *bourgeois* class, as elsewhere in Europe, was growing stronger, richer, and more influential. The heaviest burdens fell on the shoulders of the peasantry and the lower classes.

Madame de Pompadour died in 1764, and for a few years Louis was without any strong attachments. She was replaced as mistress of the ageing King by Marie Jeanne

Gomart de Vaubernier, Comtesse du Barry,* reputed daughter of a Customs official, and mistress of the Comte du Barry. She attracted the attention of Louis some time before her introduction to Versailles, but her origins made it difficult to induce the Court to accept her. The matter was arranged by a marriage to Guillaume du Barry, and she subsequently appeared at Court in 1769, almost universally detested. She had most of the vices of Madame de Pompadour without her grasp of affairs and strength of character, and soon she was the centre of intrigue. Despite this, she eased the King's closing years which were more peaceful than France had known for many decades.

Louis was taken ill on April 27th, 1774, with a fever. He saw the increase in the severity of his illness with something approaching terror, and the Court lived from day to day in apprehension of what would follow from his death and the fall of the du Barry. On May 3rd Louis sent her away to avoid the risk of infecting her, and died on May 10th.

The passing of Louis XV left a situation even more chaotic than that which attended the death of his great-grandfather. Debts were enormous, and there was no way of paying them. Revolution was nearer—almost at hand; and a diplomat of the time wrote, 'We young nobles walked on a carpet of flowers which covered an abyss.' The abyss was to yawn for his successor.

VI

Louis XVI, who succeeded in 1774, was a grandson of Louis XV.† His father, the Dauphin, had died some years before. In 1770 he married Marie-Antoinette, daughter of

---

*A biscuit portrait of Mme du Barry was made after Pajou in 1772. Pl. 75b.

†An allegory of the Coronation of Louis XVI and Marie-Antoinette was modelled by Boizot for Sèvres in 1775.

Maria Theresa, with the object of cementing the alliance between France and Austria.

Their accession to the throne was well-received. Changes were made at Court and corrupt ministers dismissed. Turgot was appointed to take charge of finance, and at once suggested sweeping reforms which were little to the liking of the aristocracy or the Church. Turgot was dismissed and replaced by the banker, Jacques Necker, whose remedy was a measure of inflation. But French intervention in the American struggle drained the Treasury faster than it could be filled. England recognized the independence of the United States in 1782, and the Treaty of Versailles concluded the war between England and France and guaranteed the autonomy of the new republic.

Necker disappeared from the scene in 1781 after an incautious attempt to restrain the spending classes, and was followed by a succession of Ministers who owed their appointment to the influence of Marie-Antoinette. Despite the courage with which she went to an ignominious end, she did much to provoke her ultimate fate. The King looked with favour on measures of reform, but she dissuaded him, forming a Court party and interfering with the appointment of Ministers. She spent money recklessly on display at a time when retrenchment was essential, and it is probably not too much to say that, although the Revolution was inevitable, her actions both brought it more quickly and increased its violence.

Particularly when the American War had exhausted the Treasury did she use her influence against any diminution of spending by the Court, and she endeavoured to restore the aristocracy to the position of influence which it held before the days of Louis XIV. Her protégé, Calonne, the Minister of Finance, performed miracles in raising money for her to spend until 1787, when the monarchy was bankrupt.

To raise more money Calonne attempted a capital levy on landed property. The aristocracy demanded the summoning of the States-General, a legislative body whose existence had been suspended since 1614. This met eventually in 1789.

Originally the States-General had been divided into the Clergy, the Nobility, and the Commons, and the first two had invariably succeeded in outvoting the third, but the Commons now included a *bourgeoisie* which was well-versed in affairs, and which had the example of the American colonists before it.

The meeting was held at Versailles, and the Court attached so little importance to it at first that the venue was chosen because of the hunting. For six weeks the disputes went on, the deputies demanding a constitution and control of taxation. The King tried to disperse the States-General by force, but the soldiers mutinied. Marie-Antoinette took the provocative step of having regiments largely composed of foreign elements moved to Paris, and the capital revolted. The flame caught, spread to the provinces, and the National Guard was formed for use against the regular troops.

A great hailstorm in July, 1788, destroyed growing crops, and starving peasants had since been moving into Paris in search of food. They formed the explosive mixture which eventually tore the monarchy apart. On July 14th, 1789, the Bastille was stormed, *châteaux* near Paris and in the provinces were burned, and some members of the aristocracy—the farsighted—fled abroad.

Government of the country was taken over by a National Assembly who, by a series of resolutions, abolished serfdom, tithes, feudal courts, tax exemption privileges, and other medieval survivals, and proceeded to formulate the Declaration of the Rights of Man.

Louis appeared in Paris wearing the *tricolor* cockade in

an attempt to placate the people, and he was given a good-humoured reception. At this time, and later, it is possible that he could have become a constitutional monarch, but Marie-Antoinette decreed otherwise. In October, 1789, at a time when thousands were starving, a great banquet for anti-Revolutionists was given at Versailles. The National Guard, followed by a large crowd of which the majority were women, marched to Versailles, broke into the Palace, and compelled the King, the Queen, and the Dauphin* to return to Paris.

The royal family were now virtually imprisoned in the Tuileries, whilst the deputies strove with the gigantic task of giving France a constitution. The Assembly had behaved generously towards the King, voting him a handsome civil list, and treating him with marked respect, but his belief in the divine right of the Bourbons to rule France gradually lost him support. The *rapprochement* broke down entirely when the Assembly attacked the clergy, and proposed to expropriate their property. This was a measure of rough justice, since the Church had always avoided its share of taxation. Unable to accept this, Louis started to negotiate with most of the kings of Europe, asking for help.

Mirabeau endeavoured to keep the situation from complete disaster, and La Fayette, Colonel-General of the National Guard, added his influence on the side of moderation. But power was gradually falling into the hands of the extreme Left, represented by the Jacobins' Club, which soon rivalled the Assembly in influence. The death of Mirabeau in 1791 finally tipped the scales against Louis, and in June he left the Tuileries disguised and at night, accompanied by

*The birth of the Dauphin had been commemorated by an allegory of Marie-Antoinette as Venus seated on a dolphin offering the newly-born infant to France. It was modelled by Pajou in biscuit porcelain in 1781.

the Queen and their two children, *en route* for the Army of Eastern France which was reputed to be loyal.

The royal party was recognized by the landlord of a posting-inn at Sainte-Ménéhoud, and the coach was intercepted at Varennes, near Verdun, within a few miles of safety. The King surrendered to force, and was taken back to Paris. Even now, no move was made against him, although his action had greatly strengthened the hand of the Jacobins' Club and its leaders—Robespierre, Danton, and Marat.

In the meantime an anti-Revolutionary movement had been growing in Europe, and with the blessing and help of the King of Prussia and the Emperor of Austria, an *émigré* army had mobilized near France's eastern frontier. A declaration of war against Austria followed, and France suffered severely in the early stages. The cause of Louis was still further jeopardized by the Duke of Brunswick, who let it be known that he was preparing to invade France to restore the monarchy.

On the June 20th, 1792, the Jacobins rose against the Assembly. They broke into the Palace, and Louis was forced to wear the red cap to appease them. His only hope, now, was to gain time and wait for rescue by Brunswick. But the threats of foreign intervention united France behind the Jacobins, and on the August 10th the men of Marseilles moved on Paris. The mob, led by Danton, was irresistible. The Guards of the Tuileries refused to fire. The Swiss Guards resisted, were killed to a man, and the Tuileries looted. Mob courts were set up. Prisoners were briefly questioned, and either turned loose or hacked to death.

On September 21st, 1792, a republic was proclaimed, and among the first things to be discussed was the trial of Louis. Attempts were made to save him from execution, but death was decreed by the comparatively narrow majority of fifty-three votes. He was guillotined in the Square of the Revolution in January, 1793. 'The kings of Europe would challenge us', snarled Danton. 'We throw them the head of a king'.

Danton's challenge at least showed courage, and courage was needed. The Prussians had reached Argonne, and Brunswick was barely stopped by Kellermann at Valmy. Only French victories in Alsace succeeded in buying a brief breathing time abroad.

There was, however, no such period at home. The idea of a machine with a weighted, falling knife to decapitate its victims was by no means new, but a more effective design by Dr. Guillotin was adopted in 1791, and brought into use in 1792. It was an invention singularly appropriate to the fanaticism of Robespierre, which was reinforced by the patriotism of Danton.

The Reign of Terror began, and from May, 1793, until August, 1794, the thud of the falling knife was heard more and more often. Decapitation was the penalty for almost anything and everything. Royalist insurrections, notably that of La Vendée, provided a steady stream of victims. The tumbrils bearing the Queen and the aristocracy rumbled through the Paris streets until even Danton's stomach turned, and he protested against the endless killing. In turn, he passed under the knife.

There seems little doubt that by 1794 Robespierre was mad. He made vague threats against everybody, and the government was finally compelled to arrest him. He was trapped in the Hôtel de Ville with some of his supporters, and shot in the jaw whilst trying to escape. The next day he was thrust on to the guillotine, and the Reign of Terror was at an end.

Despite these events, a fresh spirit had been infused into the armies of France. They began to win victories on all fronts, and only in Italy were they temporarily contained. But, in 1794, the name of a new commander began to be heard—that of Napoleon Bonaparte.

The Buonapartes were descended from an Italian family who settled in Corsica in the twelfth century. Napoleon was born in Ajaccio in 1769, and was placed by his father in the military school at Brienne in 1779. In 1784 he became a cadet in the military school of Paris, and was gazetted to an artillery regiment in the following year. In 1793 he was promoted to the rank of Lieutenant-Colonel in another artillery regiment, and was sent to Toulon. In consequence of successes there he was raised to the rank of General.

At twenty-four he was sent to command the artillery in Italy, and by brilliant generalship brought the campaign to a successful conclusion in a matter of months. He achieved this by sheer poverty of equipment. His troops, having nothing to carry but weapons, lived off the country, and moved at what was then a fantastic speed.

His successes brought him to the notice of the authorities in Paris, and when a reliable artillery officer was needed in the capital in 1795, Bonaparte was given the task.

By this time executive power was in the hands of a Directory of five members, who ruled with the aid of Councils charged with the duty of initiating legislation. The royalists tried to overthrow it in October, 1795, but they saw their hopes vanish as the thunder of Bonaparte's guns swept the approaches to the Tuileries. The Directory was saved, and remained in power for the next four years.

Bonaparte went on to consolidate his victories in Italy, and loot began to pour back into Paris. In 1798 he occupied Malta, and landed an army in Egypt. This campaign was the origin of the interest presently taken in Egyptian art and antiquities, and the use of Egyptian motifs in decoration.*

The French fleet was caught by Nelson in Aboukir Bay,

*A *cabaret* made by Sèvres for Napoleon in 1810 has views of Egypt in panels, over-lavish gilding, and meaningless hieroglyphs. It is in the Louvre.

and shot to pieces. Napoleon was then marooned in Egypt. A Turkish army, despite defeats, checked his hope of further advances into Asia, and he returned to France, leaving his army to be captured by the British in 1801.

This was his first serious reverse, although the full extent of the disaster was not apparent for almost another three years. When he returned to Paris he found that the growing interest in Roman history, fostered by the neo-classical movement which started in the middle of the eighteenth century, had suggested the idea of Consuls, and, in 1799, a conspiracy to replace the Directory with three Consuls, of whom Napoleon was the chief, was successful.

As First Consul, Napoleon was elected for a ten-year term of office. His two colleagues were there only for consultation. They had no executive power. Napoleon appointed a Council of State, a Senate of eighty members, a Legislative Body, and a Tribunate, but the effect of this elaborate structure was merely to concentrate power in the hands of the First Consul, a situation overwhelmingly confirmed by a plebiscite. Negotiations with the Pope enabled him to fill the Church with his nominees.

A victory at Marengo gave him control of Italy, and, in 1802, the Treaty of Amiens led to peace with England, and the next phase of his career was devoted to strengthening France internally. Schemes of reconstruction and development were started. The *émigrés* were allowed to return upon pledging support for the new *régime*, and the legal system was reconstructed under the *Code Napoléon*. He manoeuvred a permanent appointment as First Consul in 1802, with the power of appointing his own successor, and from this point the step to the throne of France was short.

In 1804 Napoleon was declared Emperor, and caused himself to be crowned in the Cathedral of Notre-Dame in Paris. The ceremony was performed by Pope Pius VII, but, characteristically, the Pope was pushed aside at the last moment, and Napoleon placed the crown of France on his own head.

The new Empress was Marie-Josèphe Rose Tascher de la Pagerie, better known as Joséphine, by which name she was invariably called. She was born in Martinique in 1763, her father being an officer of the garrison, and captain of the port of Sainte Pierre.

She came to France and married the Vicomte Alexandre de Beauharnais in 1779, when she was only sixteen. There was a son, Eugène (later Viceroy of Italy), and a daughter, Hortense, who was to become Queen of Holland and mother of Napoleon III. The marriage was not a success, and at one point was the subject of an action for judicial separation.

The Vicomte was arrested in 1794 and subsequently guillotined. Joséphine was arrested at the same time, as the result of her attempts to obtain his release. She was saved only by the fall of Robespierre.

She married Napoleon in 1796, and exercised great influence over him, holding court at the Luxembourg and the Tuileries. She bought the Château of La Malmaison, near Paris, in 1799 for her husband and herself. The house is small, and the gardens are no longer as extensive as formerly, but the cedar planted by Joséphine to commemorate the victory of Marengo in 1800 is still to be seen, as well as numerous relics of Napoleon.

Her reputation during Napoleon's absences was the subject of much scandalous rumour at the time, but the extent of her unfaithfulness is controversial. She spent heavily, and accumulated large debts. Much of the money went to improve the gardens at Malmaison since she was an enthusiastic gardener.

In 1807 Napoleon considered the question of divorce,

principally because Joséphine's birth was not fitting to her new position as Empress. Eventually he married Marie Louise of Austria, and Joséphine retired to Malmaison, where Napoleon was an occasional visitor. He corresponded with her up to the time of her death in 1814.

Napoleon's aggressions in Hanover, and his diplomatic *démarches* in Europe, aroused English suspicions. These speedily turned to certainty when it was known that he was preparing for an invasion of England, and hostilities broke out in 1803. England, in a manner all too familiar, frantically repaired its defences, part of which were the Martello towers familiar on the coast of Kent and Sussex. But Napoleon's hopes of a successful invasion vanished with the Battle of Trafalgar in 1805—a defeat which was hidden from the French people by an ambiguous *communiqué*.

His attention then turned to Germany. The victories of Ulm and Austerlitz* in 1805 ended the Holy Roman Empire, and Austria was forced to sign the Treaty of Pressburg. Prussia declared war to save the Province of Hanover, and was utterly routed at Jena in 1806. A trade war on Britain was declared as an alternative to invasion, and the British retaliated with a blockade of Continental ports in the classical manner of British strategy. This seriously undermined Napoleon's position.

Like the Bourbons before him, Napoleon eventually made a fatal and irretrievable error. In 1808 he seized Spain and deposed the King, uniting both Spain and Portugal. The Spanish people rose against him, starting a bitter and vicious guerilla war which sapped the strength of his forces,

---

*A large vase at Malmaison commemorates this battle. Severely classical in form, it has a central frieze of a war-chariot in the late Greek style. It bears the inscription 'Bataille d'Austerlitz', and the pompous 'Veni, Vidi, Vici' (I came, I saw, I conquered) originally attributed to Julius Caesar. It was made at Sèvres.

whilst a British army under Wellington landed at Corunna. The Peninsular War was primarily one of attrition in which the French armies were slowly exhausted.

By this time both Austria and Prussia had recovered from earlier defeats, and Russia was beginning to suffer severely from the limitations placed on her commerce by the blockades, and particularly from the cessation of her trade with Britain. In 1811 the Czar withdrew from his treaties with Napoleon, who then gathered an army of 600,000 men for a march on Moscow. In 1812 he occupied Moscow, but instead of surrendering, the Czar merely withdrew further into the country, contenting himself with attacking Napoleon's extended lines of communication, and waiting for 'General Winter' to move against the French forces.

In October Napoleon decided to return. The orderly withdrawal turned first into a retreat, and then into a *débâcle* of a kind repeated nearly a century and a half later at Stalingrad. His disciplined armies became a mob of starving men and horses fighting for survival. The road back was littered with frozen corpses and equipment, and the ever-diminishing remainder staggered on with frost-bitten feet, whilst the Russians cut out small groups from the main force and dispatched them at leisure. Only a handful of men lived to reach Posen in Germany, and Napoleon's power was finally broken.

He reached Paris and gathered fresh armies, but everywhere Europe was rising against him. Wellington decisively defeated the French at Vittoria, bringing the Peninsular War to a close, and Napoleon abdicated and went into exile on the Island of Elba.

Now began the Congress of Vienna under Metternich, the astute Austrian diplomat. The Bourbons returned to France. The Dauphin, who would have been Louis XVII, was dead, and the throne was occupied by the brother of

Louis XVI, who took the title of Louis XVIII. Like those who had gone before, Louis XVIII had learnt nothing and forgotten nothing, and, in 1815, Napoleon judged that the time had come for his emergence from exile.

A meeting of the Vienna Congress was interrupted by the news that Napoleon had landed near Cannes and was marching on Paris. The Hundred Days had begun. The Army hailed their Emperor, and gathered round him in increasing numbers as he proceeded. Marshal Ney* joined him with his army, and Louis fled to Ghent. When the Emperor arrived in Paris he was acclaimed by the people amid scenes of rejoicing, but there was no rejoicing elsewhere in Europe. Hastily the nations gathered armies for the final struggle.

The Prussians under Blücher marched to join the army of Wellington which had landed in Belgium. A clash with the Emperor's advance-guard at Ligny caused Blücher to withdraw temporarily, and Wellington fell back on the village of Waterloo. Here, on June 18th, 1815, Napoleon and Marshal Ney attacked a combined British and German army. The struggle in the morning was inconclusive, with Wellington fighting off determined attacks by the French army, but, in the afternoon, the first elements of Blücher's Prussians arrived and tipped the scale.

Napoleon fled, first to Paris, and then to Rochefort. He surrendered to the English cruiser, *Bellerophon*, to avoid capture by his disillusioned countrymen, and died a prisoner on the Island of St. Helena in 1821.

VII

This brief historical sketch of events in France covers the

*The top of a porcelain table made in 1810, and now at Malmaison, has a central portrait of Napoleon from which radiates a star. The border has portraits of his Marshals.

period spanned by this book. Amid foreign wars, civil wars, and revolutions, the artists and craftsmen of France found opportunity to do some superb work in both the fine and the decorative arts, and it is proper to consider at this point the various styles and influences to be observed.

During the seventeenth century the two principal architectural styles were the *baroque* and the Palladian, represented by the work of Giovanni Lorenzo Bernini [1598–1680] and Andrea Palladio [1518–1580]. The former is best known for his work on St. Peter's in Rome, and he unsuccessfully submitted designs for additions to the Louvre. Palladio was a notable exponent of the styles suggested by the work of classical Greek and Roman architects, and particularly of the principles laid down by Vitruvius. He was a precursor of neo-classicism which is later discussed. In England the *baroque* style made but slight impact, and it is only to be seen in the work of Vanbrugh. The Palladian style is represented by the work of Inigo Jones, and, to some extent, by that of the Earl of Burlington.

Palladian classicism is a style which depends on the proportional relationship between the various parts. *Baroque* is much more exuberant and decorative. It is essentially dramatic, and made much use of statuary in lively poses, as well as fountains and similar water displays. It appealed particularly to kings and princes with money to spend on the external trappings of pomp. It is evident in many of the late Renaissance ceiling- and wall-paintings, which are framed with characteristic *stucco* ornament, and the *baroque* architect used this kind of painting freely for decorative purposes. In painting, the style can be seen at its most serious in the work of El Greco, whose peculiar distorted rhythms are essentially *baroque*, but in a less serious vein, the work of Tiepolo is also *baroque*.

In the decorative arts the style is characteristic, and can be seen in such motifs as the German *Laub- und Bandelwerk* (leaf- and strap-work) which is a symmetrical arrangement of interlacing scrolls, strap-work, and conventional leaf-forms. This is analogous to the French *lambrequins*, which appear alike on *faïence* and porcelain, and are a type of formal ornament first used for this purpose by Louis Poterat of Rouen. *Lambrequins* are a mixture of pendant lace-work, drapes, and scrollwork of various kinds, derived from the ornamental stamps used for leather book-bindings, from lace-work, and from wrought iron-work, and to these were sometimes added swags of fruit and flowers. Equally *baroque* are such motifs as the *baldacchini* (canopies) to be seen in the designs of Jean Bérain.

During the seventeenth century, as I have already recorded, Chinese art became extremely fashionable in Europe. Mazarin spent large sums on a collection, and Louis XIV did the same. In 1687 the Dauphin furnished an apartment at Versailles with tapestries with Chinese motifs. The state tapestry workshops of Gobelins and Beauvais, under the direction of Jean-Baptiste Oudry, used Chinese subjects, and François Boucher, who exerted an enormous influence on the decorative arts of France during his lifetime, found inspiration in the art of the Far East.

In 1705 the Compagnie Royale de la Chine was established to trade with China and the East, and enthusiasm grew, particularly in Court circles. A shop called *à la Pagode* in Paris, kept by a dealer named Gersaint, was a place of resort for women of fashion and taste. He sold lacquer screens, silks, embroideries, porcelain, and such things, brought to Europe in the ships of the East India Companies. Watteau painted the picture for his sign and Boucher engraved the trade card.

Jean-Antoine Watteau was responsible for decorations in the Chinese manner executed for the Pavillon de la Muette, and Boucher's own *Suite de Figures Chinoises* became the inspiration for porcelain figures made by various European factories. Careful distinction must always be made between direct copies of Chinese things made in Europe, and those decorated in the Chinese manner. Numerous books of engravings of Chinese subjects were published, some of which were reasonably authentic as to costume and done either by people who had travelled to China, or under their supervision. Many others, however, came from people who had no direct knowledge of the country or its people and, to them, China was a dream-world of fantasies which were often extremely circuitous derivations from Chinese art. The latter are termed *chinoiseries*, and are a most important manifestation of the vogue.

They are, perhaps, best seen in the porcelain of Meissen, in Saxony, where the early *chinoiseries* were taken from engravings executed by the *Obermaler* to the factory, Johann Gregor Höroldt. Probably the earliest engravings of this kind are in Nieuhof's *Embassy to the Grand Tartar Cham*, published in England in 1669, of which an occasional copy can still be found, whilst the latest are represented by the engravings of Jean Pillement [1727–1808] who framed his fantasies with *rococo* scrolls, and whose work was freely used by some English decorators, notably the engraver, Robert Hancock.

Despite the popularity of Meissen porcelain in France, the French factories did not develop the fantasy element in quite the same way, nor to the same extent. The self-contained world of the Höroldt engravings passed them by, and most things of the kind are more direct copies. They are analogous to the class of Chinese porcelain which copied European engravings with an often comical intrusion of the Chinese idiom, best seen, perhaps, in such subjects as the *Judgement of Paris*, in which the nude goddesses are drawn with a ruthless realism never to be seen in European versions of the same subject.

The fashion had more or less run its course by the middle of the eighteenth century, and the use of Chinese subjects at Vincennes and Sèvres is rare. Most such things came from St. Cloud and Chantilly, where *chinoiseries* and imitations of Japanese styles were comparatively common.

Japanese porcelain was as influential as Chinese if we consider Europe as a whole, although it was rather less frequently used in France than in Germany. The earliest imports were decorated in blue underglaze, and date from the middle of the seventeenth century. Confusion with Chinese porcelain is not unusual. Japanese porcelain decorated in enamel colours began to arrive in Europe towards the end of the century, and in some places it exceeded Chinese porcelain in popularity. When Augustus the Strong bought a palace to house his collection, he called it the Japanische Palais, and not the Chinesische Palais. This leaves hardly any doubt as to which he preferred.

These Japanese imports were nearly all made at Arita in Hizen Province, a very small quantity coming from Kutani in Kaga Province. The style of decoration was particularly associated with the name of a decorator, one Sakaida Kakiemon, and 'Kakiemon' has become a generic name for work in his style. Experts on Far Eastern porcelain distinguish between Arita decoration and that thought to be by the hand of Kakiemon himself, but for the present purpose no such differentiation need be made.

These wares have a characteristic palette of iron-red, bluish-green, light blue, and yellow. The rim is often outlined with chocolate brown, and a little gilding is occasionally present. Very early specimens have underglaze blue in place of the enamel blue.

Typical motifs of decoration are asymmetrical, and a

careful balance is maintained between the pattern and the relatively large areas of white porcelain.

Most Arita porcelain is octagonal, hexagonal, fluted, lobed, or of square section, the latter applying in particular to vases and *saké* bottles. These shapes were probably first used by the Japanese to overcome difficulties in firing the body, which seems to have been prone to distortion during the firing process. The avoidance of wheel-thrown forms commonly used by the Chinese was not unattractive to early European potters, particularly those using a soft paste, since they were facing similar problems. To some extent, therefore, this may account for the popularity of Japanese porcelain as a source of inspiration.

These, then, were some of the influences modifying the *baroque* style of the period of Louis XIV and the succeeding Regency. During the early part of the reign of Louis XV the *baroque* style entered on its final phase, represented by the *rococo*. The transition took place during the period of the Regency, and early examples of the *rococo* are sometimes said to be in the Régence style.

It is difficult to trace the origin of *rococo*, but a considerable part in developing and popularizing it was certainly played by Juste-Aurèle Meissonier, an architect and designer to the King in succession to Bérain, who, in 1725, became a Master of the Paris Guild of Goldsmiths by the intervention of Louis. His designs were characteristic of the style— asymmetricality,* and scroll-work.

*The asymmetrical *rococo cartouches* used by Meissonier and others, as well as the designs for mirror frames which are always excellent examples of the style, may have originated in the *baroque* designs of Paul Decker and the German designers. They published books of symmetrical *cartouches*, and, to save space, showed two separate designs juxtaposed, since (with symmetrical designs) it was unnecessary to show both sides. When invention ran dry, it seems that both sides were used as one design.

In porcelain the earliest examples are much concerned with the theme of water. A typical example is the well-known 'Swan' service of Meissen, the ornament of which was entirely of aquatic motifs, but applied marine shells and such things were not at all uncommon.

After the early period we see the scroll-work, already popular in silver, repeated on the bases of porcelain figures, and in the shapes of vessels. In Germany this scroll-work developed into elaborate arbours which sometimes dwarfed the figures, to be seen for instance in the work of Bustelli at Nymphenburg. This was made possible by the superior plasticity and stability in the kiln of the body used, and the soft porcelain body of the early French manufacturers was not suited to this kind of work. The custom of mounting figures, vases, and vessels with gilded bronze (sometimes called *ormolu* or *or moulu*)* was adopted instead. Mounting porcelain in gilded bronze was a common practice during the reign of Louis XV, but a little work of the kind was done during the early years of the eighteenth century. These mounts are often of superb quality and most elaborate. Those used for figures sometimes have leaves and stalks surmounted by porcelain flowers, and this practice will be discussed in more detail later.

Fundamentally *rococo* differs from *baroque* in being more concerned with ornament than with the thing itself. *Baroque* figures, for instance, are always three-dimensional, and can be viewed from every side. *Rococo* figures and groups

---

*The word *ormolu* has now become such common currency in English to describe the kind of metal used in France for furniture and porcelain mounting, that it is not always realized that it is not strictly correct. The French usually refer to it as *bronze dorée* (gilded bronze), which is precisely what it is. *Or moulu* refers to powdered gold used in conjunction with mercury in the fire-gilding process, and was probably later applied to the fine brass castings by colour analogy.

tend to be very limited in the points from which they can be viewed, the back often being sketchily finished. During this period much use was made of engravings as inspiration for figures and groups, and this is usually fairly obvious. The copy is reasonably faithful in front, but the back reveals the fact that the modeller had nothing to copy.

This apart, *baroque* ornament is always symmetrical. The complicated elements of the *lambrequins* are always balanced by something similar on the other side. *Rococo* ornament, on the other hand, is rarely symmetrical, the elements of one side of a frame, for instance, being different from those of the other.

During the *baroque* and early *rococo* periods French porcelain in particular was greatly influenced by that of Meissen, in Saxony,* and some attention to the work of this factory is therefore essential.

The secret of Chinese porcelain was discovered by a member of the Saxon Court, Ehrenfried Walther von Tschirnhaus, with the assistance of an alchemist, Johann Friedrich Böttger. The factory was supported by Augustus II (known as August der Starke, or 'the Strong') who was Elector of Saxony, and who had, in addition, supplanted Stanislas Leczinski as King of Poland. The work of the period which ended with the death of Böttger in 1719 is markedly *baroque* in style. In 1720 Johann Gregor Höroldt joined the factory, and introduced new styles and a greatly improved palette. He soon became *Obermaler* (chief painter), and Court Painter in addition. A school of decoration developed under his guidance which included *chinoiseries* of a kind not excelled or equalled elsewhere in Europe, both for quality of design and execution. Meissen also took the lead in other directions. Harbour scenes taken from engravings of Italian

*The origin and work of this factory is discussed in detail in my *Eighteenth Century German Porcelain*.

ports, for instance, were particularly successful. The early flower painting was based on Oriental sources, and referred to as *indianische Blumen* because most Far Eastern porcelain was imported through the various East India Companies. This was followed by the representation of natural German flowers, called *deutsche Blumen,* which were taken from various books of engravings.

Starting about 1733 the factory began to produce small figures of cabinet size (*Kleinplastik*) which were used at the time for decorating the banqueting table, as well as enormous centre-pieces made in sections. Much of this work was designed by the Court Sculptor, Johann Joachim Kändler, as well as by others hardly less skilful.

The factory made many superb services, of which the best known is the 'Swan' service made at the orders of Augustus III for his Minister, Count von Brühl, who was also director of the factory. Large objects for decoration such as mirror-frames and small console tables were made, and a mirror of this kind for Louis XV was brought to Paris by Kändler himself. It was destroyed during the Revolution.

Contemporary feeling can be judged from the following extract, the remarks of a lady of the French Court: 'Meissen is certainly rather expensive, but I have eight complete dinner services, quite apart from what I have spent on having my mirrors, candelabra, clocks, toilet-sets, and wardrobes mounted in Saxe. In fact, I have a passion for it which is almost adoration—I am Saxe from head to toe!'

Meissen porcelain is usually referred to as 'Saxe' in France, just as it is nearly always miscalled 'Dresden' in England.

Eventually the *rococo* style was replaced by the *neo-classical.* This began when the ruins of Pompeii were discovered beneath some vineyards near Naples in 1755. The town was destroyed in A.D. 79 by an eruption of Vesuvius, but the falling ash acted as a kind of plaster, encasing the houses, and in some cases the inhabitants, and preserving them. The actual bodies were not entirely preserved, but, here and there, the consolidated ash provided a mould from which a cast could be taken. The art of Roman Italy became extremely popular throughout Europe, and first becomes evident towards the end of the Seven Years War. Its first years in France appear to have started in the 1750s, and, despite the fact that he did not succeed to the throne until 1774, transitional things of this kind are often referred to as being in the *Louis Seize* (Louis XVI) style. Neo-classicism became the fashion towards the end of the century, and it is apparent in an increasing severity of line, as well as in the adoption of classical models, particularly in the decorative arts.

The course taken by the neo-classical style was influenced by a number of factors, not the least being some of the writings of Goethe on which I have commented elsewhere, and the uncompromising hostility of Winckelmann, the German art historian, to the *rococo*. The latter was the chief prophet of the new movement.

The transitional *Louis Seize* style contained some elements of the *rococo* which became less noticeable as the new style took firmer hold. During the Revolutionary period work became extremely severe and the absence of earlier luxury is marked. This was followed by the *Empire* style. The adoption of Consuls and the *Code Napoléon* is sufficient to show the influence of Roman institutions in the political sphere, but the same influences were also at work in the decorative arts. Roman furniture, in particular, was copied with some fidelity, mural paintings at Pompeii, and Greek and Italian vase paintings being used as models. The influence of the Egyptian campaign can be seen in the use of such motifs as the sphinx and scarab.

VIII

Little is known precisely of the composition of the earliest French porcelain from Rouen, a factory established by Louis Poterat in 1673. The same position exists with the products of St. Cloud, founded towards the end of the seventeenth century. Appearance leaves little doubt that they were principally of clay and ground glass.

Some differences are to be observed in the porcelain of Chantilly, a factory founded about 1725 by the Prince de Condé, because the body of the early wares, until about 1750, was disguised to a great extent by the use of a *faïence* glaze. Normal glazes are analogous to a layer, or 'flashing', of clear glass. The addition of tin oxide opacifies glass, and turns it into a dense milky-white substance. In this condition it was commonly used for glazing red or buff earthenware bodies, which are then referred to as *maiolica*, *faïence*, or *delft*.

The Chantilly factory experienced some faults of body colour in their porcelain and adopted this glaze to cover them. Slight traces of iron, for instance, in an otherwise white clay causes it to burn in the kiln to a pale buff, or to assume a slightly reddish tint, and this is, in fact, extremely common. Much Chinese porcelain will show it on unglazed parts, such as the footring, although the fact that, unlike European soft porcelain, body and glaze were fired in one operation prevents the same effect from being seen on glazed parts.

The use of a tin-glaze was an obvious solution for faults of this kind, and whilst it is true that it was a makeshift, such expedients were frequently employed during the eighteenth century in early wares.

The porcelain of Mennecy, established in 1734 under the patronage of the duc de Villeroy, reverted to the technique of Rouen and St. Cloud, with a glassy body and a clear glaze, despite the fact that a limited amount of *faïence* was also made at the same place, so it is evident that they experienced no such trouble with body colour.

The first information of any consequence we have about the actual composition of early French porcelain refers to what was to become the Royal factory of Sèvres. The method of manufacture was to make a glass frit composed mainly of Fontainebleau sand and saltpetre, to which were added small proportions of grey sea salt, alum, soda from Alicante, and gypsum. This was crushed and taken in the proportion of 75% of frit to 12.5% of white chalk, and 12.5% of a chalky clay from Argenteuil. This body, as can be deduced from the small quantity of clay, must have been difficult to handle. It lacked plasticity, and would have been difficult to work by ordinary pottery methods. A proportion of soft soap was therefore added, to the extent of about one-eighth, and this was later replaced by gum tragacanth. The latter is a thick white mucilage which is used for dressing fabrics, and in some kinds of hair-cream.

This body was, obviously, highly unstable, and is, in fact, virtually glass. It was fired in the kiln at about 1,000 degrees Centigrade, and emerged from this process in an unglazed, or *biscuit*, state. The *biscuit* was then sprayed with the glaze material suspended in water. This contained about 38% of lead oxide and 38% of sand, the remaining 24% being fluxes added to promote melting. The glaze melted at the comparatively low temperature of 500 degrees Centigrade, and it is possible to deduce that a glaze of this kind would be thick and unctuous, and likely to remelt in the enamelling kiln to some extent, allowing colours applied to it to sink in. This deduction is confirmed by observation.

The result of these processes was the famous Sèvres *pâte tendre* (soft paste), which produced the finest porcelain of the kind ever to be made. But manufacturing difficulties were great, the proportion of 'wasters' high, and the factory found it impossible to regard this as a material in itself, but only as a substitute for the Chinese secret.

Hard paste porcelain (*pâte dure*) had been manufactured in Germany since 1710, and in Austria since 1720. German porcelain made after about 1720 is, on analysis, practically indistinguishable from the Chinese. Manufacture of this body had also been started in 1752 in Strasbourg (Alsace) by Paul Hannong, who had the assistance of a German technician, by name J. J. Ringler. The consequences of edicts designed to protect the Royal factory caused Hannong to shift across the border to Frankenthal, in the Palatinate. Offers to sell the secret to Sèvres in exchange for permission to keep the factory at Strasbourg were refused because suitable materials could not then be found in France. After the death of Paul Hannong, the secret was sold to Sèvres by his son, Pierre-Antoine, in 1763 in return for an annual pension which was never paid.* Numerous other attempts were made to find a way of making hard porcelain, but these were unsuccessful, and it was not until 1768 that deposits of both *kaolin* (china clay) and *petuntse* (feldspathic rock) were found in France. The hard paste body was introduced in 1769.

The following years show the progressive replacement of soft porcelain by the new hard porcelain, and, in 1800, when Alexandre Brongniart was appointed director of the factory by Napoleon, the manufacture of the former was completely discontinued, and the undecorated stocks sold.

The history of French porcelain, therefore, can be divided into three parts, according to the body used. The first, from its inception until 1769, was a period during which only soft

---

*Pierre-Antoine was given permission to start a *faïence* factory at Vincennes in 1765.

porcelain was used. From 1769 to 1800 both types of body were used. From 1800 onwards the making of soft porcelain was discontinued, and only the hard paste body remained.

This makes the ability to discriminate between the soft and hard pastes of some importance to the student, and the principal tests are appended:

(*a*) Soft porcelain can be cut with a file. This is a crude test, and it is rarely justified. A small file of triangular section, of the kind used for saw-sharpening, is the best tool to use, and the angle should be drawn gently but firmly across the un-glazed base. Only a small cut is necessary, and if the file can be felt to 'bite' instead of sliding across the surface, the test is complete. Deep file cuts are unnecessary, and do not add anything to the information gained. If a cut from a previous test can be seen, repetition is superfluous.

(*b*) Soft porcelains often have air bubbles trapped in the body. Held to the light they appear either as circular patches of greater translucency, or as bright pin-points and specks of light. The larger ones are the so-called 'moons' which can be seen in a number of English soft pastes, but are not so often seen in the French varieties. They are to be seen parti-cularly in plates and dishes that have been thrown on a wheel with the aid of a jolley—a template used to fashion the reverse side of a dish, which is revolved on a wheel for the purpose. They appear very occasionally in some hard porcelains, and are not, in themselves, a certain indication.

(*c*) Firecracks (i.e. splitting of the body due to unequal contraction during cooling) and warping (i.e. sagging out of shape) are both fairly common faults in early wares, which appear much less frequently in hard porcelain than in the soft variety. At important factories, such as Sèvres, if either of these faults was serious, the piece was discarded as a waster. True firecracks are not accidental damage, and are only a detraction in the sense that a specimen is more de-sirable without them. They should not lead a collector necessarily to reject a very early specimen merely on this account, since they are commonest in the earliest things, and rarely to be seen in the work of an established factory. The term sometimes applied to them, 'age cracks', is a misnomer. No porcelain develops cracks as the result of age.

(*d*) Much soft porcelain is slightly porous. A little stain touched on an unglazed part is often difficult to wipe off. On hard porcelain it wipes off immediately. Underfired specimens of soft porcelain, where the body is not completely vitrified, will absorb ink like blotting paper, but this is unusual, and it is more or less confined to the English bone-ash porcelains, such as Bow and stray specimens of later Chelsea. Dirt on unglazed soft porcelain is often very difficult to remove. On hard porcelain it can be washed off without trouble.

(*f*) The body of soft porcelain was fired first, and the glaze added afterwards at a much lower temperature. The body and glaze of hard porcelain were fired in one operation as a general rule, but even when they were not, the hard porcelain glaze is feldspathic, and made of a similar substance to an important ingredient of the body. Hard porcelain glazes, therefore, are thin and glittering, and appear to be homogeneous with the body. Soft porcelain glazes are thicker, richer, and inclined to run in drops, to pool in hollows, to crack, and to craze. Where it is thickest it is often greenish or yellowish in colour. Soft porcelain glazes often collected under the base, which had to be ground in consequence. The effect of such grinding is always obvious.

(*g*) The glaze is soft on soft porcelain, and will often show multiple scratches as the result of wear and tear. Hard porcelain glazes scratch much less easily, and only by something harder than themselves. Since they cannot be scratched by a steel knife, the reader can judge how frequently they are likely to have been in contact with something hard enough to leave a mark.

(*h*) Enamel colours often sink into a soft porcelain glaze at least to some extent. Enamels on hard porcelain will lie on top of the glaze, and can be felt with the finger tips.

(*i*) Where there is a chip, most soft porcelain will exhibit a granular texture akin to icing sugar, whereas hard porcelain chips and flakes like glass or flint.

French porcelain during the period under review was decorated either by painting or by relief-work. The latter is fairly common in the early wares, particularly on those from St. Cloud. The style of ornament was copied, for the most part, from the *blanc de chine* of Tê Hua (Fukien Province), and usually took the form of flowering prunus sprays. Towards the end of the century some relief work in the manner of Wedgwood was undertaken.

By far the greater number of specimens have been painted, and two different methods of applying pigments are to be seen. The first is cobalt blue painted before the glaze was applied. For this reason such decoration is referred to as 'underglaze'. Underglaze blue was in common use on Chinese and Japanese porcelain, but it gave much difficulty to the German potters who were using a similar body. It was not introduced at Meissen for almost fifteen years after the founding of the factory. No such difficulties appear to have been experienced by soft porcelain makers, and in France it was the first colour to be used, whilst, in England, it was in common use before the application of colours over the glaze had been mastered.

Most French porcelain was decorated in overglaze or enamel colours, and during the mid-century the underglaze colours were only used for porcelain intended to cater for the cheapest market. Enamels are a kind of glass paste, and the *faïence* glaze is, itself, a white enamel, such wares being sometimes referred to as 'tin-enamelled'. The art of enamelling on copper was by no means a new one in France, the enamels of Limoges, for instance, being held in great esteem. Enamelling on a porcelain glaze is similar in many ways. The pigments—metallic oxides—are the same although there are differences in the vehicles and the fluxes used. The iron, copper, and manganese oxides, between them, provide a palette of considerable diversity, especially when they are blended. Copper, itself, provides varying shades of blue and green according to the manner of use, and the type of glaze on which it is painted. The vehicle is merely to make application easy, and fluxes lower the melting point to a temperature below that of the glaze to which they are applied.

For the most part, the colours develop in the kiln, and the painter could not, therefore, see the final effect of his work until it had been fired. Sometimes four or five firings were necessary to fix successively applied colours. The low temperature kiln in which this was done is called an enamelling or 'muffle' kiln.

I once had an eighteenth-century enamel painter's guide. This was painted with samples of all the shades available on the palette, each of which was numbered. The guide, of course, was fired so that the numbered colours developed the correct shade and intensity, and the colours on the palette were also numbered. The artist first referred to the guide for the colour he needed and noted the number. He then took colour on his brush from the appropriately numbered pot on his palette. In this way he was able to paint a picture on prepared copper or porcelain without seeing the actual colours until they had been fired.

Although these colours were painted on the glaze of soft porcelain, this sometimes remelted slightly in the enamelling kiln, allowing the pigments to sink into the glaze, and in some cases they appear almost to be below the surface. It must be remembered that only blue and manganese (a colour varying between purple and brown) were ever used under the glaze during the eighteenth century, and any example of true underglaze colours other than these must be nineteenth century or later.

Much use was made at Sèvres of coloured grounds, and these are discussed in more detail later. At this point it is sufficient to say that porcelain with coloured grounds (in German, *Fondporzellan*) has areas of unbroken colour with, usually, some panels left in white (reserved panels) which were used for decorative painting. These panels had a ragged edge, and this was generally disguised by gilding. Colours were applied in various ways—with a sponge, or blown on in powder form, for example—and in eighteenth-century porcelain are often uneven in density and application, whereas nineteenth-century and modern grounds are usually flawless and of perfect density. Ground colours can be over or under the glaze. Cobalt blue and manganese grounds are underglaze, the others were applied after glazing.

Much use was made of gilding at Sèvres, although it is not often seen elsewhere until towards the end of the eighteenth century.

Most figures from Vincennes and Sèvres are in *biscuit*, or unglazed porcelain, and these were a speciality of the Sèvres factory. A few glazed and coloured figures were made, but specimens are very rare. Glazed figures from the other French factories are also comparatively scarce in the early period, and not particularly frequent later. The greater part of French production was devoted to service-ware and such decorative items as vases.

The method adopted in the manufacture of figures is similar to that used elsewhere. An artist of repute first made a model in clay or wax. This was dissected, and each part was moulded. Arms, legs, heads, torsos, and any attributes, were all moulded separately, and a cast taken in the porcelain body. These parts were then assembled and 'luted' (or cemented) together with slip, which is clay diluted to a creamy consistency. The workman who did this was called, in England, a 'repairer', and his intervention led to distinct but minor variations in the pose of models. Lead master-models were sometimes cast so that fresh moulds could be taken of popular figures. In this way figures could be repeated, and the number of repetitions varied with the popularity of the model at the time, or the purpose for which it was made. Some models were made in greater quantities than others.

CHAPTER I

A Survey of French Decorative Art in the Seventeenth and Eighteenth Centuries

IT would be difficult to write an appreciation of French porcelain, and in particular that of Sèvres, without some reference to its background, since much of it was intimately connected with the Court, and it is, in any case, an integral part of the interior decoration of the period.

Until the death of Mazarin there was little that could be regarded as a style peculiarly French. Indeed, almost everything had at least some traces of Italian, Flemish, or Spanish influence, and the style which we now associate particularly with France seems to have stemmed from the Manufacture royale de la Meuble de la Couronne already mentioned.

The initial impetus which led to the national style was due to Simon Vouet, who was Court Painter to Louis XIII from 1627. Le Brun was his pupil, and the influence of Le Brun was predominant in the design of many of the furnishings and decorations of Versailles and other royal residences. The furniture of the period of Vouet was massive, and architectural details of interiors elaborate. As an example, chimney-pieces generally framed a painting, and the surrounding carving was extremely rich. Usually, there was a *cartouche* surrounded by symmetrical *baroque* ornament, and doors, similarly, had elaborately-carved cresting, the stiles being decorated in the same way. Plaster-work by imported Italian craftsmen assumed considerable importance in the decoration of ceilings and walls, and panels were left in which decorative paintings were executed.

Furniture, too, was architectural in form, oak and walnut being extensively used. Very little was left uncarved, but the work was always coherent and appropriate. The influence of architecture is obvious in such things as pediments and supporting pillars to cabinets, whilst panels were carved in relief or inlaid with metal. Acanthus foliage was a frequent motif, and *grotesques*, such as winged animal bodies with human heads, or human bodies terminating in pedestals or foliate scrolls, are not uncommon. The human mask, too, is often to be seen, and was usually surrounded by foliate scrolls. *Grotesques* have a long line of descent from Roman decorative art by way of Raphaël, and they appear quite commonly on Italian *maiolica*—in an early variety at Deruta, and drawn more light-heartedly at Urbino later in the sixteenth century.

In passing, it is interesting to note that the elaborately-carved chairs with high backs and cane seats popular in England during the Restoration were derived from very similar chairs of the time of Louis XIII, whilst chairs having slung leather backs and seats held into position by brass nails with large hemispherical heads, to be seen during the Commonwealth period, also came from France, although they were originally Spanish. Upholstery became the vogue in France during the first part of the seventeenth century, and such exotic materials as silks from Lyons and Venice, as well as velvets from Genoa and Utrecht, were used for the purpose.

One of the first mirrors of Venetian glass to be seen in France was installed by Henry IV [d. 1610] at Fontainebleau, and the use of mirrors later developed into the magnificent 'Galerie des Glaces' at Versailles.

Undoubtedly the most influential designer of the period, who epitomizes the *baroque* style, was Jean Bérain (*père*) who was born in 1638. His first appointment was as designer to Louis XIV in which capacity he was responsible not only for interior decoration, but for scenery and costumes for Court *fêtes*, balls, masquerades, and *ballets*. His son was also a designer of no little merit in the same tradition who did some excellent work for the Gallery of Apollo in the Louvre. The designs of these two men were much used for furniture, *faïence* and porcelain decoration, silver, tapestries, such small items as fire-dogs, and so forth, and for the architectural details of interiors. Even sedan-chairs decorated in their characteristic style exist.

The most outstanding feature of many Bérain designs is a central motif, usually of a figure or a figure-subject under a *baldacchino*, or canopy. *Grotesques* are common. Half-figures terminating in architectural detail or in twisted fish-tails, a head terminating in a single leg, a crouching sphinx with the head and breasts of a woman, and masks surrounded by foliate ornament, are typical, and they are drawn with the lightness of touch comparable with the later *grotesques* of Urbino *maiolica*. The *grotesques* were usually accompanied by more naturally-drawn figures of *putti* and such things, as well as swags of flowers and fruit, and the elements of the design were joined by typically *baroque* strap-work, which is not only characteristic of much *Louis Quartorze* ornament, but appears, for instance, in the *Laub- und Bandelwerk* (leaf- and strap-work) to be seen on some early Meissen and Vienna porcelain.

The designs of Bérain were used for much of the cabinet work of André Charles Boulle which, apart from being massive and well-proportioned, was decorated with an elaborate marquetry executed in tortoiseshell and brass. In addition to the principal design, the brass was engraved with such Bérain details as *grotesques*.

Typically *baroque*, too, are the designs of Daniel Marot [1650–1700] who was also architect to William III of England, some parts of Hampton Court Palace being attributable to him. He designed for Boulle, and clock-cases of the period in the characteristic brass and tortoiseshell marquetry are often his work. His architectural details—chimneypieces and overdoors—are typical of the period, but although he made much use of elaborate strap-work, he was less inclined to the use of *grotesques*.

Lambrequins properly so-called, belong to the seventeenth century, and Marot designed many of them. Originally *lambrequins* were bed-valances, and hangings to the canopy. Early hangings had been plain, although the fabrics used had been decorated and fringed, but *lambrequins* were looped and tasselled. *Lambrequins* used on porcelain and described in the Introduction were derived, in part, from these drapes.

Beds were important items of furniture, since it was the custom to receive friends whilst in bed, and the King gave audiences to his subjects before rising. The King's bed was known as the *Lit de Parade*, which is sufficient indication of its position.

Ceiling-painting was of considerable importance, and some of the work of this kind at Versailles was done by Le Brun. These paintings were given a rich surround of plaster ornament, and gilding was often added lavishly. The effect of this kind of interior decoration, added to the sumptuous Boulle cabinets, which were still further ornamented with gilt bronze castings, and to Gobelins tapestries as wall-hangings, gave an effect of incomparable luxury and splendour.   Grandeur was, indeed, the effect at which the decorators of the period aimed, and this they attained partly

Plate 17 (a). Miniature teapot painted with the Quail pattern after Sakaida Kakiemon. Chantilly. c. 1735. (V&AM.)

(b). Teapot painted with cranes in the Kakiemon style. Chantilly, c. 1735. (Bedford-Cecil Higgins Colln.)

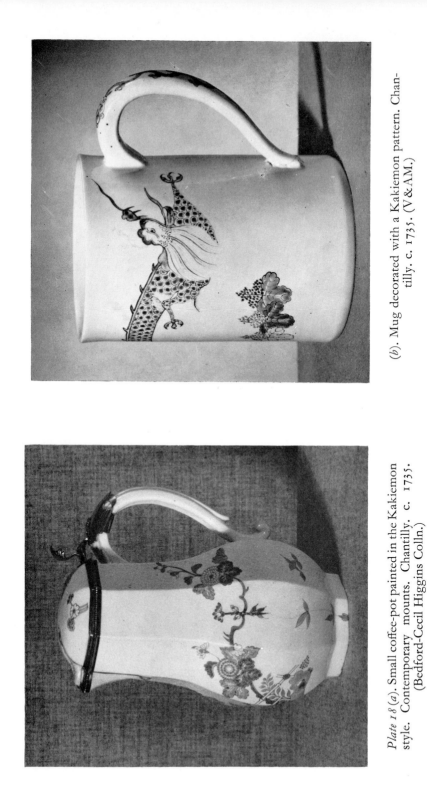

Plate 18 (a). Small coffee-pot painted in the Kakiemon style. Contemporary mounts. Chantilly. c. 1735. (Bedford-Cecil Higgins Colln.)

(b). Mug decorated with a Kakiemon pattern. Chantilly. c. 1735. (V&AM.)

Plate 19 (*a*). Tureen, cover, stand and ladle painted in the Kakiemon style with *indianische Blumen*. Chantilly. c. 1735. (V & A M.)

(*b*). Flower holder painted in the Kakiemon style. Chantilly. c. 1735. (Ashmolean-Andrade Colln.)

Plate 20 (a). Apothecary jar. Chantilly. c. 1735.
(V&AM.)

(*b*). *Cachepot* bearing the Arms of Condé with the order of
Saint Esprit. Chantilly. Hunting horn and 'LP' monogram in
blue. After 1752. (V&AM.)

Plate 21. Cachepot decorated with a boy in a landscape in purple monochrome. Chantilly. Hunting horn mark in red. c. 1755. (V&AM.)

(b). Plate with the Cipher of Louis-Philippe, duc d'Orléans, from a service made for his chateau. Mark: hunting horn and *Villers cotteret* in blue enamel. c. 1755. (V&AM.)

Plate 22 (a). Plate painted with flowers in blue, the basket-work border inspired by Meissen *ozier* patterns. Chantilly. Hunting horn mark and 'L' in blue enamel. c. 1755. (V&AM.)

Plate 23. Pair of figures, the woman in European costume, the man in Chinese robes decorated with Kakiemon flowers. Chantilly. c. 1735. A white pair in the Chavagnac sale were marked with the letter C. (V&AM.)

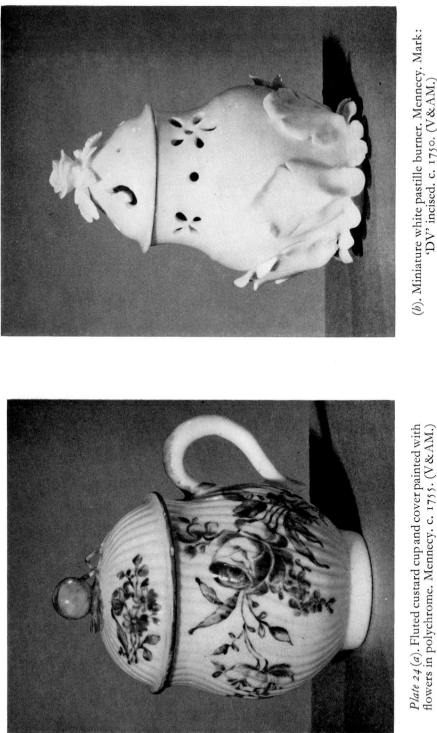

(b). Miniature white pastille burner. Mennecy. Mark: 'DV' incised. c. 1750. (V&AM.)

Plate 24 (a). Fluted custard cup and cover painted with flowers in polychrome. Mennecy. c. 1755. (V&AM.)

Plate 25. Vase painted in polychrome. Mennecy. Mark: 'DV' incised.
c. 1755. (V&AM.)

Plate 26. Sucrier painted with flowers in polychrome. Mennecy. Mark:
'DV' incised. c. 1755. (V&AM.)

Plate 27 (a). Dish with polychrome flower sprays.
Mark: 'DV' incised. c. 1755. (V&AM.)

(b). Tureen in the form of a rabbit. Mennecy. c. 1755. (Ashmolean-Andrade Colln.)

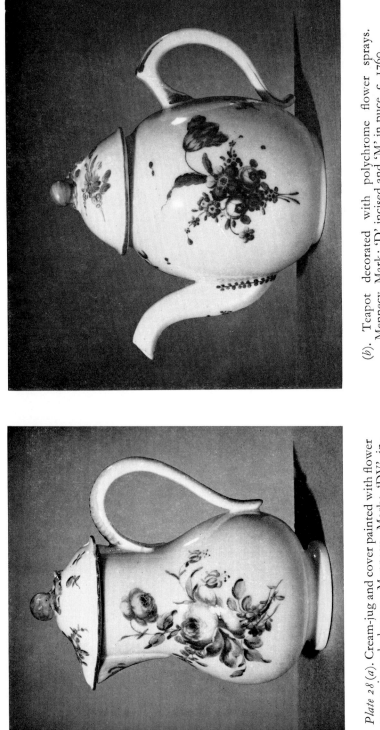

(b). Teapot decorated with polychrome flower sprays. Mennecy. Mark: 'D' incised and 'M' in puce. c. 1760. (V&AM.)

Plate 28 (a). Cream-jug and cover painted with flower sprays in polychrome. Mennecy. Mark: 'DV' incised. c. 1760. (V&AM.)

Plate 29. Coffee-pot of *faïence* form painted in enamel colours. Mennecy.
Mark: 'DV' incised. c. 1755. (V&AM.)

Plate 30 (a). Pair of toilet-pots in the form of boars' heads in contemporary leather case in the form of books entitled *Bail* (lease) *des Fermes.* Mennecy. c. 1750. (BM.)

(b). Pair of dwarfs after Jacques Callot. Rue de Charonne. c. 1740. (Ashmolean-Andrade Colln.)

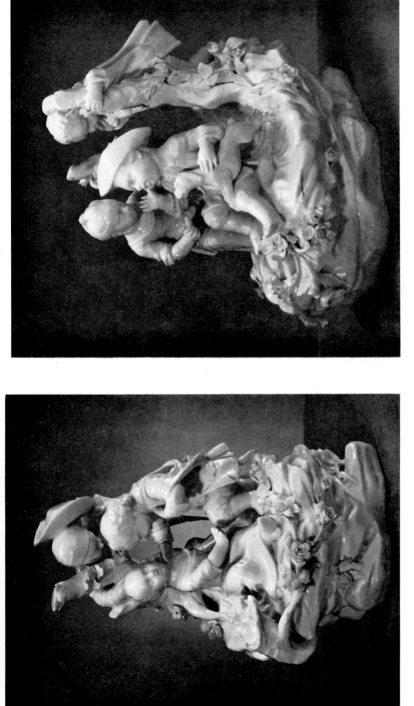

Plate 31 (*a*). Child group on a rockwork base. Mennecy (probably Rue de Charonne—see page 97). Before 1748. (V&AM.)

(*b*). Child group on a rockwork base. Mennecy (probably Rue de Charonne—see page 97). Before 1748. (V&AM.)

(*b*). An actor, decorated in colours, from a comedy part. Mennecy. c. 1755. (Metropolitan.)

Plate 32 (*a*). Figure in Eastern costume. Mennecy. c. 1750. (V&AM.)

(*c*). Zeus and Hera mounted on a cloud-scroll base. Mennecy. c. 1760. (Ashmolean-Andrade Colln.)

by the use of exotic materials, and partly by displays of virtuosity in craftsmanship.* To do this they trod a perilous path, on one side of which yawned a precipice ready to engulf them in a *parvenu* style of little merit. Most conscious attempts to achieve grandeur end precisely in this way, and it is a tribute to the skill of Le Brun in particular that the danger was nearly always avoided.

Exotic materials by themselves were not enough. Much thought and skill went to the designing of ornament. In turn this led to the use of combinations of materials to achieve the desired effect. The mounts of gilded bronze used for furniture, porcelain, porphyry, and things of the kind are an example. Tapestry, too, was used for upholstery, and panels of lacquer were popular for use in the making of cabinets. These lacquer panels came from the Far East, and were made by repeatedly painting the gum of the tree, *Rhus Vernicifera*, suitably dyed with pigments, over wooden panels until a sufficient thickness had been achieved. These panels were decorated in various ways—by carving and incision, by painting with lacquer, and with gold and silver. Red lacquer is particularly sumptuous in appearance. Later,

*Dr. Martin Lister, writing in 1698, has this to say:

'As the Houses are magnificent without, so the Finishing within side and Furniture answer in Riches and Neatness, as with Hangings of Rich Tapestry, raised with Gold and Silver Threads, Crimson Damask and Velvet Beds, or of Gold and Silver Tissue. Cabinets and Bureaus of Ivory inlaid with Tortoiseshell, and Gold and Silver Plates in a 100 different manners: Branches and Candlesticks of Crystal; but above all most rare Pictures. The Gildings, Carvings and Paintings of the Roof are admirable. . . . You can come into no private House of any Man of Substance but you see something of them: and they are observed frequently to ruine themselves in these Expences. Here as soon as ever a Man gets any thing by Fortune or Inheritance he lays it out in some such way as now named.'

imitation lacquer panels were made in *Vernis Martin*, an extremely durable varnish invented by a coach-painter named Martin. His specially-prepared panels were painted on by such artists as Lancret and Boucher, and many such things as snuff-boxes, *étuis*, and so forth, were made and decorated in this way.

Tapestries played a large part in the total effect. The best came from the Gobelins factory and from Beauvais. Le Brun was a director of the Gobelins manufacture, and the designs of the period are of the utmost magnificence, many being provided by him. Colbert supported the project lavishly with money, and the best work was done during his tenure of office. Many tapestry designs after Bérain were done at Beauvais, which was also supported by Colbert, whilst Jean-Baptiste Oudry was a later director of Gobelins who supplied it with his characteristic designs.

Floor-coverings were not forgotten. Oriental carpets from Persia and Turkey were imported, and a factory for the manufacture of carpets in the Turkish style was established in Paris on the site of a disused soap-factory, which is the reason for the peculiar name of 'Savonnerie' given to them. These products are of the finest possible quality, with designs in keeping with the period.

Much use was made of marble, both now and later. The earlier black and white marbles of the first part of the seventeenth century gave way to marbles of various colours, some from re-opened French quarries, and others from Italy and Africa. Apart from walls, staircases, pillars, and so forth, marble was used as tops for commodes, side-tables, and cabinets. Glass chandeliers, too, were extensively employed in all the State apartments, as well as numerous mirrors handsomely framed.

The *baroque* style by no means ended with the coming of the Regency. This can be seen in the work of Nicolas Pineau

[1684–1754] who was a pupil of the architect, Mansard. Pineau did much woodcarving, and some of his designs for mirror frames about this time are perfectly symmetrical, although they are also extremely elaborate. Some have a mask more or less in the *baroque* style, others a pecten or scallop shell ornament which foreshadows a later *rococo* motif. The work of the cabinet-maker to the Regent, Charles Cressent [1685–1765], is also typical of the Regency style. Much of his work was carried out in rich woods with gilt bronze mounts, but symmetry was still the rule, and it is not until the advent of Juste-Aurèle Meissonier that we see any important changes.

Meissonier had a wide reputation as a designer which extended beyond the frontiers of France. He did many designs for the nobility of Poland and Portugal, an example being interiors for the Count Bielanski in 1734. His earlier designs show but slight departure from symmetry, but, in furniture for Count Bielanski designed in 1735, the *rococo* scroll-work is fairly well-marked. Meissonier's later designs for silver table-ware and centre-pieces show the early *rococo* theme of water particularly well, the salts being in the form of nautilus shells, whilst the triple salts are distinctly reminiscent of those to be seen slightly later in French porcelain, and from the English factory at Bow about 1750. The centre-pieces have such motifs as dolphins (perhaps to be expected), lobsters, and other marine animals, on a base of typical *rococo* scrolls of a kind also to be seen in the gilt-bronze mounts of Duplessis used for the early porcelain of Vincennes and Sèvres.

The work of François Boucher, because of his particular connection with Sèvres, is discussed at length in the chapter on that factory, but he had considerable influence on the development of the *rococo* style.

The first move away from the extravagances of the later

rococo can be seen in the work of Jacques François Blondel, appointed architect to Louis XV in 1755. The work of Charles Etienne Briseaux [1680–1754] is also, for the most part, notable for its avoidance of the wilder kinds of *rococo* ornament. The grand manner which had been the key-note of decoration during the reign of Louis XIV and the period of the Regent slowly gave place, first to scenes of gallantry, and then to contrived pastoral scenes typified by Boucher's shepherds and shepherdesses.

Despite the occasional indications of coming change, the furniture of the mid-century was still notable for its marquetry and for the quality of its gilt-bronze mounts by Jacques Caffiéri [1678–1755] and others. This tendency reached its apogee in the *bureau du Roi* made for Louis XV, which was begun by Oeben in 1760 and completed by Riesener in 1769, with mounts by Duplessis, the Court goldsmith, and others. Marquetry of the finest quality was done in the latter part of the eighteenth century both by Riesener and Roentgen, whilst during the same period the mounts of Gouthière were greatly esteemed. Much furniture was decorated with porcelain plaques made at Sèvres.

The *Louis Seize* style is marked by plainer, more severe designs, although the materials are often as rich and exotic in quality and kind. Such motifs as classical urns, and swags of husk ornament, appear on candelabra and things of the sort. This tendency to severity of line increased as the end of the century drew nearer, and a tendency for the relationship of width to height to alter is apparent. The furniture of *Louis Quatorze* and *Louis Quinze* is, on the whole, considerably wider in proportion, whilst *Louis Seize* cabinets are often taller and narrower, thus reducing the massiveness of appearance. Trophies of arms, musical instruments, and implements appropriate to the arts, appear as inlays, and the use of classical figures in decoration was common. The influence of Marie-Antoinette was undoubtedly in favour of former magnificence, but contemporary fashions were against it.

Chairs and settees no longer had the *rococo* scroll-work of former times, and the frames tended to simplicity of ornament with tapered and fluted legs. The practice of covering them with tapestry from Beauvais and elsewhere, commonly with designs after Watteau, still continued, however, and relieved the severity.

The neo-classical style took firmer hold on French taste after the wars in Italy and the Egyptian campaign. Even during the reign of Louis XVI we notice walls painted with motifs reminiscent of Pompeian wall-paintings, and now the bas-reliefs and vase paintings of ancient Italy were also pressed into service by designers. Thus, we find the use of the sphinx for the arms of chairs and so forth as evidence of the Egyptian campaign, whilst caryatids, and human and animal heads terminating in a single foot, were used as supports for tables. Graeco-Roman busts were used as adornments for cabinets, and candelabra were decorated with *chimerae* in the manner of those excavated from Pompeii. Some hint of the earlier *grotesques* can be seen in the mural designs of Charles Normand [1765–1840], whilst Percier and Fontaine, the architects to Napoleon, designed furniture and decorations which included classical features.

In comparison with the earlier exercise in the grand manner to be seen in the work of the period of Louis Quatorze, that of Napoleon is heavy and pompous, and the revived Greek and Roman decorations never seem to come to life. In between we have the styles of *Louis Quinze*, and to some extent those of *Louis Seize*. *Rococo* has been well described as playful, and the Court turned from serious things to the masquerade, the pastoral entertainment, and to innumerable amorous intrigues amid the endless corridors of Versailles. The death of Madame de Pompadour in 1764 may have had something to do with the gradual supersession of *rococo* by neo-classicism, and with the change of mood noticeable in the work of the reign of Louis XVI. The Revolution led to still greater severity of treatment. Customers no longer existed for the more exotic things. Either they had no money, or they had been decapitated, and many craftsmen perforce had to turn their hands to something else.

It is important to remember the very different status of the artist during the period under review from that of the artist today. Contemporary taste did not place a painter above a master cabinet-maker in importance because of their differing functions. One provided the furniture, the other decorated the walls, and the final result was achieved by a collaboration between all kinds of artists and designers, often with someone like Le Brun acting as co-ordinator.

The painter or the sculptor, therefore, occupied a position in society completely different from that of the present. He did not produce records of a state of mind, or attempt to communicate his moods. His job was to fulfil the customer's requirements. The patron did not take what he was given and try to understand it. He placed an order with the artist and specified his requirements. He chose an artist because he preferred the style in which he knew his order would be executed.

It is not my intention to discuss the validity of these two points of view, merely to record their existence, but I am by no means unsympathetic to the artist of today in his dilemma. Had he lived in the eighteenth century, his customer would have been a man of taste whose requirements would have been congenial. During the nineteenth century, as the result of wars, revolutions, and industrial progress, money and taste became widely separated in many cases, and since the artist of spirit could not please both his customer and himself, he chose to please himself. Now that freedom has been won, the artist, quite often, does not know what to do with it. He produces introspective pictures because he no longer works under a discipline. No doubt he would have been a happier man in the eighteenth century, and it is one of the principal causes of bad design in the making of things for contemporary use and ornament, that the artist is rarely called upon to make them.

Porcelain in France did not reach its full stature until the mid-century with the rise of the Vincennes-Sèvres factory.

The earliest wares were mainly imitations of Oriental porcelain, of motifs copied from *faïence*, and of metal-work. These things they replaced. The first truly original French style adapted to the interior decoration of the period can be seen from Vincennes soon after 1750, where the earlier copying of Oriental and German styles was speedily abandoned.

Manufacture was principally aimed at supplying the Court, and the services, and decorative wares generally, are particularly noted for superb ground colours, painting in reserves, and lavish gilding. The use of white *biscuit* porcelain for figure-work provided an effective contrast to the magnificence of the remainder of the interior, with its exotic furniture, pictures, painted and moulded ceilings, and tapestry-hung walls. The taste of the time can well be seen from the extract quoted from the travels of Dr. Martin Lister earlier in this chapter, and circumstances remained unchanged almost until the end of the eighteenth century.

Although Sèvres sometimes made serious errors of taste, there can be no doubt that its porcelain was the most luxurious ever to be produced, and many of the objections which might otherwise be advanced on purist grounds, must necessarily disappear when it is considered in relation to the setting for which it was intended.

The later porcelain of the Paris factories was, for the most part, but a distant echo of Sèvres magnificence, made for people who wanted to follow Court fashions at a price within their means. Inevitably it assumed the vices of all such things. Nothing is more tawdry and meretricious than an object which apes a luxury product in cheap materials with inferior workmanship.

CHAPTER II

The Earliest French Porcelain

THE history of the beginning of porcelain manufacture in France is a complicated and contradictory tangle. Most writers have been content either to avoid discussion, or to record the facts without an attempt to reconcile them. Possibly I should be wiser to do the same, but I have a particular dislike of loose ends, and what follows is offered as a possible solution.

The difficulty is two-fold. Some conflicting facts about the beginning of the St. Cloud factory have to be resolved, and some attributions to these early factories need to be re-examined in the light of these facts.

In 1664 a privilege was granted to Claude and François Révérend for the manufacture of porcelain. The Révérends were Paris merchants who imported tin-glazed *faïence* from Delft, in Holland, and the privilege allowed them the sole right to make porcelain in the Chinese manner in and around Paris for the term of fifty years.

In 1670 Louis XIV built the Trianon de Porcelaine at Versailles for his mistress, Madame de Montespan. This, of course, was not of porcelain. Quite obviously *faïence* must be understood here, and Révérend supplied some of the

73

tiles, others coming from Rouen. Unfortunately this edifice no longer exists. It was pulled down in 1687.

It is a matter of common observation that the term *porcelain* was frequently used in Germany, Holland, and elsewhere in place of *faïence*. It is not always clear exactly what was meant. It could, of course, have been used of *faïence* generally, or, later, of *faïence* decorated in enamel colours in the manner of porcelain, and in many cases it seems fairly obvious that the latter explanation is correct.

There is a record that François Révérend employed Dutch workmen in 1667 at a factory at St. Cloud, between Paris and Versailles, and no doubt the tiles they supplied came from here. This factory was under the direction of one Morin, almost certainly to be identified with François de Morin who read a paper to the *Académie des Sciences* in 1692 on the manufacture of porcelain.

The type of porcelain made during the early period by Révérend, probably with the assistance of Morin, cannot be identified with certainty. A few experimental pieces marked with the initials 'A.P.' and a star have been conjecturally attributed to him. They are poor in quality and resemble contemporary *faïence*.

In 1698 Dr. Martin Lister, later physician to Queen Anne, came to Paris with the Duke of Portland, and on his return to London wrote a book about his travels. He mentions seeing M. Morin at St. Cloud, referring to him as the proprietor of the establishment who had, for twenty-five years, experimented with porcelain, but had only reached a successful conclusion three years before, leaving us to infer a date of about 1695 or a little earlier.

He also writes:

> 'I saw the potterie of St Clou with which I was marvellously well pleased, for *I confess I could not distinguish betwixt the pots made there and the finest China ware I ever saw*. It will, I know,

be easily granted me that the painting may be better designed
and finished (as indeed it was) because our men are far better
masters of that art than the Chineses; but the glazing came
not in the least behind theirs, not for whiteness, nor the
smoothness of running without bubbles. Again, the inward
substance and matter of the pots was, to me, the very same,
hard and firm as marble, and the self same grain on this side
vitrification. Farther, *the transparency of the pots the very same.*'*

*This account of the factory is extremely interesting, apart from
the light it throws on porcelain manufacture at the time, and I have,
therefore, given the remainder of it below:

'I see them also in the Mold, undried and before the Painting and Glazing was applied, they were as white as Chalk, and
melted upon the Tongue like raw Tobacco Pipe Clay, and felt
between the teeth soft like that, and very little gritty; so that I
doubt not, but they are made of that very Clay.

'As to the Temper of the Clay, the Man freely owned to me,
it was 3 or 4 times well beaten and wet, before it was put to
work on the Wheel; but I believe it must first be melted in fair
Water, and carefully drawn off, that the heaviest part may first
sink; which also may be proper for Courser Works.

'That it requires two, and sometimes 3 or 4 Fires to bake it,
to that height we saw it in the most finisht Pots: Nay, some of
them had had 11 Fires.

'I did not expect to have found it in this perfection, but
imagined this might have arrived at the Gomron [Gombroon]
Ware, which is, indeed, little else, but a total Vitrification, but
I found it far otherwise, and very surprising, and which I
account part of the felicity of the Age to equal, if not to
surpass the Chineses in their finest Art.

'As for the Red Ware of China [Yi-Hsing stoneware], that
has been, and is done in England, to a far great perfection
than in China, we having as good Materials, viz. the Soft
Haematites, and far better Artists in Pottery. But in this
particular we are beholding to two Dutchmen Brothers [the
Elers] who wrought in Staffordshire and were not long since
at Hammersmith.

'They sold these Pots at St. Clou at excessive Rates; and for
their ordinary Chocolate Cups askt Crowns a-piece. They had
arrived at Burning on Gold in neat Chequer Works. He had
some Furniture of Tea Tables at 400 Livres a Sett.

The italics are mine, but his words are important to a hypothesis advanced later. The reference to transparency makes it quite obvious that Lister was well-acquainted with porcelain, and since all the porcelain hitherto attributed to St. Cloud has a creamy or ivory tone, he has been reproached with poor powers of observation in suggesting that it so closely resembled Chinese. The remainder of his remarks are sufficiently acute, however, and I suggest that, in fact, he was not looking at the porcelain now called St. Cloud, but at something which, in the colour of its glaze, more nearly resembled Chinese porcelain of the period of the Emperor Wan Li with which Lister was most probably familiar.

Contemporary records suggest that another *faïence* factory existed at St. Cloud at the same time. A reference in 1691 says: 'There is a *faïence* factory at St. Cloud where they can make anything you like.' It seems probable that this was under the direction of Henri Charles Trou, bailiff to the Duc d'Orléans. He is recorded as a master-*faïencier* in 1679, in

---

'There was no Molding or Model of China Ware which they had not imitated; and had added many Fancies of their own, which had their good effects, and appeared very beautiful.

'Mons. Morin in Conversation told me, that they kept their Sand as a Secret to themselves, but this could not be for other purposes than Colouring: Also he said they used Salt of Kelp in the composition, and made a thing not unlike Frit for Glass to be wrought up with White Clay; neither could this be, for I did not taste it in the Raw Pots.

'The Ingenuous [sic] Master told me, he had been 25 years about the Experiment, but had not attained it fully, till within this 3 years.'

Comments in brackets are mine.

It is perhaps significant that we find, on an earlier page, the following:

'I visited Monsieur Morin, one of the Académie des Sciences a man very curious in minerals, &c.'

which year he married Berthe Coudray, widow of one Pierre Chicanneau.

In 1702 Louis XIV granted a privilege to 'Berthe Coudray, widow of Pierre Chicanneau, and to Jean-Baptiste, Pierre, and Geneviève Chicanneau, brothers and sister, the children of the before-mentioned Coudray and Pierre Chicanneau, undertakers of the *faïence* and porcelain works at St. Cloud.'

This goes on to attribute the discovery of porcelain to Pierre Chicanneau, and refers to the family having continued manufacture after his death, until, before 1693, they had arrived at the point of making porcelain of perfect quality.

There is no reason to suspect that the terms of this privilege depart seriously from the truth, and it indicates that the manufacture of porcelain had been carried on for a considerable time by Chicanneau and his family.

We are thus faced with two sets of circumstances, apparently contradictory. We can choose between the privilege on the one hand, or the evidence of Lister on the other, as a correct representation of the facts, or we must suppose two factories. Personally, I think the weight of the evidence is in favour of the latter. Had Lister provided the only evidence for the part played by Morin, it could quite well have been dismissed as a misunderstanding, but, to my mind, Morin's paper on the manufacture of porcelain is good corroboratory evidence of Lister's statement.

Among the marks of the Chicanneau factory we find '*St. C T*'. It is assumed, but without certainty, that the letters stand for 'St. Cloud Trou' and refer to a period from 1722 onwards when Henri Trou II became proprietor, but *faïence* made by the elder Trou before his death about 1705 is also marked '*S C T*', and I suggest that the porcelain mark may, in fact, be earlier in some cases, and was used to differentiate the wares of the Chicanneau family, now universally re-garded as St. Cloud, from those of Morin.

If the hypothesis is correct so far, it remains to determine what became of Morin's factory. Trou was the owner of a *faïence* factory, and I think it is obvious that Mme Chican-neau would regard him as a good match after the death of her husband, since a factory for the manufacture of porce-lain to her husband's formula would then be in the family. He was also bailiff to the Duc d'Orléans, afterwards the Regent, and it is likely that Orléans intervened to get them the privilege of 1702, despite the earlier privileges granted to Révérend and Louis Poterat at Rouen. The terms of the privilege were sufficient to secure the suppression of the Morin factory, and we know from the later history of French porcelain factories that, without a powerful protector, such factories were quite likely to be suppressed in favour of their more fortunate competitors. Morin died in 1707, five years after the granting of the Chicanneau privilege.

The hypothesis advanced would serve to explain one more contradiction which has puzzled writers who have examined the subject—the complete omission of the name of Morin from the surviving St. Cloud archives. If he was there at all, then his position was a responsible one, even if Lister was mistaken in thinking him the proprietor, and one would expect to find him mentioned. If, however, he was the proprietor of another factory, then he would, quite obviously, not be mentioned.

It is necessary at this point to turn to the question of porcelain-making at Rouen. In 1673 Louis Poterat, a *faïence* maker of St. Sever, near Rouen, applied for a privilege for the manufacture of porcelain in the Chinese manner. This was granted. It suggests that Révérend had made little, if any, progress with the manufacture of porcelain, and, assuming my reading of the known facts to be correct,

Morin did not start his own experiments until about 1675.

Little porcelain, however, was made by Poterat. In 1694 he applied for the renewal of a *faïence* privilege, and the whole question of porcelain manufacture was then discussed with the official making the inquiry, M. Lefèvre d'Ormesson. His report stated that although the secret of porcelain making was well-known to Poterat, little use was made of it. Louis Poterat said that the secret was known only to him, and that he made porcelain by himself without any assistance. His mother and her youngest son, however, both claimed to be able to make it too. The new privilege extended the right to make porcelain to the whole family, and a law-suit resulted which was brought to an end when Louis Poterat died in 1696. The making of porcelain was soon afterwards discontinued.

The privilege granted to Mme Chicanneau has a word to say on the subject:

> Previously a privilege had been granted to the Sieur de Saint-Etienne (Louis Poterat) to found a works at Rouen, but that the Sieur de Saint-Etienne had at most only approached this secret, and had never carried it to such a pitch of perfection as it reached at St. Cloud; that since his death neither his wife nor anyone belonging to his family has made anything in porcelain, and that thus, without wronging the heirs of Saint-Etienne, it is possible to grant the monopoly to St. Cloud, as much for the good quality as for the beauty and the perfection of the porcelain made by Chicanneau.

A connection of the Rouen factory with that of Chicanneau at St. Cloud has been surmised, but cannot be established with any degree of certainty. For the most part these surmises rest on the presence of a painter named Chicanneau at Rouen during the early part of the eighteenth century. The name is not common, and it is possible that the family came from Rouen or the neighbourhood, and that Pierre Chicanneau obtained some information from Poterat.

To return to the St. Cloud factory of Chicanneau: the fact that it must have been established for some years before the granting of the privilege in 1702 is proved by a visit from the Duchesse de Bourgogne in 1700. An extract from a contemporary account follows:

> . . . Madame la Duchesse made her carriage stop at the door of the house where Mme Chicanneau and her family have established for some years now a manufactory of fine porcelain, which without doubt has not its like in all Europe. The princess found pleasure in seeing several pieces of very good shape made on the wheel. She saw some others painted in patterns which were more regular and better done than those of the Indian porcelain. Then she went to see the *faïences* made in the manufactory, and afterwards Mme Chicanneau conducted her into their office, where she saw quantities of porcelain in its perfection. She was so pleased that she promised to come again.

The suggestion that the porcelain formula remained the secret of the Chicanneau family, and that Berthe Coudray kept it even from her husband, is, to say the least, most unlikely. As a maker of *faïence* Trou would have had an extremely good idea of what went into porcelain, and if it was, as seems probable, fired in his *faïence* kilns, it would have been virtually impossible for the Chicanneau family to have kept it from him.

Nevertheless the name of Trou does not appear until 1712, when the renewal of the privilege of 1702 mentions him by name, and, in 1722, the privilege was again extended for another twenty years to the heirs of Chicanneau and Trou. Here, indeed, we find evidence of the intervention of Orléans, now the Regent, since the privilege sets forth that the King has decided 'after the opinion of our dear and beloved Uncle, the Duc d'Orléans.'

In 1722 the family quarrelled, and Marie Moreau, widow of Pierre Chicanneau *fils*, founded a factory in Paris at the rue de la Ville l'Evêque, Faubourg St. Honoré. In this she was helped by her cousin, Louis-Dominique-François Chicanneau, who took over the enterprise from her in 1731.

In 1742 Henri Trou became the proprietor of both factories, and, at the same time, let it be known that he had obtained a new porcelain secret from his patron, Louis, Duc d'Orléans.

In 1745 he took his son, Henri-François, into partnership and died in 1746. The factory then went steadily downhill, and in 1764 Henri-François Trou was compelled to take a partner. Circumstances were against them, however, and liquidation followed in 1766.

A factory is reputed to have been conducted by the husband of Marie-Anne Chicanneau, François Hébert, in the rue de la Roquette, in Paris, and it has been suggested that some rare specimens in the style of St. Cloud which are marked with crossed arrows may be his manufacture, since the Hôtel des Arbalétriers was not far away. Hébert, who was a dealer in pottery, appears to have had some connection with Gilles Dubois of Chantilly and Vincennes, but since the family secret was not revealed to his wife until 1741, it is unlikely that anything was made before this date.

Since this chapter is primarily concerned with *incunabulae* it is a convenient point to discuss some of the other attempts to make porcelain during the early period.

One such was made by Louis, Duc d'Orléans [1703–1752], the only son of the Regent, who succeeded him in 1723. Unlike his father he was pious, cultivated, and studious. He held the post of colonel-general of infantry for eight years, and retired into private life in 1730. He entered the abbey of Sainte-Geneviève in 1742, and there experimented with the manufacture of porcelain, with the aid of the chemist,

Jean-Etienne Guettard. The *kaolin* deposits of Alençon were well-known to them, but whether they ever succeeded in making porcelain with it is something which cannot now be determined, since no identifiable specimens have survived.

A factory was started in Paris in the Faubourg St. Antoine by the physicist, René-Antoine Ferchault de Réaumur, sometimes called the 'Pliny of the eighteenth century', who is best known now for the thermometer scale which bears his name. His first experiments were undertaken about 1717, and at first were aimed at making a porcelain substitute by de-vitrifying glass, that is to say by causing it to assume a crystalline structure instead of the usual amorphous structure. He had access to the letters from China written by the Jesuit missionary, Père d'Entrecolles, in 1717 and 1724, but from the nature of his experiments it would seem that he had not understood them. A contemporary reference suggests that he succeeded in making small quantities of porcelain, but no recognizable specimens have survived. François Hébert, already mentioned, was established near the Faubourg St. Antoine, but no record of a connection with Réaumur can be traced.

An attempt to make porcelain was made at Lille about 1711 with the aid of the municipality. This appears to have had some success, and the undertakers were Barthélemy Dorez, and his nephew, Pierre Pelissier. Dorez stated that, apart from Chicanneau, he was the only potter who knew the secret, and for this reason he was given financial support. For what his evidence may be worth, Dorez said at the time that Louis Poterat sent porcelain to Paris to be sold as St. Cloud, but that his productions were so inferior that he was compelled to cease manufacture.

Pelissier withdrew in 1716, and was replaced by the two sons of Dorez, François and Barthélemy, and the manufacture was continued until about 1730. In 1720 an offer was made to sell the works to Louis, but since Orléans was already taking an interest in St. Cloud, it came to nothing, although some privileges were given to them, no doubt because they were too far away to interfere seriously with Chicanneau. Most surviving specimens claimed for Lille could equally be given to St. Cloud.

*　　*　　*　　*　　*

When we turn to a consideration of the objects themselves we find, on the one hand, a fairly coherent group of wares which, because of the number surviving, must have come from a factory with a large and varied production over a long period. On the other hand, there are several small groups of ware which cannot be attributed so easily, if at all, and a number of factories from which they might have come.

So far as the work of Rouen is concerned, we must remember that, although little porcelain was made, there was a large and flourishing business in *faïence* which extended far beyond the confines of the city, and a great deal is known about it. Rouen popularized the *lambrequin* decoration, for instance, and a variant called the *style rayonnant* (a radial arrangement of the *lambrequins*) came into use about the end of the seventeenth century. We should, particularly in the circumstances existing, expect the decoration of porcelain made at the same time and in the same place, to resemble that of the *faïence*. At the same time, it would be unwise to place too much stress on this because of the wide distribution of Rouen *faïence* at the time. Factories were always ready to copy popular patterns, whatever the material.

As W. B. Honey so rightly commented, most attributions to Poterat depend on local opinion, and the value of this must be distinctly variable. Local patriotism is certain to play a part, and the porcelain collector is not immune from the endemic disease of wishful thinking.

Some marks, notably the 'A.P.' already mentioned as perhaps being used on Révérend's porcelain, have been claimed for Rouen, as well as a number of things obviously from St. Cloud. Less doubtful are some pieces with local armorial bearings. Particularly well-known, and frequently quoted, is a small mustard pot in the Musée de Sèvres which has the arms of Asselin de Villequier of Rouen in blue, the rest of the decoration being in a typically *baroque* style. This, together with a sugar bowl which is a smaller version of the large St. Cloud *jardinière*, and which bears the same arms, are the most likely surviving examples.

The glaze of most of the pieces attributed to Rouen has a greenish hue, and the decoration is in a dark blue which sometimes assumes a greyish tone. Forms are typically *baroque*, and owe something both to *faïence* and metal-work. A few examples which have the addition of red and green enamel of a primitive variety are also claimed for Rouen. The translucency has a slight coppery tinge.

These things are quite different in the colour of the body and glaze from the work of the Chicanneau factory. The slightly greenish tone in the glaze does, in fact, approach more nearly the glaze colour of late Ming porcelain—the variety with which Dr. Martin Lister would, perhaps, have been most familiar. No marks have been observed or recorded which are of the slightest assistance in attributing specimens to Rouen, and it is doubtful whether the present position can be regarded as final in many cases.

When we come to the work of St. Cloud we find a proportion of surviving specimens painted in blue in a *baroque* style very close to that used at Rouen. Most designs of the kind, in fact, can usually be traced either to Rouen or to Bérain, and scrolls, *lambrequins*, and arabesques, together with animals and *chinoiseries*, are all to be seen. The *style rayonnant* appears as late as 1730, and *lambrequins*, generally, seem to have been fashionable until at least 1735.

Another group is decorated in relief, of which an example appears on Plate 6. The open-mouthed masks which form the handles of this *jardinière* are typical of a whole group, either decorated in relief or painted in blue or polychrome. The reliefs are sometimes of the European type, as in the illustration, and sometimes fairly direct copies of prunus blossom and such things from the *blanc-de-Chine* of Tê Hua (Fukien Province) of which large quantities were imported into Europe at the time. Tê Hua was, in fact, a very common source of inspiration, here and elsewhere.

The *jardinières* were also painted with Oriental figures in polychrome which are a mixture of Chinese and Kakiemon styles, the 'banded hedge', for instance, being used with figures which are much more Chinese in drawing. These hardly have the quality of fantasy possessed by the true *chinoiserie*, but fall midway between them and a direct copy. The colours are an approximation to the Arita palette.

A large group of wares are moulded with an imbricated pattern—a series of overlapping scales—which sometimes covers the object completely, and, more rarely, appears in bands at top and bottom. This pattern was used for cups and saucers, the tall cups, without handles, tapering to a smaller foot-ring, whilst the saucers were given an inner ring to hold the cup in position—the so-called *trembleuse* type. A moulded pattern of gadrooning appears at the base and rim of many vessels.

Teapots were given amusing animal and bird heads to both spout and handle, and animal heads appear as handles to the rare tureens. The forms, generally, appear to have been modelled on contemporary silver. All the jugs and small pots have covers (and some should have stands), and

these were often silver-mounted. The hall-marks, where
they exist, are useful for dating. It is reasonable to infer,
therefore, that the factory had some connection with a
silversmith, and possibly he acted as designer.

A particularly interesting type which is both rare and
probably peculiar to St. Cloud is the spice box, made with
three separate compartments joined in the middle, the whole
box having a single cover. Another type has two compartments, the cover being hinged in the middle to allow either
side to be opened. Both these are very much the sort of
thing that the silversmith would make, and specimens in
my experience are decorated only with *lambrequins*.

A small group of figures was made, of which the best
known type is represented by a smiling Chinese in the
Victoria and Albert Museum. Most later figures are no more
than copies of Meissen, and are not especially important
although they are usually valuable.

Many small porcelain 'toys'—such things as snuff-boxes,
cane-handles, and so forth—were made, most of which
were mounted in silver, and a particularly interesting variety
have raised gilding of *baroque* strap-work, now rarely to be
found entirely unrubbed, because of its vulnerability. This
kind of work probably reached St. Cloud by way of the
enamels of Alex Fromery at Berlin, and has distinct affi-
nities with the much earlier work of C. K. Hunger, the
Vienna arcanist, as well as resembling some of Fromery's
enamels. At St. Cloud this gilding was sometimes used in
conjunction with translucent enamels, and some moulded
porcelain has been given a wash with a translucent green
enamel, probably in imitation of Chinese celadons.

The ivory-toned porcelain body is soft and glassy in the
early period, and is analogous in some ways to Chelsea of
the raised anchor period. It has a good glaze, with a surface
resembling the peel of an orange, but of course to a much

slighter extent. The same effect can be seen on some Arita porcelain. Many things are heavily potted, a quality to be noticed in most experimental soft porcelains, and inseparable from the nature of the material. Slight firecracks, and a little warping, can both be observed on some specimens. The later body and glaze deteriorated markedly, and there are often signs of slight discoloration of the glaze. The early blue is variable in colour, sometimes being a clear blue, and sometimes a little greyish in colour.

Precise dating, or even approximate dating, is almost impossible, and the marks, of which there are many, do not help very much. The earliest mark of the sun-face appears to refer to Louis XIV in his rôle of *le roi Soleil*, and a *fleur-de-lys* appearing on two recorded specimens was probably a decorator's mark. The initial letters '*St. C*' appear on a few early examples by themselves, but nearly all have the addition of a '*T*', presumably for 'Trou'. Honey says, somewhat doubtfully, that this might imply a date after 1722, when Trou is said to have been admitted to the secret, but, for the reasons stated, I do not believe it. Numerous additions of initials, numbers, and crosses, appear to be workmen's marks. There is no other possible explanation. Many examples are unmarked. The sun-face is always painted in blue. The other marks are incised (commonly), in blue, or (very rarely) in red enamel.

Few writers on the subject have attempted to date the productions, but there is general agreement that the sun-face places a specimen before 1722. Purely as a matter of opinion, I should be inclined to group *lambrequins* in the Rouen style as among the earliest, with specimens of the *style rayonnant* somewhat later. The latter appears on some of the rare surviving plates from this source. I consider that the use of prunus blossom in relief is also an early practice, and one which was probably discontinued after a few years, since this undoubtedly happened at other factories doing the same thing, but the analogy may not be valid in this case. The moulded scale patterns no doubt were used before 1722. The moulded *jardinières* also appear to be comparatively early, and relief-work generally was probably the first kind of decoration used. No experiments with lacquer colours would appear to have survived, although many white specimens which survive from some other soft paste factories were undoubtedly first made to be decorated in this way, and the present appearance is due to the unfired pigments having worn off with generations of cleaning. Polychrome examples are later, but are a little difficult to place in point of time. It seems doubtful whether they were made much before 1730. Derivations from Meissen most probably belong to the period of 1740 or thereabouts, and the small 'toys' likewise are comparatively late. There may be stylistic details in some pieces which would enable an approximate date to be assigned.

There remains the vexed question of Morin. The wares described as coming from St. Cloud may safely be attributed to the Chicanneau family, but there is a large interrogation mark behind some of those attributed to Rouen. Perhaps, in future, further research will confirm or deny the suppositions relating both to Rouen and to this second factory, and give a lead which will result in the more positive identification of some of these wares.

The porcelain of Lille cannot be identified with any degree of certainty. A monogram 'FB' has been suggested as perhaps standing for François and Barthélemy, the sons of Dorez, but there are other possible explanations, and at present this is purest supposition. Auscher* remarks that most of the pieces attributed to Lille are so designated because they are thicker and more rustic-looking than those

History and Description of French Porcelain.

of St. Cloud, and that the Lille potters confined themselves to imitations of the metropolitan factory, but there is obviously no real evidence for such a statement. It is merely an example of trying to find a convenient pigeon-hole for an unknown group of wares. With so many competitors in the field for a small number of doubtfully attributed specimens, a positive attribution of any surviving porcelain to Lille appears a little reckless.

CHAPTER III

The Chantilly Factory

L OUIS-HENRI DE BOURBON, seventh Prince
de Condé, had a large and important collection of
Japanese porcelain from Arita, principally that with
Kakiemon decoration, in his *château* at Chantilly. I have
described this porcelain at some length on page 46, and
an example from the Chantilly factory is to be seen on
Plate 15.

Kakiemon decorations were particularly popular in
Europe during the first decades of the eighteenth century;
at first the imported Oriental wares, and later the fine
copies and derivations of Meissen. It is certain that the collection of the Prince de Condé must have included some of
both, and Meissen derivations also appear on Chantilly
porcelain. The type is called, in France, by the misnomer of
à décors Coréens, in consequence of the mistaken assumption
that they came originally from Korea.

Like many princes of the period, Condé wanted his own
porcelain factory, and when, in 1725, fate threw in his way
a man with the secret, named Ciquaire (or Sicaire) Cirou,
who had been at the St. Cloud off-shoot in the rue Ville
l'Evêque, a new factory was established at Chantilly.

At the time it is doubtful whether permission would have been granted officially, since the influence of the late Regent and his successor was sufficient to protect the interests of St. Cloud. An application for a privilege in 1735, however, was successful, although provision was made for the rights of the Chicanneau and Trou families. Cirou, in his application, refers to his experience of porcelain-making extending over the previous ten years, and to his successful attempts to copy the Japanese wares. He expressed his intention to sell his wares in France, Germany, and England, and for this he was given a privilege for twenty years.

Apart from its production of porcelain, Chantilly is important as a link between St. Cloud and Vincennes-Sèvres. Cirou learned to make porcelain from his work at St. Cloud, and, in 1738, two Chantilly workmen named Gilles and Robert Dubois were discharged for misconduct. They went to Vincennes, and took with them a Chantilly kiln-master, named Humbert Gérin who designed and built the first Vincennes kilns. Accompanying these three men was a potter, François Gravant, who had been a grocer at Chantilly. It is extremely doubtful whether the brothers Dubois possessed the porcelain secret, at least in a form which would have enabled them to make it, and it is likely that Gérin was, at this time, the most important of the four. By 1741 the Dubois had proved themselves as worthless to the Vincennes directors as they had been to Cirou, and their place was taken by Gravant, who had probably worked with Gérin in the construction of the new kilns. The fate of Gérin is unknown.

The son of Gravant, Louis-François Gravant, who was also in charge of mixing bodies at Sèvres in succession to his father, returned to Chantilly as proprietor in 1776, and was succeeded by his wife after his death in 1779.

Cirou died in 1751, and the management of the factory

was afterwards in a number of hands, none of which were particularly important. Finally, it was bought by an Englishman with the curiously appropriate name of Christopher Potter, who also owned a factory in the rue de Crussol in Paris. Chantilly closed about 1800 in consequence of Potter's financial difficulties. The manufacture of porcelain was discontinued before the Revolution, and it is unlikely that anything of the kind was made afterwards.

Throughout its life, Chantilly productions were mainly derivative, and the work of Arita, and such factories as Meissen and Sèvres were freely copied. The Arita copies are remarkably fine and much sought after, but the wares made after Cirou's death in 1751 are rarely of much interest to the discriminating collector.

*   *   *   *   *

The most characteristic Chantilly productions are those with designs taken from Arita porcelain, and until 1740 these appear to have occupied the factory's entire attention.

A few have been identified by name. The 'quail' or 'partridge' pattern (*caille* or *perdrix*) was popular at Meissen, and at the English factories of Bow, Chelsea, and Worcester. This, and the 'banded hedge' (*haie fleurie*), are probably the most frequent of all Arita patterns. The 'flying squirrel' pattern (in French, '*écureuil*'), which is the German '*fliegender Hund*', is another of the same kind. The *rote Drache* (red dragon) of Meissen, a derivative pattern in the manner of Arita mainly executed in iron red and gilding, was copied and referred to as the 'Prince Henri' pattern.

The elements of these patterns were sometimes recombined to make new ones. Probably the most successful are the sprays of *indianische Blumen* used to decorate some lobed bowls of Japanese form. These possess the characteristic asymmetry to be noted in the early Arita wares, and this style is probably more particularly to be associated with the work of Kakiemon himself. The use of patterns of this kind in association with a yellow ground is particularly effective, although this is a development not to be seen in the Japanese wares. Generally, the palette is a very close approach to the original, and, in some cases, Chantilly wares are, without fairly close examination, difficult to distinguish from those of Arita. The flowers, and other elements of the design, are outlined in red or black, the colours being filled in with washes. The normal palette included red, light blue, a good green, brown, yellow, and black, with, very occasionally, a little gilding.

Mention must be made at this point of the German decorator, Adam Friedrich von Löwenfinck, who fled to Chantilly from Bayreuth at some time between 1736 and 1740. He was accompanied by his brother, Carl Heinrich von Löwenfinck, also a painter. The von Löwenfincks returned to Germany in 1740, and obtained employment at Ansbach. Adam Friedrich will be mentioned hereafter in Chapter VII which is devoted to the work of the Strasbourg factory, but he has been credited, at Meissen, with a later type of *chinoiserie* which is, in fact, much more Japanese than Chinese in origin, although he appears in the factory records only as a flower painter. At present his hand has not, I believe, been definitely traced on Chantilly porcelain, but the possibility ought not to be overlooked. He may, of course, have been employed entirely as a copyist of existing patterns.

The early Chantilly forms were derived from those of Arita, described on page 47, and lobed examples were particularly popular. Oriental figures, with a strong Japanese flavour, were also made at the time, although they are extremely rare, and much sought after. The robes are usually decorated with *indianische Blumen*. Some later figures of good quality were probably modelled by Louis Fournier, who came from Vincennes in 1752 and remained until 1756.

The Japanese period ended about 1740, and some derivations from Meissen followed, particularly specimens painted with *deutsche Blumen*—the natural German flowers which had been introduced at the Saxon factory a few years before. To the same period belong some naïve decorations drawn in black and filled in with green.

Chantilly received an unpleasant blow in October, 1752, when, by royal edict, the manufacture of porcelain was forbidden for a period of twelve years to any person, whatever his title or position, and it was, at the same time, forbidden to paint any white pottery in colour, or to import pottery or porcelain so painted from abroad. This was to secure the position of the Vincennes factory in which the King had an interest, and whilst it was not always applied with full severity, Chantilly reverted to the use of monochromes, some cupids after Boucher painted in crimson *en camaïeu* being an example. A few polychrome pieces, which seem to date before 1766 when the prohibition was relaxed, suggest a measure of evasion, but Condé was a member of the King's family, and a powerful protector.

One of the reasons for the edict may have been the copies of Vincennes porcelain which were being made at Chantilly, but suggestions that the ground colours of the former factory were reproduced do not appear to be well-founded.

Later, decoration tended to become very slight. Plates, for instance, commonly had a central flower spray with, at most, a diaper pattern on the ledge. Much porcelain with a transparent glaze (see below) is decorated thus. A decoration of small flower sprays at intervals is known as the 'Chantilly sprig', and, at a later date, the 'cornflower sprig' was painted in much the same way, but in green, blue, and pink enamel instead of in underglaze blue. These sprigs were much copied elsewhere on unambitious wares.

'Toys' were not commonly made at Chantilly, although misattributions are not uncommon. Snuff-boxes, often mounted in silver, are scarce but of fine workmanship, and good specimens are especially desirable.

The Chantilly body resembles that of St. Cloud, although the glaze used makes close comparison difficult. The body was made with clay from Luzarches and white sand from la butte d'Aumont, with some potash as a flux. The precise potting of Chantilly wares suggests that the body was more tractable than that used at St. Cloud.

From 1725 until the death of Cirou the body was covered with a *faïence* glaze which greatly enhanced the vividness of the colours used on it. Whilst other soft porcelain factories occasionally added a little tin oxide to their glazes to modify faults of colour, only Chantilly used a completely opaque tin enamel which is comparable to the *faïence* glaze. Chantilly products between 1725 and 1751, therefore, can be identified with comparative ease and safety. Viewed by transmitted light the body shows a yellowish-green colour, called by the French *citronné*, whilst the body, when it is not covered by the tin enamel, shows much the same colour. 'Moons' (see page 55) are present occasionally.

In 1751, to meet competition from the Mennecy factory, a change was made to the normal type of transparent glaze, and a cheaper ware decorated with blue underglaze then became possible. Specimens are comparatively common. It is not certain if a tin glaze was used occasionally after 1751, but, of course, there were no technical difficulties in the way of firing an occasional batch of this kind.

Unmarked Chantilly porcelain is fairly common, but the mark of the hunting horn often appears and is extremely well-known. During the period of the tin glaze it was in red, and in blue under the transparent glaze. The mark in enamel blue also appears occasionally in the later period. Initials probably refer to workmen, and the mark *'villers cotteret'* in full, appears on items from a service made for the Duc d'Orléans. It refers to the *château* for which the service was made.

Plate 33. Characteristic group of children painted in enamel colours.
Mennecy. c. 1760. (V&AM.)

Plate 34. Group of children in *biscuit* porcelain. Mennecy. Mark:
'DV M'. c. 1760. (V&AM.)

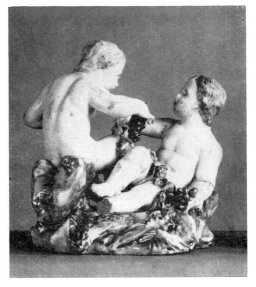

Plate 35 (a). Group of two boys, somewhat in the style of Mennecy and marked 'DCO' incised. c. 1765. See page 105. (V&AM.)

(b). Jar, one of a pair, painted with polychrome flowers. Strawberry knob. Mark: 'DCP' incised. c. 1765. See page 105. (V&AM.)

Plate 36. Jardinière in two parts, decorated with a tavern scene and figures ??? is polychrome. Sceaux, *c.* 1760–1771. (V&AM.)

Plate 37 (a). Bowl decorated with river scenes in the manner of Meissen. Vincennes. c. 1745. (V & AM.)

(b). Bourdaloue painted with flower sprays. Vincennes. c. 1750. (Ashmo-lean-Andrade Colln.)

Plate 38. Teapot, *sucrièr*, and cup and saucer, *gros bleu* ground, decorated in reserves with exotic birds in gold silhouette. Vincennes. c. 1753. (Wallace Colln.)

Plate 39 (a). Jardinière, *gros bleu* ground, rich gilding, and birds in gold silhouette in reserves. Vincennes. c. 1753. (V&AM.)

(b). Powder-horn, turquoise blue ground; on one side, a stag hunt; flowers and hunting trophies on the other. Made for Marie Josèphe, Dauphine of France, daughter of Augustus the Strong of Saxony, and mother of Louis XVI. Vincennes. c. 1753. (Metropolitan.)

Plate 40. Covered cup and saucer decorated with relief gilding on white porcelain. Vincennes. c. 1750. (Fitzwilliam.)

Plate 41. Cachepot painted with classical subject. Vincennes. c. 1753. (BM.)

Plate 42. Casket, turquoise blue ground with flower painting in reserves. Silver-gilt mounts with the Paris hall-mark for 1754/5. (Wallace Colln.)

Plate 43 (a). Pot-pourri vase, the applied flowers painted in colours. Contemporary mounts. Vincennes. c. 1750. (V&AM.)

(b). *Plateau* with apple-green ground and children by Vieillard. Sèvres. 1758. (Wallace Colln.)

Plate 44 (a). Ewer and basin, turquoise blue ground and flowers painted
by Binet. Sèvres. c. 1758. (V&AM.)

(b). Ewer and basin painted in reserves with birds by Aloncle, the
gilding by Prevost. Contemporary mounts. Sèvres. 1780. (BM.)

Plate 45. Part tea and coffee service. *Rose Pompadour* ground, rich gilding, and painted with trophies by Buteux *aîné*. Sèvres. c. 1760.

Plate 46 (a). Tray, green ground, the centre painted with *L'Education de l'Amour* after Carl Vanloo. Gilding by Nöel. Sèvres. c. 1760.

(*b*). Covered cup and saucer decorated with drops of enamel, simulating rubies, turquoise, pearls, etc. Sèvres. c. 1785. (V&AM.)

(*c*). Coffee-cup, *bleu de Roi* ground, with a portrait of Benjamin Franklin. Decorated by Le Guay. Sèvres. c. 1780. (V&AM.)

Plate 47 (a). Part of a toilet set, painted by Parpette. Said to have been used by Louis Seize. Sèvres. (Wallace Colln.) c. 1775.

(b). Tea-set decorated with *oeil de perdrix* on blue, painted with trophies by Chulot. Sèvres. 1775. (Wallace Colln.)

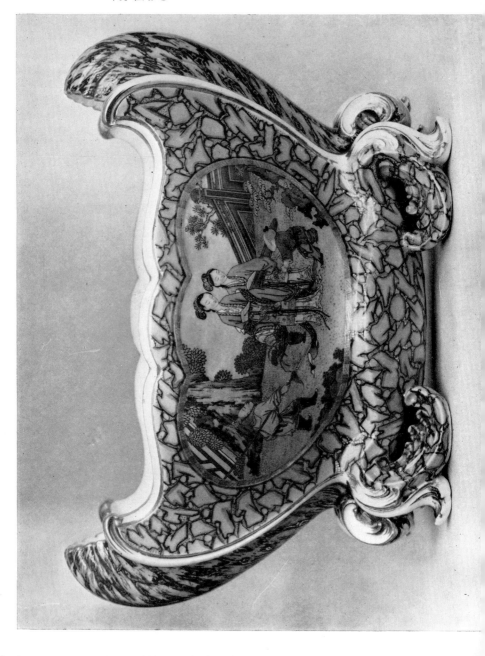

Plate 48. One of a pair of Sèvres *jardinières*, marbled pink ground. Chinese subjects by Dodin. 1761. (BM.)

CHAPTER IV

The Later Soft Porcelain Factories

LOUIS-FRANÇOIS DE NEUFVILLE, Duc de Villeroy, son of the Marshal who was defeated by Marlborough at Ramillies, had a small *faïence* factory as early as 1734. An inscribed specimen dated 1738, and decorated in the Rouen style, is in the Musée de Sèvres. The manufacture of porcelain was first at the rue de Charonne, in Paris, but was later transferred to the Neufville estates at Mennecy, on the northern outskirts of the City, in consequence of the privilege granted to Charles Adam at Vincennes.

The de Neufville factory was managed by François Barbin, and the manufacture of porcelain was added without official sanction about 1735. No action was taken until 1748, when Barbin was forbidden to copy or imitate Vincennes porcelain, or to employ anyone who might have worked at the latter establishment. When we take into account the extent of his temerity in making porcelain at all in such circumstances, it says much for the influence of de Neufville that the factory was not closed altogether.

Barbin was joined by his son, Jean-Baptiste, in 1751. The latter became a partner in 1758, the elder Barbin retiring in 1762. Three years later both men died suddenly.

Not much is known of the workmen during this period. One, Charles Dubray, appears in the Mennecy parish records for 1741. There was one man, however, who is of some importance, and who apparently started his career at Mennecy during the period of the Barbins—Pierre Berthevin. Since he was at Copenhagen in 1765, he probably left because of the death of the Barbins. He arrived at Marieberg, in Sweden, in the year following, and his presence here accounts for many resemblances between the style of Marieberg and that of Mennecy. The reeded custard cup and cover, one of the most commonly surviving examples of the work of the latter factory, was also repeated at Marieberg.

Nicolas-François Gauron was responsible for some characteristic Mennecy figures. His actual period of service was short, since he became chief modeller at Tournai in 1758, remaining until 1764, and he may have been at Vincennes in 1754. He was later in England.

Gauron is reputed to have modelled an allegorical group at Tournai representing Charles d'Oultremont, Prince-Bishop of Liège, which was presented to him by the magistrates of Dinant to commemorate his consecration in 1764.

A large *Pietà* in *biscuit* porcelain, made at the same factory, is almost identical with a Chelsea example, and is sometimes claimed for Gauron, but on stylistic grounds alone I feel it is much more likely to be the work of Joseph Willems, also at both factories. The hand seems to be the same as that of the *Roman Charity*, *Una and the Lion*, and other well-known Chelsea models in this class. *Una*, in fact, is a well-attested Chelsea model by Willems, an example of it being found among his effects at Tournai after his death. A likely class of Tournai figures may be found in the groups of children on a rock-work base, which are similar in style to groups modelled at the Chelsea-Derby and Derby factories, and first appear at Mennecy about the time at which Gauron was modelling for them. Examples appear on Plates 33 and 93 which are characteristic of this interesting class.

In 1766 the Mennecy factory was advertised for sale, together with a stock of porcelain which included 'cups, saucers, antique vases, groups, pedestals, mustard-pots, gravy-boats, dishes, covered dishes, cruet stands, powder-boxes, sugar-boxes, sugar-bowls, and fruit-baskets', which is some indication of the scope of manufacture, although the popular custard cups are not mentioned by name.

The undertaking was bought by Joseph Jullien, a painter, and Symphorien Jacques, a sculptor, who were also potters at Sceaux, to the south of Paris. The factories were run jointly until 1772, when they sold their interest in the works at Sceaux. The Mennecy factory, itself, was moved to Bourg-la-Reine in 1779, where it came under the protection of the Comte d'Eu.

Joseph Jullien was succeeded by his son, Joseph-Léon, after his death in 1774. Charles-Symphorien Jacques joined the factory in 1780 when his father retired, and he became sole director in 1790. In 1804 he filed a petition in bankruptcy. In this way the original Mennecy undertaking came to an end. It is doubtful whether any porcelain was made after 1780, and the last years were probably devoted to making creamware (*faïence-fine*) in the English manner. In 1778 Jacques lodged a complaint with the Minister of Commerce on the subject of the harm being done to the factory by imports of English creamware, presumably that of Wedgwood.

There are one or two factories related in one way or another to the undertaking at Mennecy which it is convenient to consider here.

One of these is that of Crépy-en-Valois which was founded in 1762 by Louis-François Gaignepain [1739–1770] who had been a Mennecy workman. Most surviving examples seem to be glazed white figures. Some things made here may be misattributed to Mennecy; there is a fairly close resemblance, and separation is not easy in the absence of marks.

The factory at Sceaux owned by Jullien and Jacques was founded in 1748 by an architect named de Bey, with the assistance of a chemist, Jacques Chapelle, as manager. Chapelle has been well-described as a 'universal genius' who had some skill as a sculptor, painter, chemist, and physicist. It is probable that the early experiments in the manufacture of porcelain were made by Gilles Dubois, and a workman named Chanou who had been at the St. Cloud factory in the rue Ville l'Evêque. The death of its patron, the Duchesse de Maine, in 1753 no doubt had an adverse effect on the fortunes of the Sceaux factory, and its attempts to make porcelain were frustrated by the already mentioned edicts in favour of Vincennes. The principal manufacture in the early period was described, at the time, as *faïence iaponée*, which may have been a clandestine porcelain decorated in the style of Arita.

Until 1763, when Jullien and Jacques became the proprietors, it is likely that only token amounts of porcelain had been made, and no identifiable specimens survive. Jullien and Jacques, however, were obviously attracted to porcelain as a material, and the force of the earlier edicts was lessening. Moreover, the factory found a new protector in the Duc de Penthièvre, High Admiral of France, and some porcelain (later discussed) was manufactured. They disposed of their interest, however, to Richard Glot in 1772, and, in 1780, the latter applied for permission to use colours and gilding which appear subsequently on both *faïence* and porcelain.

The Duc de Penthièvre was also the patron of a factory at

Orléans. A privilege was given in 1753 to Jacques-Etienne Dessaux de Romilly to establish a *faïence* factory. It was granted for a term of twenty years, and allowed the manufacture of *faïence* and a material termed *'terre blanc purifée'* [sic.]. The latter may have been a type of soft porcelain, otherwise the term appears meaningless.

The factory was taken over later by Claude-Charles Gérault d'Areaubert, and, in 1767, it was described officially as the Manufacture royale de porcelayne d'Orléans. The widow of d'Areaubert closed it down in 1783, but it was reopened by Bourdon de Saussay in 1788, closing finally about 1812.

Employed here, as well as at Sceaux, Strasbourg, and Tournai, was a modeller named Jean-Jacques Louis, perhaps to be identified with a modeller of the same name at Ludwigsburg, in Germany. Another modeller, one Huet, who had been at Sèvres, probably worked at Mennecy and Crépy-en-Valois, as well as at Orléans.

*   *   *   *   *

The early porcelain of Mennecy resembles that of St. Cloud. It is covered with a clear lead glaze which lacks the orange-skin effect of the St. Cloud ware already noticed, and the body is frequently of a dark ivory tone which is characteristic. Differentiation is usually fairly easy to anyone acquainted with the porcelain of both factories.

Suggestions that an opaque tin-glaze, similar to that of Chantilly, was used occasionally are not well supported, but the possibility cannot be entirely excluded, and a good deal of early ware was apparently painted with the popular Japanese patterns.

Wares copied from St. Cloud include such reliefs as the prunus blossom, and cylindrical jars with this decoration are sometimes confused with Chelsea porcelain decorated

in the same way. The form, however, was never used at
Chelsea, and is an obvious derivation from Tê Hua. The
lambrequins of Rouen, painted in blue underglaze, were also
taken from St. Cloud, and used to decorate knife handles,
some of which have been excavated on the site of the old
factory in the rue de Charonne. These are not uncommon in
England, and are sometimes misattributed to the Bow
factory. Their nature makes differentiation a little difficult.
A few painted with Japanese patterns bear the mark, '*DV*'
(for *de Villeroy*) and these, and the excavated examples
mentioned, help to identify the whole group.

Perhaps the commonest survivals are small custard cups
and covers which are moulded with a spiral reeding and,
usually, painted with characteristic flower sprays of the
deutsche Blumen type. A pinkish-purple (or rose) and a purple-
brown were commonly used, and are peculiar to the factory.
The prohibition relating to the use of gilding led to its
replacement by blue, pink, and (very rarely) yellow, particularly for the lining of the rims of various articles, whilst
mouldings on vases and such things, which would normally
have been gilded, were similarly treated.

Mennecy flower painting is distinguished in quality, the
purplish-brown being used for the flower stems. The work
was, apparently, much admired at the time, and appears on
Sceaux *faïence* at a much later date. I have observed it on
examples with the late gold anchor mark, adopted in consequence of the position of its patron as High Admiral.
Bird painting, too, is excellent in quality, and can also be
observed on later *faïence* from Sceaux. Figure painting after
Watteau and Lancret is also to be seen, but is rare.

Many attempts were made to copy the wares of
Vincennes-Sèvres, and decorations such as the *bleu de Roi*
ground with *oeil de perdrix* gilding exist, although examples
are very rare. The crimson and blue monochromes of

Vincennes, later described, were also copied, and the crossed *L's* mark has been recorded in conjunction with the usual Mennecy mark of *DV* incised.

Rare too are the *pot-pourri* jars copied from Chantilly and Vincennes, which can be seen occasionally. Shapes were sometimes fantastic and elaborate. Some vases in the Vincennes style were ornamented with small applied flowers, but flowers for mounting in *ormolu* do not seem to have been made at Mennecy. Early work of this kind is relatively crude, but that of the 1750s is of distinctly better quality. Flower knops were used for teapots and coffee pots.

Small boxes were a common item of manufacture, and are much sought after today. Some are in the form of animals. Certain identification is often extremely difficult, but miniature painting of high quality can be attributed to Mennecy without doubt.

Numerous figures were made. I have already mentioned, earlier in this chapter, the groups of *putti* on rock-work bases which can, perhaps, be tentatively attributed to Gauron, although a group of this kind is marked *DV Mo* in reference to Christoph and Jean-Baptiste Mô who were probably 'repairers' rather than modellers. The date awarded to this class is about 1760 which would, of course, make it impossible for Gauron to have modelled them, but there is no certainty in the matter, and the rock-work bases—an early *rococo* theme—suggest that they might well be a few years earlier. By another hand some Italian Comedy figures are worth recording, as well as some adaptations from Meissen models, and some rare small figures of fine quality with Mennecy colouring may properly be attributable here.

A small quantity of *biscuit* figures were made, as well as some portrait medallions in relief.

Figures, particularly uncoloured examples, are sometimes difficult to separate from those of Crépy-en-Valois where figures appear to have been the principal manufacture. These often have a considerable resemblance to known Mennecy types. The same factory made a speciality of small boxes, often in the form of such animals as the cat, the sheep, and the dog, as well as of small scent-bottles, and similar toys.

The wares of Bourg-la-Reine are hardly to be separated from those of Mennecy, since it was a continuation of the parent factory with the same proprietors, and, presumably, in many cases, the same workmen. Not much porcelain appears to have been made here, and some of it was marked with the letters *BR* incised. Painting on some attested examples is a little inferior to that of Mennecy, whilst preserving the same general style.

Specimens of early Sceaux porcelain, made before the acquisition of the factory by Jullien and Jacques, cannot be identified. Under their control, however, a certain amount of porcelain was made, and paste and glaze much resembled that of Mennecy. Since the earlier prohibitions were then being relaxed, some good painting of birds and flowers, as well as of *putti* in a pink monochrome, can reasonably be attributed to this period. The addition of gilding would suggest a date after 1784, when permission to paint in colour and to use gilding was granted. The earlier examples were treated in the same way as at Mennecy, and the enamel blue was a common substitute on parts which would otherwise have been gilded. Suggestions that hard porcelain was made at Sceaux have not received definite confirmation.

The wares of Orléans are extremely difficult to identify. A few specimens of a soft porcelain marked with an *O* under a coronet in blue are probably referable to the Dessaux period. It seems that soft porcelain was made until a year variously estimated as between 1764 and 1770, and a hard porcelain thereafter. Records of a visit by Monsieur, the King's brother, in 1777 suggest that manufacture was on a

II. *Jardinière* in the Louis Quinze style with *rose Pompadour* ground and rich gilt scrollwork surrounding the reserves, which are painted with cupids and trophies. Sèvres. 1757. (Wallace Colln.)

large scale, but since *faïence* was made as well, the amount of porcelain produced may not have been very great.

Honey refers to two figures, crude in execution, in the Franks Collection (British Museum) inscribed *Louis* (for Jean-Jacques Louis) and *Pierre Renau* as likely examples of Orléans figure work. Other writers mention the characteristics of Orléans porcelain without reference to examples, which makes their evidence of doubtful value.

In the absence of marks, attributions in most cases must inevitably be a matter of personal preference based on whatever evidence may be present. Even the marks assigned to this factory are controversial. There is little doubt that some *biscuit* figures were made, and a class of this kind obviously not from Sèvres, is sometimes awarded to Orléans.

Since identification of documentary specimens depends to some extent on marks, some attention to these is essential. The name, *de Villeroy*, appears on a few pieces in full, but usually this is contracted to *DV*, in blue, red, black, or incised. In painted form the mark is early, later it is incised. The marks, *D, C, O*, and *D, C, P*, are sometimes found on porcelain in the style of Mennecy. They have been attributed to Crépy, although, if they are to be taken from Mennecy, Orléans would appear to be the more likely. A few specimens marked *crepy* or *c.p.* are obviously from the former factory.

Bourg-la-Reine porcelain is marked with an incised BR. In this case there can be no doubt, since the mark was registered at the time with the police in accordance with the law. The *O* surmounted by a coronet in blue is generally regarded as the mark of Orléans, and was so registered at the time. A later mark (p. 216) is not as certain, and it has been suggested that it would be better given to Chantilly.

Sceaux porcelain, when marked, usually bears an incised *SX*, or, less often, an anchor. The anchor also appears on *faïence* in a painted form.

CHAPTER V

Vincennes-Sèvres

THE royal factory of Sèvres had its beginning at the Chantilly factory of the Prince de Condé.

Orry de Fulvy, brother of Orry de Vignory, the Minister of Finance, was fond of gambling heavily, and his losses were often spectacular. To recoup himself he engaged in speculative enterprises, and was, for some reason, attracted to porcelain manufacture. Whilst porcelain was, to use the words of the Herzog Karl Eugen of Ludwigsburg, 'a necessary appanage of lustre and prestige', it was hardly profitable, and it would be difficult to select any European factory of the period which was not to some extent dependent on subsidies from the Government or a ruling prince for its existence.

De Fulvy deputed a relative who was a member of the Society of Jesus to ask Père d'Entrecolles, a Jesuit missionary in China (whose earlier letters on the subject of porcelain-making in that country were well known), for additional information, but, in the absence of suitable deposits of the necessary raw materials, nothing could be done.

In 1738 some workmen from Chantilly, Gilles and Robert Dubois, and a kiln-master and enameller, Humbert Gérin, left the factory and started to experiment with porcelain-

making in Paris. They may have been accompanied at this
time by François Gravant, the potter who had been a
grocer in Chantilly. If they were not, he joined them shortly
afterwards.

With difficulty they managed to make a few experimental
pieces which were sold in Paris, and de Fulvy heard of this
through the Marquis de Chatelet. He visited them, and
thought their work sufficiently promising to secure permission for the use of some buildings in the disused *château*
of Vincennes. A sum of 10,000 livres* was advanced to
enable them to make a start.

Their knowledge, however, was defective, and both the
Dubois were addicted to alcohol. The number of kiln-
wasters was inordinately high, at times reaching five-sixths
of the production. The Dubois were, therefore, discharged
as incompetent in 1741, and their place taken by Gravant
who had copied their notes on the mixing of the bodies and
the firing. He obtained additional help from Chantilly and
St. Cloud, and, in 1745, a practical porcelain body was produced. Gravant remained in charge of the mixing of the
body until his death in 1765.

De Fulvy had formed a company consisting of himself,
Verdun de Martchiroux and a M. Beaufils, which had a
capital of 100,000 livres. His brother, de Vignory, used his
influence to obtain a privilege from the King, which was
granted on July 24th, 1745, in the name of Charles Adam.
This was for the term of twenty years, and refers to the
manufacture of porcelain after the style of the Saxon.

*It is almost impossible to fix the value of eighteenth-century
French currency in terms of the £ with any degree of accuracy. Its
value, of course, fluctuated at the time with variations in economic
conditions, as it does today. A fair equivalent to the value of the
livre at the mid-century is probably about two shillings and sixpence
(about thirty-five cents, U.S. currency). On this basis 10,000 livres
would be equivalent to about £1,250. (1960).

Little is known of Charles Adam, but a curious sidelight on early porcelain manufacture is thrown by his communication to the King in 1745, in which he says that 'a new factory has just been established in England for the manufacture of porcelain more beautiful than that of Saxony owing to the nature of its composition'. The factory mentioned could only have been Chelsea, which was probably started with the assistance of a migratory workman from St. Cloud.

The financial position was still difficult. Mme de Pompadour found Orry de Vignory too mean with money, and procured his dismissal. This meant that de Fulvy lost his brother's support, and the new Finance Minister, Jean-Baptiste de Machault, was not, at first, entirely favourable to the project, although, in 1747, he issued orders which forbade the manufacture of porcelain elsewhere in France. This was not strictly enforced, but this and later edicts caused Hannong a great deal of trouble at Strasbourg. The situation was saved by Verdun de Martchiroux, who managed to secure the help and interest of Mme de Pompadour. She, in turn, persuaded the King to intervene, and to grant an annual subsidy of 20,000 livres.

Expenses mounted, and insufficient sales were being made to provide for them. The Company borrowed heavily in 1749, and again in March, 1750. In December of the same year it was decided to make a large increase in capital, which was fixed at 550,000 livres, divided into two hundred and twenty shares of 2,500 livres apiece. At this time about a hundred workmen of all kinds were employed.

Some important appointments were made in 1745. Boileau de Picardie, from the office of taxes, was put in charge of administration; Jean Hellot, Director of the Academy of Sciences, was appointed chemist to the factory; Claude-Thomas Duplessis, goldsmith and bronze-worker to

Louis XV, was given the post of designer, both for porcelain and for bronze mountings; and a certain Hulst (or Hults), of whom little is known, acted as general adviser and organiser. The decoration of the factory's products was looked after by Jean-Adam Mathīeu, enameller to Louis XV, but in many ways the most important appointment was that of Jean-Jacques Bachelier who took charge of painting and modelling, and later introduced the use of *biscuit* porcelain for figure modelling.

Bachelier was born in Paris in 1724, and, in 1747, he was appointed director of studios at Vincennes, in which capacity he helped to engage the artists. His salary was, at first, only forty-eight livres a week, with food provided in addition, but he had scholarships to the school of painting to the value of 1,400 livres per annum.

Hulst asked Bachelier to aim at 'novelty, variety, and prettiness'. Prettiness was to be interpreted as lightness of touch—like a pretty woman, smiling and agreeable.* Bachelier took his advice to heart, and, with the encouragement of Mme De Pompadour, rose steadily, becoming Art Director in 1751 and remaining in this position until 1793. He was largely responsible for the characteristic Sèvres style. His death occurred in 1805.

The chemist, Hellot, with the help of a staff of enamellers experimented with various colours. Jean-Mathias Callat worked on various blues, Meissen green, yellows, reds, and purples, whilst Bailly, who was in charge of the colour-making department, experimented with yellows and derivative colours. Taunay, who is represented in the Musée de Sèvres by a cup dated 1748 painted with trial colours, did

---

*'Gentilesse, nouveauté, variété doivent être sa devise. Qui dit gentilesse dit choses légères. On ne lui demande que des éternuements de sa génie, semblables à ceux d'une jolie femme, c'est à dire riants et agréables.

research on carmine and violet, and a formula for gilding was bought from Brother Hippolyte, a Benedictine friar of Notre-Dame des Champs, which was perfected by Louis-Pierre Massuë, in charge of the gilding shop, who had formerly been a painter at St. Cloud.

De Vignory died in 1750, and his brother in the following year. This caused a fresh financial crisis, since the factory was bound to repay their interest in the Company to their executors, whilst large sums were still owing to the King. The undertaking was, for this reason, reorganized, the privilege being transferred to a new company in the name of Eloi Brichard. The capital was fixed at 800,000 livres, of which 200,000 came from the King, who was also entitled to a quarter-share of any profits. At the same time, the Company was given the status of Manufacture royale de porcelaine. The royal cipher of the crossed *Ls*, occasionally used before this date, was confirmed to the factory as its mark.

The new privilege, had it been strictly enforced, would have ended porcelain manufacture elsewhere in France. It was forbidden to make or sell porcelain, and even to paint *faïence* in colours. Brichard was empowered to inspect factories suspected of infringements, and could enter private residences for the same purpose, not excluding the royal palaces. The import of porcelain from abroad was forbidden under heavy penalties, and permission to use the buildings at Vincennes was confirmed until a new factory could be built. The secret formulae were to be the property of the King, and the persons mixing the bodies were to be appointed by him. Workmen were given many special privileges, including remissions of taxation, but were forbidden to leave without giving six months' notice, whilst those in positions of trust had to get special permission from the King. All workmen were expressly forbidden to engage in making porcelain elsewhere. Finally, all existing privileges to other factories were revoked.

In 1752 the porcelain of Vincennes made its appearance in Paris as a competitor to that of China and Meissen. Among the early products were artificial flowers of porcelain which quickly became fashionable, and *bouquets* for Louis and Maria Leczinska were mounted in *bronze dorée* by Duplessis. Whilst its first reception was a little lukewarm, the Dauphine, who had hitherto been convinced of the supremacy of Meissen, was quickly won over, and admitted that the new porcelain was equal to that of the Saxon factory. This was not only a great encouragement to the directorate, but helped to establish the popularity of the wares.

The Paris dealers in porcelain, who had hitherto bought heavily from Meissen, supported Vincennes, even to the point of suggesting new styles. The most prominent of them was Lazare Duvaux,* formerly a large customer of the Saxon factory, who paid 36,000 livres for Vincennes porcelain in 1753 and no less than 102,000 livres in 1756. Duvaux bought for both the King and Mme de Pompadour, about one-third of his purchases being made on the King's behalf. In 1753 he sent the porcelain flower bouquets of Mme de Pompadour to Vincennes to be cleaned, and for the broken ones to be replaced. These Paris merchants not only bought and sold porcelain, they were also responsible for mounting it in gilded bronze in the same way as they had previously mounted Oriental and Meissen porcelain.

The advent of Mme de Pompadour had not been without influence on the arts generally. Boucher had been called to the Court to help her in working out her ideas, and such sculptors as Falconet and Coustou were also working for her.

Livre-journal de Lazare Duvaux, marchand-bijoutier, 1748–1758. Ed. J. Courajod. 2 vols. Paris, 1873.

François Boucher had such influence on the styles adopted by the factory that he needs to be discussed in more detail. Born in 1703, the son of an obscure painter who also designed upholstery, he was apprenticed to François Lemoyne, who decorated the *Salon d'Hercule* at Versailles. He then, at the age of seventeen, engaged himself to an engraver named Cars, the father of Laurent Cars, his duties being to draw designs for engraved printing plates. Since these ranged from trade-signs to book-plates, his experience was both varied and useful.

Boucher's genial manner won him many friends, and orders from the Baron de Thiers helped him on his way. Soon he was engaged to engrave the work of Watteau, and at twenty-five Boucher went to Rome. Here he stayed for about three years, but was ill for much of the time. In 1733 he returned to Paris, and married Marie Jeanne Buseau, who later worked in his studio as a copyist. His election to the Academy followed in 1734.

Boucher was an intimate of Juste-Aurèle Meissonier, the designer and one of the originators of the *rococo* style, who was godfather to his son in 1736, and in the same year his *Cris de Paris*, engraved by Ravenet and Le Bas, appeared. These were later modelled by Kändler at Meissen as porcelain figures. Again, in the same year, Boucher successfully submitted designs for the *Don Quixote* series of tapestries to be made by the Gobelins factory, at the suggestion of the director, Oudry, and these were the first of many equally successful tapestry designs. In 1737 two cartoons of rustic subjects for the Beauvais tapestry looms were precursors of his later pastoral style.

The work of the period of *Louis Quatorze* had been in the grand manner; now, everything was elegant and making love more important than martial glory. Boucher was taken up by the Court, and appeared in the *salon* of Mme

Le Normant d'Etiolles (later to be Mme de Pompadour) in company with such distinguished men as Voltaire. His pictures of pastoral scenes, cupids, and naked goddesses* were selling as fast as he could paint them. Principally, he was a decorative painter, and most of his work was done for particular settings.

In 1737 his friendship with La Tour seems to have caused him to turn to pastels occasionally, as a change from painting in oils. Some fine landscapes were done in the years between 1740 and 1745 which were later used by various engravers. His interest in Chinese art seems to have begun about 1740, and it was in this year that he designed the trade-card for Gersaint, already mentioned. In the same year Huquier published a book of engravings—*The Five Senses, representing various Chinese pastimes, by F. Boucher,* and in the *Salon* of 1742 he showed some sketches of Chinese subjects to be carried out in Beauvais tapestry. His *Suite de Figures Chinois* was used by the porcelain makers as inspiration for figure models.

At this time Boucher was designing *chinoiseries,* tapestries, gilt-bronze mountings and ornaments, frames for his pictures, and interiors. He was also on the staff of the Paris Opera as decorator, designing the costumes and scenery for the ballet, *Indes galantes,* in 1743.

A *List of the Best Painters,* compiled by the Director-General of Buildings in this year, refers to Boucher as 'an historic painter, living in the rue de Grenelle-Saint-Honoré, opposite the rue des Deux-Ecus, pupil of Lemoyne, excelling also in landscape, grotesques, and ornament in the

---

*These were always popular, and no doubt the goddesses of Boucher and his imitators were responsible for the directive of the Comte d'Angiviller, Director-General of Buildings to Louis XVI, which required the Academy officials to report nudes likely to be dangerous to public morals.

manner of Watteau: and equally skilled in painting flowers, fruit, animals, architecture, and subjects of gallantry and fashion'.

About 1746 the King, influenced by Mme de Pompadour, appointed her guardian, Le Normant de Tournhem, to the position of Director-General of Buildings, and Boucher then had two friends at Court. Orders from the Court increased in number, and for a time he found himself in the invidious position of working both for the Queen and for the King's mistress—a situation eventually decided in favour of the latter.

As Mme de Pompadour grew in power and influence she was both patron and pupil. His friendship gave her some relief from the unremitting intrigues of the Queen's party, and from the Minister, Maurepas, who sought to evict her from the King's bed. Their objection to her seems to have been more because of her humble origin than any kind of moral scruple. Opinion said that she was not fit to 'have the honour of the King's adultery'. Maurepas lost no opportunity of vilifying her, and of making her the subject of lampoons to be sung in the streets, until she secured sufficient influence to procure his dismissal.*

As soon as Mme de Pompadour had amassed a sufficiently large private fortune she bought works of art of all kinds, expending colossal sums on them, and her encouragement of the Sèvres factory was related to this phase of her life. She established a small theatre at Versailles, the members of the Court competing for the honour of playing in the productions. Her maid was offered an army command for a

---

*Although the standards of the Court circle of Louis XV and Mme de Pompadour were undoubtedly lax, the more scurrilous stories ought to be accepted with a good deal of reserve. There was certainly much spiteful gossip at the time, which has since been too easily accepted as fact.

relative in exchange for a part in one of these productions, and Boucher left the Opera to design stage-settings for this private theatre.

These entertainments were to keep the King from boredom—a mood which rarely left him. Mme de Pompadour knew that her power and influence depended on her ability to keep the King amused. To this end, when her own powers of physical attraction began to wane, she supplied him with a succession of temporary mistresses from the lower classes who were unable to compete with her in intellect. One of these was Boucher's model, an Irish girl named Murphy—'*la petite Morphil*', and Boucher was asked to paint suggestive pictures for the King's pleasure.

In 1748 Boucher painted *L'agréable Leçon*—a shepherd teaching a shepherdess to play a flute—which attracted the attention of a number of porcelain factories, and in 1750 he could afford to move to the rue Richelieu. He now had the use of a studio in the King's library, and had amassed a considerable fortune.

Le Normant de Tournhem, Director-General of Buildings, died in 1751, and his place was taken by the brother of Mme de Pompadour. Curiously enough, this obvious piece of nepotism was extremely successful, and the young Director proved a good friend to Boucher. In 1752 the latter was given an annual pension of 1,000 livres, and apartments and a studio in the Louvre. In the meantime, work was going on at Fontainbleau, whither Boucher was called to decorate the Council Chamber. Very soon he was occupied with the many cares necessarily facing an artist in an official position—serving on Commissions, reporting on the condition of pictures, and numerous social occasions—and the quality of his work began to deteriorate.

By 1754 Boucher had turned to pastorals—shepherds and shepherdesses, repeated as figures at almost every porcelain factory in Europe. His pictures were fantastically popular. He could sell as quickly as he could paint, and engravers issued sets of prints after his work as fast as the plates could be engraved. In 1755, in consequence of the death of Oudry, he was given the post of Director of the Gobelins tapestry factory.

The year 1758 saw the precursors of the change in style soon to come, and the picturesque ruins of Greece and Rome were making a first tentative appearance. Diderot attacked Boucher and his work, and subjects taken from classical sources began to be popular. Boucher attempted the new style without very much success.

Denis Diderot, who made numerous attacks on Boucher thereafter, was educated by the Jesuits. At first he earned a living by journalistic hack-work and the compilation of encyclopedias, but soon became a prominent member of a group of free-thinking philosophers who fought against the tyranny of the Church and the corruption of the Court. With his friend, Jean-Jacques Rousseau, he made a large contribution to the climate of public opinion which culminated in the Revolution.

Mme de Pompadour died in 1764, at the age of forty-two years, and Boucher lost his most powerful protector. Nevertheless, his popularity was not seriously affected, and her brother gained him the position of First Painter to the Court in succession to Vanloo. Although he had to relinquish his directorate of the Gobelins factory in consequence, his remuneration of 1,200 livres a year was converted to a pension. Nevertheless Diderot continued his ill-natured attacks on Boucher's work and moral character, and the health of the latter began to fail. He died in May, 1770, still seated at his easel.

The art of Boucher is important, not only for itself and for its influence, but for the way in which it exhibits, in its development, all the successive phases to be seen in the art of the *Louis Quinze* period. His influence on porcelain-making and decoration was widespread in France, and, to a lesser extent, in England and Germany. His work began when *baroque* was giving place to *rococo*, and finished a little before the transitional *Louis Seize* had culminated in the full-blown neo-classical style.

Boucher's connection with Vincennes began when Bachelier asked him for assistance. It is probable that he did, in fact, exercise some supervision over the modelling of groups and figures taken from his work. In 1754 Madame de Pompadour had eight *biscuit* figures modelled by Blondeau (Plate 73)—a modeller who was also responsible for four hunting groups after Oudry which are almost the earliest examples of Vincennes figure sculpture known. Boucher also provided sketches for the sculptor, Jean-Baptiste Fernex, who worked between 1753 and 1756, and for the modeller, Suzanne, whose principal works were children after Boucher. The work of Fernex and Suzanne is, in fact, difficult to separate. These are discussed later.

Boucher's nephew, Jacques-Louis David, was one of the more important exponents of the neo-classical style. Born in 1748, David went to Rome in 1774, where he spent the next six years studying the antique. He became a member of the French Academy in 1780, and, during the Revolution, was a member of the Committee of Public Safety. Narrowly escaping death by the guillotine, he was appointed Court Painter to Napoleon in 1804. After Napoleon's fall he was banished to Brussels for his part in the condemnation of Louis XVI. David's influence can be seen in some of the work of Sèvres during the period of the First Empire.

Vincennes was unsuitable as a site for a porcelain factory and regarded as no more than a temporary convenience, although it was again used for the same purpose in 1765 by Pierre-Antoine Hannong (See Chapter VI).

Vincennes is within the metropolitan district of Paris; it can easily be reached on the *Métro*. At first used as a residence of the Kings of France, it was discarded, and for a time, under Louis XI, it became a state prison. It was again used as a prison during the insurrection of the Fronde, and the Prince de Condé was lodged there for a time. Louis XIV stayed at Vincennes occasionally, but for the most part it was forgotten as a residence, possibly because it was situated in an unfashionable part of Paris. For a short period it was occupied by the royal factory, and again by the factory under the patronage of Louis-Phillipe, Duc de Chartres, but later reverted to a prison, Mirabeau being incarcerated here before the Revolution. Vincennes also saw the execution of Louis-Antoine de Bourbon, Duc d'Enghien, condemned to death in 1804 on a charge of conspiracy against Napoleon.

Mme de Pompadour, with the King's interest and assistance, selected a new site near her *château* of Bellevue, and not far from Versailles. Sèvres is situated to the south-west of Paris on the banks of the Seine, a few miles from St. Cloud. She employed the architect, Lindel, to design the factory, but unfortunately this was his first such assignment, and he was unused to designing industrial buildings. The new factory was badly planned, and, instead of being spaced out on a single floor, it was given three storeys, which meant that the workpeople spent much of their time climbing from one to the other. Accommodation was provided for the King, which included such luxuries as a private chapel, where doubtless he sought divine intervention on behalf of the new undertaking. A warehouse for the display of porcelain was also included. The total cost was more than a million livres.

The factory moved to its new premises in 1756, and subventions from the Crown were needed almost at once to keep it in existence. A large number of people were employed at the time of the removal to Sèvres, but production was not competitive. Complaints of high prices were numerous, and the porcelain of both Meissen and the Orient was cheaper. The cause seems to have been two-fold: the large number of kiln-wasters, and the fragility of the body.

The factory demanded a very high standard, and discarded products which other factories would unquestionably have released for sale. These rejected specimens were either smashed, or, if the defects were trivial, put on one side. Some of them were sold to decorators at the time, but this was discontinued when it was discovered that such things were being decorated and sold as the production of the factory. Even the factory's artists illegally painted this kind of white ware at home. It was, therefore, allowed to accumulate until the Revolution, when it was sold to provide the workpeople with bare subsistence, and formed the base for many of the most deceptive fakes of old Sèvres porcelain.

The fragility of the porcelain led to an unwillingness on the part of the Paris porcelain dealers to handle it. They complained that they were not allowed for breakages in transit. Moreover, they did an extremely lucrative business in hiring out services for celebrations and parties, and it was found that breakages were far greater with porcelain from Sèvres than was the case with the much tougher porcelain from Germany and the Far East. The factory, too, had curious methods of calculating charges. For example, all specimens of the same shape were charged at the same price, regardless of the quality or elaboration of the painting. This was convenient for the purpose of accountancy, but made the sale of the humbler objects difficult. Probably because of difficulties with the porcelain dealers the factory opened its own showrooms in the rue de la Monnaie, and Mme de

Pompadour proved an excellent saleswoman. The Marquis d'Argenson, ever her enemy, wrote of her as saying, 'Not to buy as much of this porcelain as one can afford is to prove oneself a bad citizen'.

Debts accumulated, and in October, 1759, the partners in the Brichard Company succeeded in persuading the King to take over the factory for himself. It remained royal property thereafter, Louis XVIII complaining bitterly to Berlin of the plundering of his factory by Blücher's Prussians in 1815.

Boileau, who had remained in his position hitherto by astute manoeuvring, despite the changes in ownership, was retained, and Bertin, the Minister of Fine Arts, and the Sieur de Barberie de Courteille, Intendant of France, were also appointed as administrators. Most of the work of rehabilitating the undertaking fell on Boileau, who immediately took energetic steps against competition. The various edicts were applied with severity, and the manufacture of porcelain or *faïence* by any but a few registered factories was totally forbidden. A few which enjoyed influential patronage were permitted to continue, but these were only allowed to make wares decorated in blue in the Chinese manner.

Reprehensible though these edicts may seem today, they were, to some extent, justified. The Sèvres factory had set itself the task of making the finest porcelain in the world, regardless of cost, and it is obvious that only an undertaking in the special position both of belonging to the King and enjoying such privileges could have done it. The other factories inevitably had to sacrifice quality to maintain profits and a large volume of sales, and Sèvres could not have competed with them on these terms, and, at the same time, sustained the very high level of attainment shown in its products. Sèvres was determined to make porcelain of a quality fit to be associated with the name of the King of France, and it could only do so if protected by rigorous measures of this kind. Indeed, despite the advantages enjoyed, it still made losses, and the King made up a deficiency of 96,000 livres in 1763. These deficiencies, large though they were, are perhaps the more understandable when we remember the kind of wares the factory was producing. In 1757 a garniture of vases cost 42,000 livres to make—almost half the total deficit of 1763.

The years following 1759 saw considerable growth in the factory's output, both in quantity and diversity. Much service-ware was produced to take the place of silver, since a great deal of the latter had been sent to the Mint for conversion into coin. Apart from service-ware, however, we find the great decorative vases and inkstands (on which much time and money were lavished), as well as humbler items of utility for the toilet and the bed-chamber—brush-backs, toilet-pots, chamber-pots, *bidets*, and so forth. Small items—always popular among those members of the nobility whose purse was limited—included such things as *bonbonnières*, tobacco boxes, snuff-boxes, sword- and cane-handles, watch-cases, *étuis*, boxes for gaming counters, and scent-bottles, whilst the factory did not disdain to make such *trivia* as thimbles, buttons, and even artificial teeth. The latter were probably popular among the ladies of the Court, since the beauty of several is recorded as having been marred by decaying teeth. The choicest pieces were brought into the sale room on New Year's Day, the King himself selling them to the nobility. As a contemporary account has it, 'He sells the pieces himself, and they are not cheap'.

The more important things were miracles of craftsmanship which have never been surpassed. Decorated sumptuously by artists of skill under the direction of designers such as Boucher, they were intended to be placed in settings of the utmost magnificence. It is true that, judged by normal criteria, it is possible to bring the charge of over-decoration, but this porcelain is a special case, and we need to remember the surroundings for which it was intended. For this reason the King's gifts of porcelain were regarded as a mark of signal favour, and almost as expensive as the silver and gold plate they replaced.

In 1766 the factory was in a sufficiently strong position for the earlier severity of the edicts to be relaxed. Figure modelling, polychrome decoration, coloured grounds, and gilding were still reserved to the royal factory, and permission to manufacture was only granted to other factories on condition that each piece bore a mark, and that the mark was registered with the police. Permitted decoration was limited to underglaze blue and to monochromes *en camaïeu*.

Figure modelling since 1757 had been in charge of Etienne-Maurice Falconet. This appointment was an extremely important one, since most of the finest work in *biscuit* was done whilst he was head of this department. Falconet was born in 1716, the son of a carpenter of the rue Poisonnier. His uncle, Nicolas Guillaume, was a carver of such things as marble mantelpieces, and young Falconet was his pupil for a time. Later, he was taken up by Jean-Baptiste Lemoyne, under whose tuition Falconet learned to be an artist as well as a craftsman. Although he was keenly interested in the excavations at Herculaneum, he did not allow himself to be swayed by extremes of opinion, such as that of Winkelmann when he said, 'Porcelain is nearly always made into idiotic puppets'. Falconet turned his attention to the portrayal of nymphs, usually undraped or partially so, in which penchant he resembles Boucher. These models were done with great artistry, the best known undoubtedly being *La Baigneuse* (Plate 76) which was copied by many European factories.

Even before his appointment to take charge of the department of modelling he had achieved recognition by the

King, who gave him a studio in the Louvre—a considerable honour—as well as an annual pension of five hundred livres. He was given another studio at Sèvres above the King's chambers, which, in time, he turned into a school for young sculptors. Here he must have worked in close touch with Boucher, who was adviser on all matters relating to painting and sculpture, and some of Falconet's own work was adapted from Boucher's designs. A collection of engravings entitled *Figures in French porcelain designed by M. Boucher in 1757* was engraved by Falconet *fils*. Some of Falconet's figures made during this period are discussed later in this chapter, but the distinctive Sèvres style in figure modelling dates from this time.

Falconet became a member of the French Academy in 1761, and produced his *Réflexions sur la Sculpture* in the same year. In 1766 he asked leave to go to Russia to work for Catherine the Great, where he was responsible for a colossal statue of Peter the Great in bronze. He returned to France in 1781, and died ten years later. Diderot was one of his friends, and did much to encourage him. A bust of Diderot in a series entitled *Galerie des grands hommes* was issued in 1766.

In 1764, Mme de Pompadour had died, and Boucher was ill and aging. Falconet left for Russia in 1766, and de Courteille died in the following year. The old order was changing, and the death of de Courteille caused the King to take the factory under his personal control.

Falconet was replaced temporarily as chief modeller by Jean-Jacques Caffiéri, son of Jacques Caffiéri, sculptor, silversmith, and bronze worker. Jean-Jacques had been a pupil, first of his father, and then of J.-B. Lemoyne, and he was admitted to the Academy in 1757. His character left something to be desired, and he pestered the authorities for a pension because of his father's services. Bachelier, therefore, was given control of the modelling department, as well as that of painting.

Bachelier was, by now, an extremely busy man. He was director of a school for teaching industrial art, he designed for the Gobelins tapestry works, and had a contract for decorating the Ministry of Foreign Affairs. He had, in fact, amassed a considerable fortune. He had some revolutionary ideas at this time, which probably stemmed from the prevailing climate of fashion. For instance, he wanted porcelain to become the rival of bronze and marble, and Plate 51b shows a porcelain vase, veined like marble and mounted in gilded bronze, which dates from this period. *Biscuit* figures, too, began to lose some of their earlier charm and spontaneity. The work put in hand by Falconet was finished, and a start was made on copies from 'the antique'.

These were the years of experiments with hard porcelain, which are reviewed in more detail in Chapter VI. The new body was first used in 1772. The soft porcelain, which was particularly suitable for painting, continued to be made, and was not discontinued until the end of the century. The painters are not so well known as the modellers, because, generally, they did little work outside the factory, but some of the more important are discussed later in this chapter.

The use of Sèvres porcelain for the decoration of furniture, later to be extremely fashionable, began about 1760. Most such work was done at the time by the firm of Poirier, although the Garde-Meuble de la Couronne also ordered plaques for this purpose. These were very commonly used for insetting into small tables, but clocks soon began to be ornamented similarly. At first the plaques were put into a gilded bronze setting, but the whole case was later made in porcelain.

Boileau died in 1772. His death brought to light a great

deal of maladministration. In the department of figure modelling, for instance, it was found that all the moulds had been thrown together in a heap after use, and everything depended on the memory of one old man who, when moulds were required, had to find them. There was, too, little discipline among the workers, whilst the directors had few thoughts beyond getting rich at the factory's expense. The new director, Melchior-François Parent, had the difficult task of bringing order into chaos and introducing systems of classification and arrangement. He took over at a time when *biscuit* was becoming hard to sell, and he did much to develop the manufacture of hard porcelain to help the factory in its difficulties. In 1778, however, he was accused of misappropriating funds amounting to 250,000 livres, and this led to his imprisonment in the Bastille. Affairs were certainly in bad shape, no less than 150,000 livres being due to the workmen for wages, and to suppliers for raw materials. It remains a point of controversy, however, as to how far Parent can be blamed for the situation. It is probable that he inherited a very difficult position which the astute politician, Boileau, had managed to conceal until his death.

Louis XV died in 1774. The place of Madame de Pompadour as a patron of the factory had never been taken by Madame du Barry, although she bought a great deal of porcelain, and continued to do so until the time of the Revolution. Services exist with her monogram, 'D' in gold and 'B' in woven flowers. Pajou, a pupil of Lemoyne, who was already well known as a portrait artist, did a bust of Madame du Barry in 1770 which was reproduced by Sèvres in *biscuit*. This was sold to the factory at half price because the sitter did not like it. She said the hair style was out of date, and ordered another without paying for the first. A third, with the hair in the style of Falconet's *Baigneuse*, was also rejected by the sitter, to Pajou's great annoyance; her *coiffeur*, Legros, was a man of considerable influence in Court circles. Another portrait of the du Barry was made after a bust by Lemoyne, who was also asked to do a portrait of Marie-Antoinette to send to her mother, Maria Theresa.

Augustin Pajou was one of the more important sculptors to model for the factory after Falconet's departure. He was born in 1730, and won the *Prix de Rome* in 1748, going to Rome to study at public expense. His *Pluto holding Cerberus in Chains* gained him admission to the Academy, and among his better known portrait busts may be numbered those of Buffon, Pascal, Turenne, and Descartes.

Another sculptor of the same period was Jacques Saly, whose work was judged by some to be even better than that of Falconet. He was commissioned by the Danish East India Company to do an equestrian statue of King Frederick V; and a statue of Louis XV at Valenciennes, which was destroyed in 1793, survives in the form of a copy made at Mennecy. Houdon, one of the greatest sculptors of the period, also occasionally contributed models to the factory. He survived the Revolution, and in his later years taught at the École des Beaux-Arts, dying in 1825.

The place of Parent was taken by the Director-General of Royal Buildings, Charles-Claude de Labillarderie, Comte d'Angiviller. He, in turn, appointed Regnier, and a Swiss chemist named Hettlinger, as administrators. The position was a difficult one. The hard porcelain factories of Paris were producing wares of good quality at much lower prices, and they were protected by princes of the blood, and, in one case (rue Thiroux), by Marie-Antoinette herself. There was a fantastic amount of corruption inherent in the situation. Years of training were given to artists in the École Royale, and, when they were about to give some return for the money spent on their education, they were lured away from the royal factory by bribes. Other workers were bribed to give details of new models before they could be finished and put on the market.

The Comte d'Angiviller, therefore, needed to take drastic action. Regnier made economies, and the King ordered Lenoir, the Lieutenant of Police, to exercise vigilance over illegal competition, but, in fact, Lenoir was protecting some of the competitors himself—of course, for a suitable reward.

The climate of opinion of the time began to question the rights of the King to these monopolies, and Necker, the Minister of Finance, who was opposed to draconian measures, tried to effect a reconciliation between Sèvres and its competitors.

In 1784 a new edict revived earlier prohibitions and referred to the fact that the restrictions previously imposed had not been entirely observed, and that the factories in Paris and the neighbourhood had become so great in number that serious damage was being done to the forests and woods round about, due to their use of wood for fuel.

Some delay was granted to factories with such powerful protectors as the Queen, the Comte d'Artois, and the Duc d'Angoulême. M. de Calonne, the new Finance Minister, requested d'Angivillers to delay action under the edict, and a year was allowed them to complete orders in hand. Advantage was taken of these concessions, and d'Angivillers was later in urgent communication with de Calonne, bringing to his notice fresh evasions of the regulations. Another edict was, therefore, promulgated in 1787, forbidding any porcelain to be made in the style of Sèvres without permission, and providing for an annual inspection by the Commissioners appointed by the King. In this way the manufacture of articles of luxury was entirely forbidden, and expressly reserved to Sèvres. This monopoly remained in force until the Revolution, when all such privileges were abolished.

The coronation of Louis XVI took place in the Cathedral of Rheims on June 9th, 1775. Louis was no less interested in the factory than had been his grandfather. Marie-Antoinette, too, had taken a good deal of interest in it. In 1769, when Paris was anticipating the marriage of Louis to Marie-Antoinette, Sèvres had worked for two years on a vast table decoration which was a reproduction of the Place Royale at Rheims. This had colonnades, steps, fountains, figures of children, merchants, and so forth, with a central reproduction of a statue of the King by Pigalle. The cost was fantastically high, although it was only a small part of the cost of the marriage celebrations. Most of this work was destroyed during the Revolution, but several copies of the statue were taken, and one or two survive.

In 1775 the new chief modeller, Louis-Simon Boizot, presented a small group called *L'autel Royale, ou le couronnement du Roi* to the King and Queen, which is preserved in the Petit Trianon. Boizot had taken over the sculpture studios from Bachelier in 1772, at the age of thirty. He had won the Prix de Rome ten years before, but did not become a member of the Academy until 1778. Boizot was the son of Antoine Boizot, who had married the daughter of Oudry, director of Gobelins, and was friendly with Pierre Gouthière, a bronze worker of great skill best known for his furniture mounts, who occasionally mounted porcelain. During the Revolution Boizot became a member of the commission appointed to protect works of art. He was extremely popular with the Court, and his appointment to the place of Bachelier was a popular one.

Like Kändler before him, Boizot conceived the idea of a life-size statue in *biscuit* of Louis XVI, for which purpose a special body was devised. This figure was not actually finished. It is, however, noteworthy that much of Boizot's work is of large size. An example is shown on Plate 78. His

Plate 49 (a). Large *jardinière* with central division, *rose Pompadour* ground with green bands, painted with peasants carousing after Teniers by Dodin. Sèvres. 1759. (Wallace Colln.)

(b). *Jardinière* painted with *Le Pêche* by J. B. Le Prince after Boucher, in blue with red flesh tints in a panel reserved on a yellow ground. Sèvres. 1763. (V&AM.)

Plate 50 (a). Covered pierced basket and stand in turquoise and white. Sèvres. 1759. Mark: a lighted candle. (Wallace Colln.)

(b). Flower-stand with *bleu de Roi* ground, the coast scene painted by Morin. Louis Seize style. Sèvres. 1772. (Wallace Colln.)

Plate 51 (a). Tureen-shaped vase and cover painted with harbour and a ruin scene on a *bleu de Roi* ground. The cover painted with figures *en grisaille*. Sèvres. 1791. (Wallace Colln.)

(b). Bowl of white porcelain marbled with grey. Contemporary mounts. Sèvres. 1763. (V&AM.)

Plate 52 (*a*). Inkstand, designed by Claude-Thomas Duplessis. The medallion of Louis XV, the monogram 'MA' and the arms of France, suggest a gift by Louis to his daughter Marie Adelaide (1732–1800). Sèvres. c. 1760. (Wallace Colln.)

(*b*). Pair of vases painted by Fontaine. Date letter for 1761. Sèvres. (V & AM.)

Plate 53 (a). Candelabra or *flambeaux* of four lights in pale blue-green and white, the elephants' heads supporting double lights, the cupids, after Boucher, painted by Dodin. Sèvres. 1756. (Wallace Colln.)

(b). A pair of bulb-holders in *rose Pompadour* and green, painted with flower-bouquets in reserves. Sèvres. Before 1764. (Wallace Colln.)

Plate 54 (a). Pair of vases and covers, turquoise blue ground, painted with shipping scenes. Sèvres. Date letter for 1757 (E). (V&AM.)

(*b*). Pair of vases of 'jewelled' porcelain, painted with subjects after Eisen from Montesquieu's *Temple de Guide*. Blue ground. Sèvres. 1781. (BM.)

Plate 55. Vase-shaped flower stand (one of a pair) with turquoise blue ground, painted with pheasants and other birds. Dolphin handles. The bases are detachable and made to hold water. Sèvres. 1756. (Wallace Colln.)

Plate 56 (a). Jardinière painted with exotic birds in panels reserved on a green ground. Sèvres. 1760. (V&AM.)

(b). Jardinière painted with a figure of Cupid in a panel reserved on a rose Pompadour ground. Flower painting by Dubois. Sèvres. 1761. (V&AM.)

Plate 57. Vase and cover with turquoise blue ground painted with *La Baigneuse* after Lemoyne. Louis Seize style. Sèvres. c. 1765. (Wallace Colln.)

Plate 58. Vase with apple-green ground, gilded tassels and acanthus leaves, and a mythological subject. On the reverse, military trophies. Gilding by H. E. Vincent *jeune*. Sèvres. c. 1780. (Wallace Colln.)

Plate 59. Vase and cover painted with floral garlands, probably by Micaud, on a blue ground with an *oeil de perdrix* design in gold. The classical medallion painted *en grisaille*. Sèvres. c. 1769. (Wallace Colln.)

Plate 60. Cylindrical vase with *bleu de Roi* ground and medallions *en grisaille* on an ormolu base. Sèvres. c. 1775. (V&AM.)

Plate 61. Pair of *cachepots* with turquoise blue ground and medallions *en camaïeu.* Richly gilt. Part of a service made for the Empress Catherine II of Russia. Sèvres. 1778. (Wallace Colln.)

(*b*). Sèvres porcelain top of a Louis Seize parquetry table by Adam Weisweiler. (Christie's.)

Plate 62 (*a*). Large krater-shaped vase with classical figures in white relief on a blue ground. Sèvres *biscuit* porcelain. End of the

(b). Wall chandelier (*bras de cheminée*) in porcelain and gilt bronze. Sèvres. 1760. (V&AM.)

Plate 63 (*a*). Cabinet by André Schuman (fl. 1779–87) inset with Sèvres plaques, the centre of which is decorated with a farmyard scene. (Wallace Colln.)

Plate 64. Vase clock with *oeil de perdrix* on green, the stand and mounts in the manner of Gouthière, the clock by Mountjoy of Paris. Sèvres. c. 1770. (Wallace Colln.)

work is always in hard porcelain. His portrait busts of Marie-Antoinette made in 1774, and of Louis XVI in the following year, no longer exist. No specimens have survived, and the moulds were smashed in 1793 when, in an excess of enthusiasm for the Revolution, the workmen destroyed all such things.

The craftsmen of Sèvres went from one triumph to another in the handling of their material. In 1783 a vase about five feet in height was made at a cost of 70,000 livres, and one still larger was made two years later. Exhibitions of porcelain, from which the public could buy, were held at Versailles, and the King himself unpacked the pieces, breaking, according to Hettlinger, not a few. About 1780 a new kind of decoration was devised which consisted of drops of translucent enamel which were sometimes put over gold foil. These imitated rubies, emeralds, and so forth, and the type was referred to as 'jewelled' porcelain. Whilst we can admire the ingenuity displayed, we may legitimately question the taste which led to its introduction.

A sumptuous dinner service and table-decoration made for Catherine the Great in 1775 led to international complications. This had a turquoise ground, and cameos in the 'antique' style, the intervening space between the cameos being filled with foliate ornament in rich gilding. Catherine paid a small amount on account, but refused to pay the balance, and the Foreign Ministers of both countries were involved in correspondence about it. It is difficult to say whether or not this was ever settled because the Revolution intervened, but Boizot became bankrupt as the result of his share in the work.

I have already mentioned that the edicts of 1784 and 1787 were promulgated in order to revive the flagging fortunes of the factory. The economic situation of the time was bad, and the factory was seriously in debt because no one could afford to buy its products. By 1789 the warehouses were full of unsold stock, and it became impossible to find sufficient money to pay the workmen, or to buy new materials. Many of the staff were discharged and went elsewhere, and unrest spread rapidly. An offer was made by a group of financiers to buy the factory, but the King refused to sell. He directed that no more debts were to be incurred, and promised subsidies to keep it in existence until things improved.

But events elsewhere overtook the King's intentions, and a decree of 1791 recognised the factory as chargeable to the King's Civil List. In 1792 Haudry, and the Minister of the Interior, Roland, were placed in charge of administration. Regnier and Hettlinger were retained at their posts, but the workmen repeatedly denounced them to the Committee of Public Safety, and ultimately they were arrested. In 1793 Bachelier, and the Assistant Art Director, Lagrenée, were discharged, the latter returning afterwards as Art Director.

A member of the factory's Revolutionary Committee, J. B. Chanou, who had been principally responsible for the arrest of Hettlinger and Regnier, was appointed administrator, and took the opportunity not only to get rid of Lagrenée and Boizot, but to embezzle the funds and to loot the stock. The cashier, Barrau, was arrested on trumped up charges, and ordered to collect all debts within a month. Perhaps fortunately, this task was impossible, and the Committee for Agriculture and the Arts brought back Hettlinger, and appointed one Salmon, as well as a chemist, François Meyer, as directors. Lagrenée and Boizot were at once re-engaged.

It is not particularly surprising that, as a result of this maladministration, the workmen were starving when Hettlinger was reappointed, and, with rare magnanimity, he sold his jewellery to get money to pay their wages, and the government gave relief in the form of flour and meat. These, however, were putrid, and could hardly be eaten, and, in 1799, a deputation interviewed various members of the government. The factory was finally given financial assistance. This was little more than its due, since the Directoire had placed orders for porcelain for which the factory had never been paid.

In 1800 Alexandre Brongniart was appointed director by the Minister of the Interior, Lucien Bonaparte, and he took immediate steps to put the factory on a better footing. Boizot and Lagrenée were both discharged, and a sale at the Louvre was held to raise money. More financial assistance was given by the new government, and, in 1806, Napoleon took the factory under his protection.

Brongniart, who took the directorship from his rival, Dihl (page 197), remained until 1847. Originally Inspector of Mines and Professor of Natural History, he was an excellent administrator. He disliked soft porcelain, and discontinued its manufacture, selling all the remaining stock to decorators. The soft glaze hitherto used on hard porcelain was replaced by a feldspathic glaze. This enabled him to develop a palette suitable for the exact copying of easel pictures on to porcelain. He introduced a system of mass-production in which artists who specialized in particular types of decoration were employed to do part of the work, the remainder being passed on to another specialist, with results which can be imagined.

In 1815 Paris was occupied by the allied armies. The Prussians looted the cash reserves of 10,000 francs, bought some of the stock at reduced prices, and packed and sent porcelain commemorating Napoleon's battles to Berlin without payment, disregarding protests that the factory was the private property of Louis XVIII.

At this date it is convenient to cease this review of the history of the Sèvres factory. The work of the nineteenth century, in common with that of other European factories, is hardly worth considering. The factory, of course, is now the property of the French Government, and it possesses an extremely important collection of French porcelain in the Musée de Sèvres. Its productions are considered in more detail in the following pages.

*   *   *   *   *

The porcelain of the brothers Dubois has only been doubtfully identified. It has been suggested that it might resemble that of Chantilly, but there is no reason to suppose that a tin glaze was used. We have the authority of Bachelier for saying that some decoration in the Kakiemon style, as well as *indianische Blumen*, was done at the time, and since Meissen was popular, some derivations can be inferred. (Plate 37a). The influence of St. Cloud is especially apparent in a few examples with raised prunus decoration.

This early body was greyish in colour, with a brilliant glaze, and forms were simple. Faults in the glaze were hidden by a flower or an insect in the same way as that used at Meissen for the same purpose.

In 1745 the body became much whiter, and the making of porcelain flowers, usually roses, pinks, jonquils, anemones, lilies, tulips, and hyacinths, was introduced about the same time. These flowers were immensely popular, the King spending vast sums on them for the decoration of his *château*, whilst Mme de Pompadour created a winter flower garden at Bellevue composed entirely of porcelain flowers. The Marquis d'Argenson* wrote: 'The King has ordered more than 800,000 livres' worth of porcelain flowers from the Vincennes factory, naturally painted, for all his country houses, and especially for the *château* of Bellevue belonging

*Argenson, René Louis de Voyer de Paulmy, Marquis d': *Journal et Memoirs*. Paris, 1861–7.

to the Marquise de Pompadour. Paris talks of nothing else, and this unheard of luxury causes great scandal.'*

According to other eye-witnesses these flowers were so deceptive as to appear natural until examined closely. By 1748, the flower studios, where forty-five women were already employed under the direction of Mme Gravant, had to be extended.

A vase of white porcelain was offered to the Queen in 1748 which was mounted in gilt bronze, and held four hundred and eighty flowers with bronze stalks and leaves. It stood about three feet high, and the bronze work alone cost about one hundred louis.† In 1749 the Dauphine sent a similar vase to her father, Augustus of Saxony, which was, for a long time, in the Dresden Collections, but which now seems to have disappeared.

The flowers were, at first, used in conjunction with vases made at Meissen, but the vases, too, were speedily supplied by Vincennes. It is noteworthy that, at this period, such decorative items as inkstands in gilt bronze were often decorated with Meissen figures, and the fashion for mounting porcelain in this way was established before the founding of the Vincennes undertaking.

In 1749 flowers formed the greater part of the factory's production, and wares were decorated with similar flowers and leaves applied to the surface, giving an appearance of great richness. This fashion, too, was much copied elsewhere, and led to such things as the naïvely-modelled vases

---

*'Le Roi a commandé à la Manufacture de Vincennes des fleurs de porcelaine peintes au naturel avec leurs vases pour plus de huit cent mille livres, pour toutes ses maisons de campagne et spécialement pour le château de Bellevue de la Marquise de Pompadour. On ne parle que de cela dans Paris, et véritablement ce luxe scandalise beaucoup.'—The Marquis was an avid collector of porcelain from the Royal factory.

†About £300 in present-day currency (1960).

of Longton Hall, in England, which are surmounted by a mass of modelled flowers. After 1755 the taste for flowers declined rapidly, although they were still made occasionally, several bouquets being ordered by the Court during the reign of Louis XVI.

The character of production began to change about 1752. The Court goldsmith, Duplessis, was responsible for many of the designs, which often show a strong resemblance to contemporary metal-work. The more elaborate shapes are represented in the Wallace Collection by the boat-shaped *vaisseau à mât* (*mât* means mast, whilst *vaisseau* can mean either a vase or a ship), and by candlestick vases with elephant heads. Both were designed by Duplessis. (Plate Frontispiece and 53a.) The *vaisseau à mât* illustrated has the banner of France, with *fleur de lys*, draped on the mast, and a bowsprit at either end.

Vases of one kind or another became the most characteristic products of the factory, and vases for the chimney-piece (*garniture de cheminée*) were made in sets of three, four, or five. Sets of this kind were made during the seventeenth century at Delft, in Holland, where they usually consisted of two beakers and three covered vases arranged alternately. Many of those from Vincennes and Sèvres were provided with coloured grounds, rich gilding tooled and chased, and panels in which paintings of various kinds were executed. The earliest painted decoration was derived from Meissen. The privilege of 1745 mentions painting in the *'façon de Saxe, peinte et dorée à figures humaines'*.*

The comparatively scarce Oriental designs, the 'banded hedge' and so forth, were taken from work by Meissen, Chantilly, and St. Cloud—very rarely from the originals. Japanese patterns at Chantilly are discussed in more detail on page 92. *Chinoiseries* are infrequent from

*'In the style of Meissen, painted with human figures and gilded.'

Vincennes and Sèvres, and, for some reason, were always expensive. Mme du Barry ordered a service in 1773, each plate of which cost one hundred and forty livres. Marie-Antoinette ordered a *service japon*, and some cups and saucers *japonnés* were made for the dealer, Lazare Duvaux, who was responsible for decorating Mme de Pompadour's *château* at Bellevue.

The greatest influence seems to have been exerted by Chantilly during the early period, and such things as the 'vase Chantilly' are indicative of the position. Many of the flower painters of the early period were recruited from Condé's factory. There is also a noticeable resemblance between the flowers of Vincennes and those of Strasbourg *faïence*, the latter enjoying tremendous popularity at the time.

An intense lapis blue enamel introduced in 1753 was used round the edges of some pieces, as well as to outline moulded shell ornament and *rococo* panels. These enamel borders were usually ornamented with gold in addition. The lapis blue was also used as a monochrome *en camaïeu* for figure painting, the flesh tints being added in pink, which was surrounded by an elaborate *cartouche* in gold. This colour was used most effectively in conjunction with a yellow ground. This combination recalls the use of black with flesh tints, particularly by the German *Hausmaler*, Seuter. The practice may have been a remote ancestor of the Vincennes decoration. Purple was also used for *en camaïeu* painting of this kind, and flowers, birds, landscapes, and figure subjects can be seen in this and the lapis blue. In particular, little *putti* after Boucher were often used.

The earliest ground colour, the *gros bleu*, was devised by Hellot, and first used about 1749. It was sponged on, and is therefore always a little uneven, but usually it is of great intensity. This blue is very dark in colour, and was always applied under the glaze. Perhaps because of the intensity, the ground was covered by patterns in gold which had the effect of reducing it somewhat. These patterns are well-defined, and include an irregular network of gilt lines—the *caillouté*, and another similarly irregular pattern, the *vermiculé*. Gold was strewn in dots over the surface as early as 1750, whilst decoration in gold silhouette over a deep blue ground can be seen in 1753 and was a logical development. Large birds, pheasants and herons, were particularly treated in this way. This kind of decoration can later be seen in England, at the Chelsea factory during the gold anchor period, and is to be noted on such things as plates from the Mecklenburg-Strelitz service.

Following the *gros bleu*, Hellot succeeded in producing the *bleu céleste*, a turquoise ground which is attributable to 1752, the earliest known specimen of which is in the Sèvres Museum. This is a prime target of the forger, but is then rarely successful. Usually it is too green in tone. The *jaune jonquil*, a yellow ground, was produced in 1753, but was rarely used. It is particularly effective in conjunction with figures in lapis blue. Violet and green were first used in 1756.

In 1753 Hellot collected all the various discoveries in the realm of colour into a volume* which is now in the archives of the Musée de Sèvres. In this he lists the colours then available—red-purple, dark purple, soft jonquil, yellow, yellowish-green, blue *'tendre'*, greenish-brown, dark greenish-brown, brown, brownish-black, *'gorge de pigeon'*, *'verte de mer'*, *'verte farcé'*, and so on. The palette was now extremely comprehensive, and shows that great progress had been made.

*Recueil de tous les procédés de la porcelain de la Manufacture royale de Vincennes décrits pour le Roy Sa Majesté s'en étant réservé le secret par arrêté du 19 Auout 1753.

III. Tureen and cover with a ground of turquoise blue, rich gilt
scrollwork, and figure subjects in reserved panels. Vincennes. Before
1753. (Wallace Colln.)

Gold was laid on thickly, burnished, and engraved with great skill. Some of the engraving was done with the point of a hob-nail, a primitive tool which was very effective for the purpose. Fine gilding was, in fact, always a speciality of the factory, more particularly on its soft porcelain. The method adopted was to grind gold with honey. This was painted on thickly and given a light firing. Such gilding is dull and rich in appearance, with none of the meretricious brassiness of the mercuric gilding process used by other factories towards the end of the century. Gilding by the latter method is done with gold dissolved in mercury which is painted on and fired. The heat of the kiln drives off the mercury, leaving the gold behind as a thin film.

The porcelain of Vincennes, after the earliest years, shows an increasing tendency towards over-decoration, and gilding, although always of the highest quality, becomes more elaborate with the passing of time. Paintings in re-served panels were enclosed within finely-tooled *cartouches* formed of palm-branches, reeds, flowers, and *rococo* scroll-work, and, in many cases, the gilding is at least as fine as the remainder of the decoration. Gilding of this kind was a factory speciality, and forgeries are frequently revealed by poor gilding, badly finished—something never to be observed in a genuine specimen. One of the early gilders, Etienne-Henri Le Guay, is particularly associated with important work.

The names of some of the painters of the period are known, although there is little detailed information about them to be had. Mutel and Etienne Evans, the latter a fan-painter, did birds and landscapes. The painter, Xhrouet, sometimes said to have invented the *rose Pompadour* ground, used the same subjects. Much of the finer work was done by Vieillard, who came to Vincennes in 1752, and who was followed in the factory's employment by his son, a flower painter, in 1784. From 1750 onwards many of the fan-painters of Paris were recruited to the enamelling studios of Vincennes. They were, of course, skilled painters of miniature decoration, and many of them were flower painters.

Flowers were a favourite subject with Bachelier, and it is hardly surprising that much of the surviving painted decoration has these for a subject. Birds were also a favourite, but landscapes and figures are rarer. The earlier flowers are less realistic than the later varieties, and are usually grouped in slight bouquets. Probably under the influence of the Meissen *deutsche Blumen* and Strasbourg floral painting, bouquets began to be richer and more elegant, although they lost some of their earlier charm. The tendency towards natural representation increased towards the end of the century, culminating in a style which was little more than illustrative of a botanical treatise. Birds, too, were at first of the exotic variety, based on natural birds but much more decorative. These gradually became more realistic, and, after about 1775, under the influence of Buffon's *Histoire naturelle des oiseaux*, even came to the point where the name of the bird was put on the reverse of plates and dishes, being, by this time, little more than illustrations to Buffon's work.

Flower painting was in the hands of such artists as Antoine-Toussaint Cornaille, who came from Chantilly; Taillandier, from Sceaux, and his wife; Jean-Baptiste Tandart and Charles Tandart; Denis and Felix Levé, and Thevenet.

The little *putti* of Boucher were popular, and were painted in monochrome. Polychrome painting was not common at Vincennes until the last year or two. The period of subjects after Boucher is subsequent to the removal to Sèvres. Subjects derived from the painter, Teniers, were probably introduced just before the removal. These were extremely popular, and their adoption led to the use of a detailed miniature style in which the whole of the surface available was enamelled, instead of the earlier Vincennes style in which a good deal of the white porcelain was left uncoloured. This alteration in the direction of a detailed rendering of an easel picture was hardly an improvement, but much ingenuity was shown in the treatment. The name of Dodin, who came to Vincennes in 1754, is associated with this kind of work at which he was adept, and Vieillard was hardly behind him.

Morin, from 1754 onwards, did shipping scenes, in part suggested by the harbour scenes of Meissen, and military subjects. The battle of Fontenoy in 1745, in which Louis XV personally defeated an English army, was commemorated in this way on a large vase.

Vincennes porcelain of all kinds, and in particular its figure-work, was often mounted in gilt bronze of the finest quality by Duplessis and others. Duvaux was certainly responsible for mounting a great deal. These mounts, in the *rococo* style, were often extremely elaborate. Of course, they have been imitated, and such mounts should always be examined carefully. They were made by casting, but eighteenth-century specimens have been very carefully chiselled and tooled afterwards to remove cast marks and to sharpen the details. This clarity and sharpness of detail is, in fact, an eighteenth-century characteristic. Mounts of poor quality must always be suspect.

Rococo ornament of the most elaborate kinds was difficult to carry out effectively in the soft porcelain body used, and this was often supplied by the mounts. This applies particularly to some of the early glazed figures and groups, but also, to some extent, to some of the decorative wares.

Vincennes porcelain usually shows a certain exuberance of form which is one of the principal characteristics of the *rococo* style, and this persisted in some of the vases until the reign of Louis XVI. The first reaction from it, however, can be seen as early as 1757, soon after the discoveries at Pompeii. The influence of Anne-Claude-Philippe, Comte de Caylus, was considerable. His illustrated works on Greek and Italian vases and antiquities were published between 1752 and 1767. The Academy of Herculaneum was founded in 1755, and published its first volume on the excavations, dealing with the *frescos*, in 1757, copies of which were eagerly sought. In 1762 Johann Joachim Winckelmann published the first of a series of *Letters* about the discoveries. One of these was particularly critical of the Naples Court, and the Comte de Caylus, a collector of considerable wealth, as well as a writer and engraver, translated a copy and had it published in France. This caused a great deal of acrimony, and as a result Winckelmann was unable to visit the sites again until 1764. Winckelmann's own *Geschichte der Kunst des Altertums* was published in 1764. It will be seen, therefore, that interest in classical antiquities had been large and growing before the influence of the discoveries became perceptible in the decorative art of the period. *Rococo* seems to have been abandoned finally with the service for Catherine the Great made in 1778. After this, everything is *à l'egyptienne*, *à l'étrusque*, or *à l'antique*.

During the Vincennes period, and later at Sèvres, service-ware was an important side of the production. A fairly frequent survival is the *écuelle*, a decorative tureen for soup or vegetables, which had a cover and stand. These were made in large quantities, both at Vincennes and at Sèvres, and were usually superbly decorated. Jugs mostly resemble those popular in contemporary *faïence*, and were made with a cover. The larger ewers were provided with a basin, and were manufactured in large numbers. The *gobelet*, a covered cup and saucer, was made in enormous quantities—two or three thousand each year—and the decoration varies considerably, one from the other. They were first made in 1753, this early version being called a *litron*. Cups and saucers were often superbly decorated, those with a *gros bleu* ground and birds in panels in gold silhouette being particularly handsome.

Complete services do not appear to have been made at Vincennes before 1753. Until this date china dealers bought plates and such things by the dozen, and put services together to order. In 1753 a large service for Louis with a *bleu céleste* ground painted with flowers was started, and the King and Mme de Pompadour began to give services to ambassadors and to foreign rulers. The period following the removal to Sèvres, therefore, was one in which table services of all kinds were extremely fashionable, and much time was devoted to them.

Porcelain, too, became popular for toilet-ware of all kinds. Barbers' bowls and a soap dish survive from the Vincennes period, but after the removal to Sèvres such things as eye-baths, spittoons, chamber-pots, *bidets*, and so forth were made, as well as pomade and cosmetic pots of all kinds. One, Demoiselle Martin, a seller of cosmetics, ordered rouge pots and similar objects at frequent intervals, and it is evident that exotic packaging for such things is by no means a modern innovation. A complete toilet set, in which even the brush-backs are of porcelain, is in the Wallace Collection (Plate 47a).

The transfer to Sèvres in 1756 was marked by some changes. The chemist, Pierre-Joseph Macquer, joined Hellot in 1757 to help with experiments in the hard porcelain body. Falconet was appointed Director of Sculpture in the following year.

Forms became distinctly more complicated, since the factory was now more proficient in handling the difficult soft paste body, and the elaborate bronze mountings of the early period were no longer so much in evidence. This tendency to complication was later modified by the onset of the *Louis Seize* style.

Vases, already an established speciality of the factory, continued to be made in a wide variety of forms, with decoration which constantly became more elaborate. Many such vases were made for *pot-pourri*, a mixture of dried petals and aromatics, which was used to scent the air. These vases were pierced at the top to allow the perfume to escape. They were frequently given modelled ornament of one kind or another.

The designs for vases were often given names, but some of these cannot be identified. The vase, '*à oreilles*', had *rococo* handles. These were made in 1757, and were still popular as late as 1783. The vase '*Hollandais*' was in the form of a fan. The vase '*Paris*', about thirty inches high, was probably the largest ever to be made in soft porcelain, being somewhat larger than any known example from Chelsea.

Equally popular were flower-bowls (*jardinières*) which took many forms, some of which have divisions in the centre. These, too, have names which are now difficult to relate to the things themselves. The vase, '*à oignons*' (Plate 53b), was specially made for the tuberose, which was grown as a bulb, and for other Dutch bulbs.

Table-ware of all kinds was manufactured in large quantities. The *déjeuner* was a small set on a tray, generally square if intended for one cup, and oval if such things as a milk-jug and sugar bowl were also supplied. If there were two cups, it became a *cabaret*. There is a distinct difference between the use of the term at Sèvres and at contemporary German factories, where the *déjeuner* tea-set, for instance, included a teapot, a cream-jug, a sugar basin, and a pair of cups. At Sèvres, trays were difficult to make,

and other materials than porcelain were sometimes sub-
stituted. So far as similar wares are concerned, teapots were
made soon after the Vincennes period, and tea-caddies first
appeared at the same time. Chocolate cups are to be seen
after about 1762, but the chocolate pot is a very rare item,
although the coffee-pot is somewhat less scarce.

In earlier services the plates were not always of porcelain.
Very large tureens were regarded as table ornaments, and
decorated accordingly, and such things as sauceboats, salad
dishes, salts, mustard pots, and so forth were provided.
Such small items as knife-handles and coffee spoons were
often included.

Dessert services consisted of plates and dishes, *sucriers*,
ice-cups and trays, and ice-buckets (*seaux*) for cooling wines,
in different sizes for bottles and half-bottles. There were
other additions to these services according to the fashion
of the times and the requirements of the customer. Mme de
Pompadour, for instance, had some labels for wine bottles
made in 1760, and the '*terrines à purée*', made in 1773, were
for the potato which M. Parmentier was then trying to
popularize in France.

The manufacture of plaques for the decoration of furniture—an important side of the factory's production—
began about 1760, probably at the instance of the firm
belonging to Simon Philippe Poirier. They were later
bought by Dominique Daguerre and his partner, Martin
Eloi Lignereux, who made a great deal of furniture for the
Court of France, and supplied the Prince-Regent and other
wealthy Englishmen.* Occasional sales were made to the
Garde-Meuble de la Couronne, and to Jean-François Leleu.
The latter was associated with the *maître ébéniste*, J. F.

---

*This firm later sold a great deal of Sèvres porcelain in London,
and Lignereux purchased white porcelain for redecoration during
the Revolution, much of which was, no doubt, exported to England.

Oeben, and worked for Mme du Barry, Marie-Antoinette, and the Prince de Condé.

Most of such work, especially at first, was done by Poirier. Circular tables, with porcelain tops and a bronze gallery, were often made by him, and were probably the first things thus to be decorated. Plaques in the form of segments of a circle were also used by Martin Carlin, of the rue du faubourg St. Antoine, who worked for Marie-Antoinette.

Clock-cases were usually in gilt bronze with the addition of plaques of porcelain, but the first such case made entirely of porcelain was done in 1750. Clocks were inset into pillars of porcelain, and vases (Plate 64) were also thus used. Later, about 1788, clocks were mounted in a combination of marble, porcelain, and bronze, one such clock for Marie-Antoinette being made by Pierre-Philippe Thomire [1751–1843] who had originally worked for Pajou and Houdon as a bronze-founder, and who, in 1783, took the place of Duplessis at Sèvres. He later founded the firm of Thomire-Dutherme et Cie which became extremely large and successful. Light fittings (Plate 63b) were embellished with porcelain, although they are much scarcer than clocks.

Turning from these important decorative objects to the smaller things, we find that porcelain boxes of all kinds were always extremely popular, and were decorated with great care and skill. The larger boxes were made up from plaques which were sent to the *bijouterie* to be mounted in gilt bronze, or more precious metals. Some of the smaller *tabatières* (tobacco boxes) were made in one piece, with the lids mounted in gold. Boxes for *bon-bons* differ little in form. Small plaques were adapted to such jewellery as bracelets, and watch-cases of porcelain are not unknown. Even sword-hilts were made, although apparently much more for ornament than for serious use. Small, but expensive, trifles included thimbles, and porcelain eggs, usually mounted in gold with perhaps a pair of scissors inside. These were intended as gifts. Of the more unusual things, telescopes, opera glasses, and even a seed-tray for a canary have been recorded. An egg-'boiler' appears on Plate 65.

Some distinct advances were made in the use of colours after 1756. The most important was the introduction of the *rose Pompadour* ground, a pink ground, inclined to opacity, which varies slightly in shade from piece to piece. The origin has been attributed both to the painter, Xhrouet, and to Hellot. It is possible to point to a payment of one hundred and fifty livres to Xhrouet which may have been in recognition of his invention. On the other hand, I do not think a specimen subsequent to the death of Hellot in 1766 is known. How much it is possible to regard this latter fact as evidence, however, is disputable, since the colour may well have been abandoned in consequence of the death of Mme de Pompadour in 1764. The most likely explanation is that the colour was devised by Xhrouet and Hellot in association, since the latter's position makes it certain that he would have been associated with whatever experiments were conducted. This particular ground was much copied in England, the claret grounds of Chelsea and Worcester undoubtedly being attempts to reproduce it. In the nineteenth century, Coalport, and several other English factories, tried to attain it under the misnomer of the *rose du Barry*.

Rose Pompadour was also used effectively in conjunction with a green enamel, the latter being usually in the form of interlaced ribbons (*à rubans*), and a marbled variety appeared about 1763. Representations of *cabochon* jewels—oval, raised, bosses—were also painted over the same ground.

About the same time the overglaze ground, *bleu de roi*,

was introduced. This, which is much more evenly laid than the earlier *gros bleu*, is also less interesting, but it was the envy of many of the German factories, who went to the lengths of introducing industrial spies to get the secret of it. Since this lay mainly in the type of glaze on which it was used, the German hard porcelain factories found it impossible to reproduce it exactly.

The transition from the *rococo* to the so-called *Louis Seize* style began about the same time as the transfer to Sèvres, but since the royal factory had been unable to adopt the more elaborate moulded and applied ornament which marks the *rococo* period at the Germany factories, the forms did not alter so much as the decoration. The most obvious differences, therefore, are in the painting. Flowers, for instance, gradually became more naturalistic. The painting of the period has, in fact, been well described as a 'preoccupation with mere fact', which slowly developed into more or less exact copies of Pompeian frescoes and such things.

Painting in reserves began to lean heavily on miniature painting, and it will be observed that many of these things (the work of the decorator, Dodin, is an excellent example) became detailed representations of mythological and similar subjects. The porcelain is, for the most part, completely covered by colour. This is particularly in evidence on vases, although furniture plaques often have a considerable amount of white porcelain surface.

Many such things were painted in the manner of Boucher —pastoral scenes, landscapes, and mythological subjects. Boucher was enjoying a great vogue at the time, as I have recorded. Teniers, too, was almost equally favoured. These paintings are to be seen on many of the vases and *jardinières*, and were particularly popular during the reign of Louis XVI. Historical subjects belong to the same class.

Gilding was much in evidence until the end of the

century, although the motifs used made the same concessions to the change in style as the other kinds of decoration.
An innovation of 1781, which was probably derived from
the earlier combination of raised gilding and translucent
enamels mentioned on page 129, took the form of drops of
translucent enamel representing jewels which were applied
over the gilding. These 'jewels' imitated rubies, emeralds,
sapphires, and pearls, and the process, attributed to Cotteau,
needed a number of firings which made it very expensive.
Genuine examples are extremely rare, although forgeries
are not at all unusual. Gold of different colours was used
later in the century, and made an effective contrast.

The introduction of hard porcelain demanded certain
changes of technique. The glaze was not at first feldspathic,
as it became later under Brongniart, but compounded of
sand, chalk, and ground porcelain fragments. It gave the
body an extremely white appearance, but the enamels which
had been used on the soft porcelain glazes were not always
suitable. Nevertheless, hard porcelain had manufacturing
advantages. Enamel painting on soft porcelain often needed
a large number of successive firings, and these could be
greatly reduced in number, with an appreciable saving in
expense. Neither grounds nor enamels, however, were of
the same quality as those used on the soft porcelain glaze,
and for this reason the two kinds were manufactured side
by side for purposes appropriate to their nature.

The development of hard porcelain proceeded slowly at
first. Much difficulty was experienced in attaining the high
temperatures necessary to fire it successfully, and the glaze
also gave trouble. This was resolved by leaving it unglazed
for the most part, and Louis ordered that the new body be
used for *biscuit* figures. It was probably his intention that it
should not be employed for other purposes, but the material
was too tempting. It made possible the manufacture of far

larger things than could have been attempted in the earlier body, and by 1783 a vase five feet in height, decorated with the subject of *Atlanta's Race*, and costing 70,000 livres, had been made. This was for the Court of Tuscany, but Louis was so impressed by it that he kept it, and ordered another. Both are now in the Louvre.

New ground colours were devised for especial use on hard porcelain—brown, black, and a dark blue. A tortoise-shell ground had been introduced somewhat earlier, and this was now adapted for the same purpose. It appears on an enormous vase—the vase 'Cordelier'—made in 1785 which was, at the time, the largest ever to be made. It was over five feet in height. This ground, a product of iron and manga-nese, with the addition of cobalt blue produced the so-called 'green tortoiseshell', which was at one time much in demand without very good reason. A purple quite often used throughout the reign of Louis XVI was intro-duced in 1773, and lilac, mauve, and puce, were brought into use at the same time. A yellow, similar to the rare Vincennes ground colour, was brought back in the 1770s and enjoyed a limited amount of popularity.

Of the decorative themes used during the later period of the *Louis Seize* style, the little rose sprays were introduced about 1768, and later became exceedingly popular. Marie-Antoinette liked *biscuit*, and porcelain with comparatively slight decoration, which is best seen in the work of her own factory in the rue Thiroux. A belated fashion for *chinoiseries* began about 1773, when Madame du Barry ordered a service of this kind. *Chinoiseries* in gold on a black ground were perhaps done by Sinsson and Le Guay about 1780. Trellised patterns and gold grounds belong to about the same period, or a little earlier.

Flower painting began to be extremely naturalistic in 1775, and thistles and daisies were brought into use about the same time. The decoration of scattered cornflower sprigs (*décor barbeau*), later so widely copied elsewhere in Paris, was devised by Hettlinger to please Marie-Antoinette, whose favourite colour was blue. Monkeys are a very unusual decorative theme, but a *déjeuner* was made in 1776 painted in this way at the cost of six hundred livres, and, in 1785, a pair of vases received bronze mounts in this form. These were repeated in the following year for the Prince de Condé.

The so-called 'Etruscan' friezes probably began about 1783, and scrolls and grotesques after Pompeian wall-paintings, and from Raphael (who got them from the *thermae* of Titus), came into use about the same time. Medallion portraits and friezes *en grisaille*, adapted from classical sources, were commonly used.

These classical decorations owe much to Lagrenée *le jeune*, who was appointed Assistant Art Director in 1785. He was associated with the Baron Vivant Denon, an artist, connoisseur, and collector, who sent a number of ancient vases from Naples to Hettlinger which are still preserved in the Musée de Sèvres.

The competition of Wedgwood at this time led to numerous attempts to imitate his jasper in Paris generally, and Sèvres used a blue *biscuit* porcelain for the purpose. The figures, as may be seen from Plate 62a, are usually in a much higher relief than in Wedgwood's own work, and the style of modelling is characteristically French. Plaques of this kind were used for furniture decoration, particularly during the Revolution.

The production of furniture of all kinds ornamented with porcelain plaques increased considerably. La Beaupré, an expensive courtesan, had a coach decorated entirely with panels of porcelain, and the use of similar panels on sedan chairs is also to be noted.

For a time the Court had a craze for playing at shepherds

and shepherdesses, and small dairies and summer houses were built which were luxuriously decorated inside, although the outside looked like a rustic cottage. The fashion was started in the days of Louis XV and Mme de Pompadour, but Marie-Antoinette had farms at the Petit Trianon and at Rambouillet where she spent much time. For these farms such things as milk-dishes, butter-dishes, churns, milk-jugs, and so forth were ordered both from Sèvres and from the rue Thiroux. A cup and saucer of this kind in the Musée de Sèvres has a cow and a calf as decoration.

Large plaques of soft porcelain were painted with imitations of oil paintings, and hung on the wall. One measured two feet square. Some hunting scenes by Asselin after Oudry are typical. The idea was popular at the time, and it was repeated again at various factories during the early part of the nineteenth century, but there is small justification for the practice.

A good deal of extremely fine gilt bronze mounting was done during the *Louis Seize* period by P. P. Thomire and others, and the large vases already mentioned are excellent examples of the kind. These mounts, of course, differ considerably from those of the *Louis Quinze* period. The *rococo* flourishes have gone, to be replaced by such motifs as cupids, and rams' heads. The vase 'Cordelier' already mentioned was decorated with bronze cupids in this way. The difference, both in style and subject matter of the decoration, makes the period obvious. Quality of mounting is still as high, the casts being carefully chiselled and cleaned up by metal-working tools, and this is often the principal indication of an eighteenth-century mount.

In 1784 the King acquired the hard porcelain factory at Limoges (see page 173), and white wares were made here for decoration at Sèvres. The Sèvres marks were added, but the initials 'CD' (for the Comte d'Artois) sometimes appear in addition, which is sufficient indication of the source. There are some perceptible differences between the porcelain of Sèvres and that of Limoges, which in the absence of a distinguishing mark, might raise some doubts as to the authenticity of a specimen.

Most porcelain made during the period of the Revolution needs little identification, quite apart from any marks which may be present. Such things as the *fasces* of the Roman lictors, Phrygian caps, and *tricolor* cockades and ribbons, tell their own story. Quality of the porcelain and its decoration was often inferior.

Egyptian motifs are subsequent to the ill-fated expedition to Egypt, and the custom of sending porcelain as gifts to important personages was revived by Talleyrand, the Foreign Minister to the Directory, one such service for the Prussian Ambassador being painted with motifs derived from Raphaël.

Soon after 1800 Brongniart discontinued the soft porcelain body altogether, and introduced a new glaze for the hard porcelain akin to that already in use in Germany. Chrome green was introduced about the same time, as well as other colours more suited to painting on the new glaze. The use of large areas of gilding became common. The Empire style was now at its height, and the battles of Napoleon were commemorated by their use as porcelain decoration by Swebach and others.

Napoleon continued the practice of making royal gifts of porcelain, sending services, and things of the kind, to the Czar, Prince William of Prussia, and other notabilities of the period. A large vase with a relief of the marriage of Napoleon and Marie Louise was made in 1810.

The general style of the period led to an almost complete covering of the white porcelain by ground colours, and by lavish gilding intended to simulate solid gold. Painted decoration was 'tight', with much extremely detailed representation in a naturalistic style. Large plaques imitating oil paintings were made which exhibit more virtuosity than taste. Forms were usually severe, and based on classical models.

The artists responsible for the decoration of Sèvres porcelain often used a sign to indicate their handiwork, and a list appears in Appendix I, together with the dates between which they worked, and the kind of work they did. Little detailed information is available about most of them, but any divergence between the sign-manual and the kind of decoration should be questioned. It is advisable to remark that all the existing lists, compiled from several sources, are not completely trustworthy, and may contain minor errors of fact. In cases of divergence, I have usually followed the information provided by W. B. Honey (*Dictionary of European Ceramic Art*). Some marks vary slightly from one example to another.

The marks on Sèvres porcelain are nearly always in blue overglaze, and consist of the royal monogram, the date letter, and (quite often) the painter's mark. The date letter, whenever present, appears in the centre of the monogram, except if double letters are used, when they occasionally appear on either side of it. On hard porcelain made between 1770 and 1793 a monogram surmounted by a crown appears occasionally, and this is sometimes in red as well as in blue. I have also seen the simple monogram in red on pieces which I considered to be genuine, but very rarely.

The date letters are listed in the Appendix, and start with *A* to indicate 1753 when the factory was still at Vincennes. The letter *D* and onwards indicate manufacture at Sèvres. In 1778 a system of double letters was adopted, beginning with *AA* in that year, and this went on until July 17th, 1793, when it was discontinued, having then reached *PP*. Another system of dating started in 1801 which is noted in the Appendix. The monograms are usually a simple pair of crossed *Ls* in script, opposed to each other, but occasionally they received slight embellishments. From 1793 to 1804 the mark was $_{Sèvres}^{RF}$ for *République Française*. The marks of the Consular and Empire periods are given in the Appendix.

Figures before 1750 can only be doubtfully attributed. Some animals and birds were made, but are exceedingly scarce. A parakeet on a tree-trunk, after a model by Kändler at Meissen, is an example, and can probably be dated to about 1745. These things were sometimes decorated in rather curious colour combinations—blue and gold or green and gold.

The Paris market was already being supplied by Meissen, and it is natural that the few things remaining from this period should resemble the work of the Saxon factory. Mostly they are allegorical groups of figures, and modelling is usually simple, the elaborate *rococo* ornament, done to such good effect in porcelain by the German factories, being replaced by the gilt-bronze mounts, in which somewhat similar motifs appear. These mounts, by Duplessis and others, sometimes took the form of candlesticks, inkstands, and such things, with recesses for the mounting of figures, and Meissen figures were also used for the purpose.

Work of this kind is now regarded as extremely important, but in its application to porcelain figures it began to fall into disuse to some extent in 1751 when *biscuit* was introduced by Bachelier.

Among the modellers of the period are Nicolas Gauron, also of Mennecy and Tournai, who did a figure of a *River God* marked *Gauron 1754*, of which an almost identical version can be seen from Mennecy. Another modeller was Louis Fournier, at Vincennes until 1749, and later at Chantilly and Copenhagen. To him is attributed an extremely rare coloured figure in the Louvre called *La Source** (which, as may be expected, represents a woman seated beside an overturned water-jar) with a superb and elaborate mount by Duplessis which not only has the typical *rococo* motifs, but the upper part represents a small tree surmounting a mound.

Another group, after Oudry, is an elaborate composition of Europe and Africa, in which Europe reclines on the back of a kneeling horse, whilst a scantily-clad female Africa stands beside her. This was probably modelled by Leboiteux.

Perhaps more important was Blondeau, a sculptor who did some animals from drawings by Oudry. His *Chien poursuivant un cygne dans les roseaux*† is an important early work of the factory.

He also did a series of eight figures—*Enfants d'après Boucher*—which were so successful that they were issued in *biscuit* in 1754. They were inspired by a popular ballet-pantomime, *La Vallée de Montmorency*, given in 1752 with Mme Favart in the part of Corydon, with a jealous Lisette and Babet opposite. From the same play was *Le Jaloux* by Van de Voorst of a girl seated, with a kneeling suitor beside her, another lover, his face distorted by jealousy, peering at them from behind a pedestal. A group after Boucher, the *Leçon de Flute*,‡ was much used at Sèvres thereafter, and copied at Chelsea and Frankenthal in reverse. At the latter factory it was given the characteristic trellised *rococo* arbours of the *Modellmeister*, J. F. Lück.

This work caught the imagination of Court circles, and orders for these charming and original figures were many. Contemporary opinion placed them above those of Meissen.

*'The Spring.'
†'Dog pursuing a swan amidst the reeds.'
‡'The Flute Lesson,' sometimes called 'The Music Lesson.'

Biscuit, too, was almost immediately successful, helped by Mme de Pompadour.

Biscuit figures were made with great care. After each one had been moulded it was carefully touched up before firing by the 'repairer', usually a skilled modeller also. Placing them in the kiln was, in itself, a highly skilled operation, the unsupported parts receiving the addition of temporary props to prevent them from sagging during the firing operation. The actual placing in the kiln had to be done with care, the *biscuit* figures being put into the lowest ovens. After firing, the props were removed, and the surface was carefully cleaned with fine sand to improve it, and to remove any traces of the mould joints. Only the finest pieces were passed for sale, any discoloured or misshapen examples being instantly rejected.

At this time Boucher was supplying many drawings which were given to various sculptors to execute. One of the most important was Jean-Baptiste de Fernex [1729–1783], an artist of great skill, whose work was extremely popular. A seated shepherdess done in 1753 was intended as a portrait of the actress, Mme Favart, already mentioned, a copy of which was ordered by the King. This marked a change from the *Enfants de Boucher*, and gallants and pastoral figures generally became much more popular, although children still continued to be made, probably by Louis-Felix de la Rue, who did many models of the kind. Fernex in 1754 did the figure of a milkmaid—*La Laitière*—which was a reduction of a statue intended for the dairy of Mme de Pompadour at Crécy. A pair to this—*La Batteuse de beurre*, also for Crécy, was modelled by Falconet.

Another modeller, named Suzanne, was—like Fernex—probably a pupil of the sculptor, d'Huez. He also resembled so many of the earlier of the factory's artists in being a member of the Académie de St. Luc, St. Luke being the patron saint of artists.* Suzanne appears to have joined the factory a year or two before 1755, and he did a number of figures after Boucher in the latter year, one of which was a girl with chickens called *La Fermière*.

Two extremely popular models were *The Little Stonemason* done in 1754 by Fernex which depicts a small boy dressing a block of stone, and *The Little Laundress* by Suzanne (1755) of a small girl kneeling and beating clothes with a paddle.

There was a vogue at this time for idealized figures of peasants and artisans, and scenes with a similar theme were played at the Court Theatre at Versailles. At the time, too, the gardens of the Tuileries were being reconstructed. This palace and its gardens was situated in the centre of Paris. The use of the site dates from the fourteenth century, when it was called the Hôtel des Tuileries in reference to a number of tile-works in the neighbourhood. The Palace was built by the architect, Philibert Delorme, in the middle of the sixteenth century for Catherine de' Medici, and was burned down during the Revolution of 1871. The reconstruction mentioned included the provision of a broad walk, with an equestrian statue of Louis XV by the sculptor, Edmé Bouchardon [1698–1762], who had studied under Coustou, and was later at Rome for ten years. This statue was destroyed in 1792. The statue, and the surrounding bridges, terraces, and so forth, were reproduced in *biscuit*, together with figures of gallants, peasants, and children. The complete set was the Tuileries in miniature for the dining table in a way which had already become fashionable in Germany, where these

*The Guild of St. Luke was a rival establishment to the official Académie des Beaux Arts. After falling into disfavour during the seventeenth century, it was revived in 1706 under the protection of the d'Argenson family, and it held exhibitions in competition with the official *Salons*.

large decorations for the dessert table were extremely elaborate.

The children were in the style of François Duquesnoy (also called François Flamand), a seventeenth-century Flemish sculptor whose models of children were particularly well-liked, and the modeller has been identified with Louis-Felix de la Rue, who won the Prix de Rome in 1750. His early death necessarily limited the number of surviving models by his hand, but a white glazed group of two small boys in the Victoria and Albert Museum has been attributed to him (Plate 68b). He did a series of children at Vincennes, shortly before the transfer to Sèvres, and the factory presented Machault, who had become Minister of Marine in July, 1754, with a pair of paper-weights in the form of naked boys with such aquatic additions as fishes, nets, and so forth.

Falconet joined the factory in 1757, but, even before this date, a figure made at Vincennes has been attributed to him. This, representing friendship and called *L'Amitié*, was a copy of a statue at Bellevue which was complemented by another called *L'Amour* by Jean-Baptiste Pigalle. Falconet had been made an Academician in 1754 for his work, *La France embrassant le buste du Roi*.* He was extremely jealous of the position of Pigalle, and intrigued with the servants of Mme de Pompadour for her favour.

Twenty examples of *L'Amitie*,† which depicts her standing beside a short, flower-decked, column offering her heart to Louis, were made, and sold in August 1756, and probably as a result, Falconet was later made Director of Sculpture at the new factory. He was then in charge of a number of artists and 'repairers', and eventually he formed

*France embracing a bust of the King.
†A figure made in 1764 known as the *Amitié au Coeur*, dressed in antique drapery and offering a heart with both hands, has been confused with the earlier version.

a team of young sculptors, one of whom, Le Riche, did a large model of children reaching upwards to a column, which may have been a centre-piece. The others included Duru, Liance, Huet, Leclerc, Tristant, and Perrotin.

Falconet was much influenced by Boucher, and did a whole series of figures after the latter's designs which nevertheless have the stamp of the sculptor's style.

Probably as a reaction from the earlier grand manner of Louis XIV and the Regent, figures of artisans and peasants became popular, and it is noticeable that these are now modelled in a more realistic vein than those which had been done at Vincennes a few years before. For instance, the peasant, Sganarelle, a character in Molière's *Le Médecin malgré lui**, was modelled by Falconet from illustrations which had already been done by Boucher. Particularly liked, too, were *La Curiosité, ou la Lanterne magique* and *La Loterie, ou le Tourniquet*,† two groups which especially pleased Madame de Pompadour. The rustic scene had hitherto been unknown to sophisticated Court circles, but it was now taken up with enthusiasm as something completely new. The peasants of Piedmont and the Savoy were also modelled in the same vein, and engravings of such subjects were used for the purpose. Perhaps the best known example comes not from Sèvres, but from the hand of Eberlein at Meissen, whose model, the *Piedmontese Bagpiper*, taken from an engraving (a copy of which is in the British Museum) was reproduced at Bow in England, and elsewhere. It is, in fact, tempting to see in this a copy of a Vincennes *biscuit* figure at Meissen, but no French example is known to me.

---

*The doctor in spite of himself.

†The magic lantern is, in fact, a kind of peep-show, and not a projector. The *tourniquet* is a revolving game round which the children are grouped.

Falconet later turned to mythological subjects, and his *Nymphe qui descend au Bain* (better known as *La Baigneuse*) made in 1758 was an instant success, being copied at a number of other European factories e.g. Ludwigsburg, Zürich, Berlin, Copenhagen, and Meissen. Another—*La Nymphe qui sort du Bain*—sometimes known as the *Nymph with the sponge* was done in 1762.* *La Baigneuse* was a particularly large and ambitious figure, which probably needed a special porcelain body. Another fine group in the same vein, no doubt inspired by the growing interest in classical art, is *Leda and the Swan*, and the sketch for a model of *Cupid and Psyche* was exhibited in the Salon of 1761. Scarcely less important is the *Pygmalion Amoureux de sa Statue*, sometimes claimed, without much reason, for the modeller, Duru (Plate 70).†

In 1757 Falconet made the first bust of the King, which was taken from one by Lemoyne and given by Louis to Mme de Pompadour for her residence at Crécy in 1750. This was the first of many portrait busts of all kinds which were made between now and the beginning of the Revolution.

Dancing became very fashionable, and ballets were even inserted into the most unsuitable dramas and operas. Molière suffered in this way, and Boucher was asked to design scenes for inclusion in plays which had hitherto lacked a diversion of this kind. The ladies of the Court attended public dances in masks, and some of these dances were considered to be scandalous because they demanded such *poses amoureuses* as the clasping of waists and shoulders by the partner. A popular dance of this kind, *L'Allemande*, was represented in *biscuit* by *L'Allemande Suisse* and

*Falconet said of these models that they were '*plus noble, d'un gout plus général et moins sujet à révolution de la mode.*'
†The *ballet de Pygmalion*, presented in 1760, was very successful.

L'Allemande Français. The drama, in fact, changed from being a fairly serious pastime to what we should now call musical comedy, and amorous intrigues became the vogue among those who had the leisure for them.

Belonging to this period are three well-known groups which were, at the time, considered to be a little *risqué*. *Les Trois Contents* of 1765 was taken from *Les Rivaux heureux*— a play at the théâtre de la Foire—the story of a woman who distributed her favours between two suitors, which delighted Parisians at the time. *Le baiser donné* was taken from a play by Taconet at the théâtre des Boulevards, also in 1765, and *Le baiser rendu*, the most suggestive of the three, came from the same source (Plate 72).

Falconet left for Russia in 1766, and his departure was a serious blow to the factory. *Biscuit* figures had become exceedingly popular. The earlier decrees had lost some of their force, and in spite of all edicts to the contrary, other factories were making *biscuit* to fill the ever-growing demand. Many of these copied the models of the royal factory exactly.

Bachelier was appointed Director of Modelling, and Falconet had left sufficient designs in hand to enable work to be continued for a time. Well-known sculptors, too, were asked to make models of some of their better known work in a reduced size.

Bachelier was attracted to the classical mode, and the factory for a time became little more than a vehicle for reproducing sculpture. His ambition was, in fact, to make Sèvres a museum of contemporary sculpture by transposing it into *biscuit*. This was not unpopular. The discoveries at Pompeii, too, were part of the *Zeitgeist* and Falconet had earlier shown a tendency in this direction. Nevertheless, the value of *biscuit* as a vehicle for figure modelling was greatly diminished by it.

Plate 65. Coquetière (egg-boiler) with a green ground and painting in
reserves. Sèvres. c. 1758. (Wallace Colln.)

Plate 66. Group, possibly *Venus and Adonis*, white glazed porcelain, contemporary mounts. Vincennes. c. 1750. (V&AM.)

Plate 67 (a). Hercules and Omphale, with Cupid.
White glazed group after an engraving from a
painting by Lemoyne. Vincennes. c. 1750.
(Metropolitan.)

(b). Clock-case in white glazed porcelain.
Zephyrus and Flora. Vincennes. c. 1750. (BM.)

Plate 68 (a). *Diana*, white glazed porcelain, probably modelled by Louis Fournier. Vincennes. c. 1750. (V&AM.)

(b). A pair of groups, each of three boys, in glazed porcelain after a model by L-F. de la Rue in 1757. Sèvres. c. 1760. Mark: 'ic' incised. (V&AM.)

Plate 69 (a). White glazed group representing 'Music'.
Vincennes. c. 1750. (BM.)

(*b*). White glazed group representing 'Science'.
Vincennes. c. 1750. (BM.)

Plate 70. Pygmalion Amoureux de sa Statue, modelled by Falconet. The
Sèvres *biscuit* version may have been done by Duru. 1763. (BM.)

Plate 71 (a). *Le Sabot Cassé*, model by Falconet. *Biscuit* porcelain. Sèvres. 1760. (BM.)

(b). *Psyche*, model by Falconet. *Biscuit* porcelain. Sèvres. 1761. (BM.)

(c). Cupid, model by Falconet. *Biscuit* porcelain. Sèvres. 1758. (BM.)

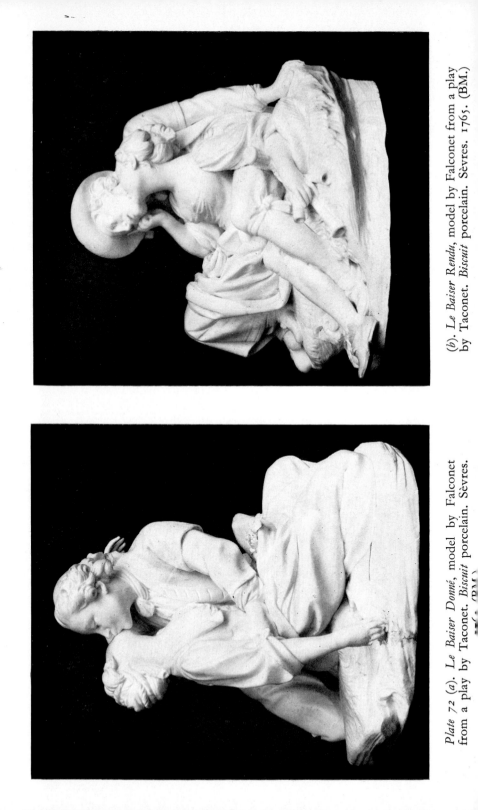

Plate 72 (*a*). *Le Baiser Donné*, model by Falconet from a play by Taconet. *Biscuit* porcelain. Sèvres.

(*b*). *Le Baiser Rendu*, model by Falconet from a play by Taconet. *Biscuit* porcelain. Sèvres. 1765. (BM.)

Plate 73 (a). Le Jeune Suppliant, sometimes called *La Protestation*, modelled by Blondeau after Boucher. Vincennes/Sèvres. c. 1755. (V&AM.)

(b). White glazed version of 73 *(a).* Vincennes. c. 1753. (Fitzwilliam.)

Plate 74. Leda and the Swan, biscuit porcelain, by Falconet after Boucher.
Sèvres. c. 1760. (V&AM.)

Plate 75 (a). Bust of Louis Quinze after Lemoyne. Pedestal by Dodin. Sèvres. 1761. (BM.)

(b). Madame du Barry, after Augustin Pajou. Medallion with the monogram 'DB'. Sèvres. 1772. (Metropolitan.)

Plate 76. La Nymph qui descend au Bain (La Baigneuse)
After a marble statue by Falconet exhibited in the
Paris Salon of 1757 with sensational success, and
widely copied at other European porcelain factories.
Sèvres *biscuit* porcelain. (V&AM.)

Plate 77. Figure of a youth writing. L. S. Boizot. 1780. Sèvres. Mark: interlaced 'LL' and 'FF' (1783) in blue enamel. (V&AM.)

Plate 78. Group of *putti*, one playing on a drum held by another.
Louis-Simon Boizot. Sèvres. c. 1780. (Hastings.)

Plate 79. Figure emblematic of Asia from a set of the continents. Perhaps by J. W. Lanz. Strasbourg. c. 1753. Mark: 'PH' impressed.
(V&AM.)

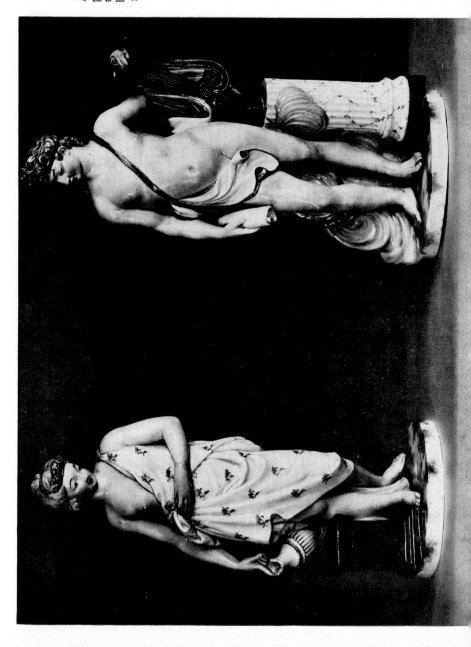

Plate 80. Apollo and *Hebe*, painted all over in flesh tints, with green washed bases. Niderviller. 1780–93. (V&AM.)

To this period belongs a *Vénus Callipygous*,* and other things of the same kind, and about the same time the sculptor, Pigalle, was asked to supply models, although there is no reason to assume that he ever had an official connection with the factory. One of these, the *Joueuse d'osselets*†, done into *biscuit* in 1769, he had used earlier to pay his fare home from Rome. A *Mercury* of 1770 is from an original in the Sans Souci Palace in Berlin, and a *Hymen—Mercure messager de l'amour*‡ of 1772 resembles it in many ways. A *Vénus assise* (Venus seated), also translated into *biscuit*, is in the Louvre. I have already mentioned, in relating the history of the factory, the adaptation of a statue of Louis XV in the Place Royale at Rheims to part of a colossal table decoration made to celebrate the marriage of the Dauphin and Marie-Antoinette.

Jacques Caffiéri, who had been at Sèvres since 1765, was tried for a while as a successor to Falconet, but proved unsatisfactory in this position. He did a number of models for the factory. A *L'Espérance qui nourrit l'amour*§, in which a small cupid is depicted in the act of suckling, is by his hand, and was done about 1770. This was thought to be rather shocking at the time, since it was unfashionable to feed infants in this way. Later, he did a portrait of Molière in a *Série de Grands Hommes*‖, to which Pajou, Clodion, and Boizot also contributed. A bust of *Rameau* can be attributed to 1768, and another of *Voltaire* to 1770. This was the second bust of Voltaire to come from the factory, an earlier version being

---

*Callipygous—Greek; a reference in complimentary terms to the female bottom. The well-known antique Aphrodite Callipygous depicts her looking backwards and downwards over her shoulder in a neck-dislocating attempt to admire it.

†The Player of Knuckle-bones.

‡Hymen—Mercury's messenger of Love.

§Hope nourishing Love.

‖Series of Great Men.

done by an ivory-carver, Dupont Rosset. This was a considerable feat, since Voltaire pretended to be coy, and objected to being immortalized in this way. Of the Caffiéri bust he wrote: 'Le meilleur buste qui ait été fait de moi.' (The best bust which has been made of me).

The work of Jacques Saly found an appreciative public at the time. His best known work is *Le Faune*, first done in marble, which is remarkable for being an unclothed version of a shepherd carrying a sheep made at Longton Hall, in England, some fifteen years earlier. It would seem that the work was not, for this reason, original, and that both this and the Longton example were derived from a common source, which was probably an Italian bronze of the seventeenth century. This is suggested not only by the style, but by the fact that Longton Hall used Italian bronzes on more than one occasion.

In 1771 a bust of the Dauphine, Marie-Antoinette, was done which, on account of its large size, was extremely difficult to fire successfully, and it was subsequently reduced in size. A bust of Mme du Barry by Pajou had been issued in the previous year.

Le Riche started a series based on the romance of Don Quixote at this time, a subject which was also used by the Gobelins tapestry factory. This was extremely popular, and the Spanish alliance also produced such things as *La Conversation espagnole* after Vanloo, which depicts a man playing a flute and a woman with a lute. Spaniards took the place of Italians in the theatre, and *Don Giovanni* provided Count Almaviva, who was done in *biscuit* by Le Riche in 1772. The year 1774 saw the issue of a standing figure of Mme du Barry as a Spanish singer.

Another large table decoration was started in 1772 which was to reproduce the ceiling decoration in the Galerie d'Apollon in the Louvre. This was a *cortège* depicting

Bacchus surrounded by vines, *amphorae,* and so forth. The modeller was, perhaps, Felix Lecomte, a pupil of Falconet, who exhibited a dancing *bacchante* in 1773, and whose *Fénélon* and *Rollin* were later reproduced in *biscuit.* He was favoured by Mme du Barry, who gave him commissions to decorate her home at Louveciennes.

The year 1770, of course, saw the introduction of the formula for hard porcelain, although it was not used to any considerable extent for two or three years afterwards, and then, for some time, only for *biscuit* models. Also, Louis-Simon Boizot took over the directorship of the sculpture studios from Bachelier in 1772, and these two events both greatly influenced the course of events between then and the Revolution.

Boizot had little of the genius of Falconet, but he was an extremely competent modeller working, for the most part, in the neo-classical style. He appears to have enjoyed the friendship of Pierre Gouthière, the bronze worker. The latter was the son of a saddle-maker, and was born in 1732. In 1758 he became a master-gilder, and began to work for the Court in 1769. He did much work for Marie-Antoinette, but was declared bankrupt in 1788, one of his debtors being Mme du Barry, who owed him three-quarters of a million francs. Very little work can be attributed to him with any degree of certainty, but he did supply occasional mounts for Sèvres porcelain.

To return to Boizot, in 1773 he made a *biscuit* group to celebrate the marriage of Charles X of Spain to the Princess of Savoy, and, in 1775, modelled his allegory of the Coronation of Louis XVI and Marie-Antoinette, previously mentioned. These two things made him very popular with the Court, and he gained a powerful position in consequence. Mere copies of the antique were no longer so fashionable, and original models of merit were, once again, demanded.

Both glazed porcelain and *biscuit* were displayed in the King's Library, which was an excellent piece of publicity for the factory, and it was the fashion to buy Sèvres porcelain, whether one wanted it or not. Boizot provided about twenty-five new models, and the modellers, Le Riche and Perrotin, something like twenty more. Even medallions were done for less affluent customers.

This was the period of Rousseau and the return to nature. Costumes assumed a slightly more rural air, and since the King was fond of hunting, Marie-Antoinette took to the horse and followed the hunt. This was a new departure from the days when the ladies of the Court used coaches for the purpose, and a *biscuit* figure by Boizot made in 1773 depicted a woman galloping to a *rendezvous*.

Another tendency of the time was the sentimental representation of family life. This is well seen in the work of Jean-Baptiste Greuze, the painter. Two of his pictures are entitled, *Le Père de famille expliquant la Bible à ses enfants* and *La Jeune Fille qui pleure la mort de son oiseau*,* after which further comment would be superfluous. One, Moreau, a publisher of prints, began a series of illustrations of the history of French costume (the *Moeurs françaises*) in 1774, and he made a particular cult of the family. His women are filled with maternal devotion, and are surrounded by young children. In 1774 Boizot modelled a young mother to whom a servant is presenting her newly-born baby, called *La Nourrice*, and children became very popular, even to the extent of supplanting the gallant. I have elsewhere commented on the rise to influence of the *bourgeoisie* during the latter part of the eighteenth century which was primarily responsible for this vogue for pseudo-sentiment. It can occasionally be seen as early as the mid-1760s. Michel-

*'The Father of the family expounds the Bible to his children,' and, 'The Young Girl weeps for the death of her bird.'

Victor Acier, who went from Paris to Meissen about 1763, was a past-master of this kind of thing, which is one of the least desirable features of the work of the time.

When the period of mourning for Louis XV was over, the Court returned to normal with a *grande fête* given at Versailles for the Archduke Maximilian. The Queen's ball was a sensation, and Le Riche modelled a set of eight figures to commemorate it. The Queen and the Comte d'Artois were both represented.

At the same time, the Comédie Française put on *Le Barbier de Seville*, a play by Beaumarchais which was later adapted to operatic form by Rossini. Le Riche modelled Figaro with a guitar, kneeling on the ground, and singing. Boizot and Mme Favart (now Mme Préville) were responsible for the renewal of the custom of representing the stage in *biscuit*. *Iphigénie*, by Glück, was produced in 1774, and commemorated in this way by four figures.

Boizot, with the help of Duru and Perrotin, continued to add many new models of all kinds. Boizot's *La Beauté couronnée par les Grâces** was an obvious portrait of Marie-Antoinette. He was particularly facile, and could turn his hand almost equally well to things in the style of Falconet, or in the new pseudo-antique style. It is important to remember that the neo-classical style of this period was, for the most part, simply a masquerade, in which eighteenth-century people were dressed in Greek costume, with, more often than not, a plentiful addition of sentimentality to please contemporary taste.

Competition from the various factories which had sprung up in Paris and its environs grew more acute. Niderviller, too, was making *biscuit* of fine quality for models by Cyfflé and others. The quality for the most part was not as good as that of the royal factory, but it was much less expensive.

*'Beauty crowned by the Graces.'

The monopoly became more difficult to maintain, and many Sèvres *biscuit* models were copied exactly.

Of the portraits done at the time, one of Joseph II, the Queen's brother and Emperor of Austria, was exhibited at the Salon, and the Gobelins factory reproduced it in tapestry. A bust of Catherine of Russia was also modelled, and one of Voltaire was copied from the famous portrait by Houdon.

Catherine ordered about forty models by Boizot in 1779, among them being an *Apotheosis of Catherine II*, and the modellers worked for months on these figures. The table decoration alone was valued at 22,000 livres, with another 300,000 for the service which was ordered at the same time. The eventual quarrel over payment has already been mentioned.

The birth of the Dauphin in 1782 called for commemoration, and Pajou did an allegory of his birth entitled *Vénus sortant de l'aide portée par des Dauphins et tenant l'Amour dans ses bras*. Pajou made the semi-nude Venus look too much like the Queen, which was regarded as not being particularly respectable for one in so exalted a position, and he was ordered to change the features, and to remove the *fleur-de-lys* from the drapery. These alterations were done, and the original models no longer exist.

The birth of the Duke of Normandy in 1785 was commemorated by Boizot with a group entitled *The French Monarchy, on the stem of which the Genius of Fertility plants a third shoot*. This child was regarded by the Legitimists as Louis XVII, and the group depicted a baby presented to the seated figure of its mother by a winged Genius.

In 1782 Boizot made an equestrian portrait of Frederick the Great, as well as one of Catherine of Russia's son, later the Czar Paul, and his wife. The custom, in fact, grew up of modelling visiting royalty in this way, which is not without its interest to historians, although it added little to the ceramic art. To this category perhaps belongs the Series of Great Men, which was added to until the Revolution. They were not particularly popular at the time, and some difficulty was experienced in selling them. Of these, *Racine* was by Boizot; *Tourville* by Houdon; *Bossuet*, *Descartes*, *Pascal*, and *Turenne* by Pajou; *Corneille* and *Molière* by Caffiéri; *La Fontaine* by Julien; and *Montesquieu* by Clodion.

The year 1784 saw the *Nymphes redressant la statue de Dieu Pan* by Claude-Michel Clodion, one of the more important French sculptors of the eighteenth century, who was born at Nancy in 1738, and studied in Rome from 1762 until 1767. He became popular almost immediately after his return to France. He was son-in-law to Pajou, with whom he appears to have disagreed, although the reason for it is not known. Much of his work takes the form of nymphs, fauns, and things of that sort. Some of these were reproduced in Sèvres *biscuit*, and he is also said to have furnished models to Niderviller.

The same year saw a new sensation which demanded commemoration in *biscuit*—the realization of man's age-old desire to fly. Montgolfier succeeded in making a practicable fire-balloon, and Sèvres did a *Groupe de l'Aerostat* which represented a balloon on a pedestal, whilst a winged Genius passed a torch of truth and light to a figure representing Physics.

In the year 1785 a taste for *biscuit* reliefs in the manner of Wedgwood becomes noticeable. The adaptation of this fashion at Sèvres was a little belated, the other Paris factories having copied it some years before.

This year saw also the production of the *Marriage of Figaro* by Beaumarchais, with the actress, Olivier, in the part of Cherubino, and Mlle Contat as Susanna. Boizot modelled her as the Muse of Comedy, and her friend, Mlle Raucourt, as the Muse of Tragedy.

The Revolution, now, was not far away, and the great days of Sèvres *biscuit* were over. In the early Republican period such things as busts of Diderot and of Jean-Jacques Rousseau were modelled, whilst, slightly later, we find Danton, Marat, and Robespierre appearing in the same form. The Generals of the Revolutionary Armies were suitably portrayed, including Bonaparte. The latter was an extremely popular model. A few earlier groups of classical subjects were repeated. At this time an orgy of destruction went on, in which many of the moulds, and such figures and groups depicting royalty as remained in the factory's stock were smashed.

The early glazed figures occasionally bear a factory mark in enamel. *Biscuit* figures were never marked during the eighteenth century, and not, in fact, until 1860. Any such specimens bearing a factory mark are either made after this date, or are forgeries. Occasionally incised workmen's marks are to be seen, and the word *Sevres* was sometimes incised on some early nineteenth-century plaques in the manner of Wedgwood.

The collector should beware of *biscuit* figures which have been later glazed and painted in the hope of passing them off as one of the extremely rare glazed and painted figures from Sèvres. Of genuine examples, about twenty are known. The chapter on Forgeries discusses this point in more detail.

Biscuit, of course, had many imitators elsewhere in Europe, almost every factory doing some work of the kind. A number of German factories made it, and, in England, the work of Derby in this medium is well-known. The fashion was later revived in England during the nineteenth century as Parian ware.

IV. Tea-pot with *gros bleu* ground decorated with birds in gilt silhouette within a gilt scroll border. Vincennes. c. 1753. (Wallace Colln.)

CHAPTER VI

Hard Porcelain in France

DESPITE the fact that a successful soft porcelain had been made at St. Cloud, Chantilly, Mennecy, Sèvres, and other factories, French manufacturers never lost sight of the fact that it was a substitute for the Chinese porcelain body, nor did they lose the desire to emulate the Oriental productions. The difficulties in the way were two-fold—an exact knowledge of the substances required, and suitable sources of supply.

The secret of hard porcelain manufacture got beyond the confines of the Meissen factory in 1720, when it reached Vienna. Towards the mid-century Viennese workmen began to carry it to other German factories. One of these was Joseph Jakob Ringler who, in 1753, came to Strasbourg (see page 181) and helped Paul-Antoine Hannong to start the manufacture of porcelain.

The first specimens had hardly been produced when the edict of 1753 made it impossible to continue legally, and no sufficiently powerful protection was forthcoming to enable him to make it clandestinely. In these circumstances Hannong thought it best to offer the secret to the Vincennes factory in exchange for permission to continue.

A draft agreement was actually drawn up, but since the

only known source of a suitable clay at this time was at Passau, in Bavaria, and Hannong wanted 100,000 livres in cash, and an annual pension of 12,000 livres, Boileau waited until the formulae were in his possession, and then obtained a judgment in February, 1754, which required Hannong to discontinue his factory immediately. Disgusted with this chicanery, Hannong turned to the Duke Karl Theodor of the Palatinate, who gave him all the facilities required for the transfer of the factory to Frankenthal.

Whilst these negotiations had been going on, the chemist, Macquer, who was associated with Hellot, experimented with clays and various earths to find something appropriate, and contributed a paper on the subject to the Académie des Sciences in 1758.

About 1754 two arcanists from Strasbourg, Christian Daniel Busch, who had worked at Meissen, Vienna, and Neudeck, and one, Stadelmeyer, of whom little is known, came to Vincennes and were given facilities to experiment with porcelain. They had no success, although Busch ought to have known enough to produce porcelain, especially as he had been an associate of Ringler. This suggests that the fault was at least as much in the materials available.

In 1760 Paul-Antoine Hannong died. Boileau approached Joseph Hannong, but, with his father's treatment in mind, he rejected the overtures. Boileau had better fortune with the other son, Pierre-Antoine, who had failed to learn from his father's experience. He passed the secret to Sèvres in exchange for a lump sum and an annual pension. Once in possession of the information, Boileau refused to pay, on the ground that the necessary materials could not be found in France. Finally, Hannong accepted a reduced sum in settlement, but this was not paid, and, in 1781, he was awarded 18,000 livres as a final payment.

In 1767 the Ambassador to the Court at Munich, the

Chevalier de Folard, entered into negotiations with the manager of the Nymphenburg factory, Karl Joseph von Linprun. The Nymphenburg factory was not doing well at the time, and Linprun desired to safeguard his interests. The negotiations went on for some months, but came to nothing in the end. Much the same happened to negotiations with Weesp, in Holland, a factory which had been started by the Graf Gronsfeldt-Diepenbrock, with the aid of an Irish arcanist named MacCarthy, in 1757. The secret appears to have been supplied by Nikolaus Paul, who may have gained it at Wegely's factory in Berlin. The wanderings of these German arcanists are discussed in detail in my earlier work on German porcelain.*

It seems fairly certain that the secret of hard porcelain was well known in France long before its actual manufacture. In 1751, Jean-Etienne Guettard, a chemist who had worked with the Duc d'Orléans at the abbey of Sainte Geneviève, claimed to have made it.

According to Hellot, both Réaumur and Guettard advanced claims of this kind, but Réaumur's discovery was no more than devitrified glass, and that of Guettard, although it approached hard porcelain, was only an experimental success which he lacked the ability or the knowledge to turn to practical use. Guettard certainly knew all about the clay of Alençon, and he exhibited specimens of a primitive hard porcelain before the Académie.

From the same material, probably inspired by the success of Guettard, a greyish, primitive, hard porcelain was made by Louis-Léon-Felicité Brancas, Comte de Lauragais, some time shortly after 1763. A few specimens of uncertain attribution survive. De Lauragais took out an English patent for his discovery in 1766, and Sir Arthur Church mentioned (without corroborative evidence known to me)

Eighteenth Century German Porcelain. London, 1958.

that he was acquainted with Cornish *kaolin*. It is generally thought that the Comte made no use of his English patent, although some specimens attributed to him appeared in a loan collection exhibited at the Alexandra Palace, in London, in 1873. They were destroyed by a disastrous fire whilst still on exhibition, and it is now impossible to judge the accuracy of the attribution.

Most surviving specimens attributed to him are in the Musée de Sèvres, and it is difficult to regard the ascriptions as more than tentative.

In 1765 a sample of earth from St. Yrieix, near Bordeaux, was sent to Sèvres by the Archbishop of Bordeaux. The archbishop had visited the factory where he was shown various types of clay. He was given a sample of each and asked to report the presence of anything like them in his diocese. He showed these samples to a local apothecary, Villaris, who showed them in turn to the Sieur Darnet of St. Yrieix. The latter at once recognised them as similar to a kind of earth on his estate which his wife used for cleaning.

Villaris was both astute and greedy, and saw the opportunity to make a profit for himself. He sent samples of the St. Yrieix clay to Sèvres, where it was used to make specimens of hard porcelain. When Boileau asked for the source, however, he was met with evasions. Millot and Macquer were, therefore, sent to Bordeaux with instructions to find the source independently. They tried various earths in the neighbourhood, firing test samples in a locksmith's forge, but with little success. Finally they found a clay which was similar to that of St. Yrieix with which they made satisfactory tests, and Villaris, seeing his advantage fast disappearing, promised to reveal the source, asking only that he should be paid for it.

Eventually a sufficient quantity was obtained and sent to Sèvres, and specimens of hard porcelain made from the St.

Yrieix clay were shown to the King in 1769. In the same year Macquer communicated details of the discoveries to the Académie des Sciences.

The effect of the discovery was to cause the previous edicts in favour of Sèvres to fall into discard, and a number of new factories for the manufacture of hard porcelain sprang up, principally in and around Paris, which are discussed in Chapter VIII. A few of the earliest factories of this kind can, however, well be recorded at this point.

Limoges,* in the Haute Vienne, was founded in 1771, using the clay from near-by St. Yrieix. The brothers Grellet were assisted by a chemist named Fournérat, and by Massié. At first this was done clandestinely, but Turgot, Intendant of Limousin, advised them to apply to the King for a privilege, and the position was legalized in 1783, the registered mark being *CD*, incised or painted. The mark came from the fact that Limoges was within the confines of the estate of the Comte d'Artois, who extended his patronage to the factory.

In 1784 the King acquired the factory as a branch of Sèvres, and, to judge from surviving eighteenth-century specimens, it was principally engaged in making the less important kinds of service-ware. Most of the work has some slight moulding, and is painted with flower sprays of an unambitious kind. The body has an ivory tone. During this period the chemist, Darcet, who was later a director at Sèvres, was placed in charge. Many other small factories were established in the area at a later date because of the clay-beds in the vicinity.

Another factory in the same district was that of La Seynie (or La Seiné) which was established at the *château* of the same name by the Marquis de Beaupoil de Saint-Aulaire, the Comte de la Seynie, and Garreau de Grévigné, with Dembly

*A *faïence* factory was founded here in 1737 by André Massié.

as director. They applied for a privilege in 1779. Little porcelain was actually made. The mark was *LS*, either separately or intertwined in the form of a monogram, and the decoration was usually of flower bouquets and sprays. They did a large business in preparing and supplying the clay of St. Yrieix to the Paris factories.

Vincennes once more turned to porcelain-making under fresh ownership. Pierre-Antoine Hannong applied for a privilege in 1766 without success. He did, however, receive permission to make *faïence*. Permission was obtained by a mysterious individual called Maurice d'Aubiez, and it has been suggested that d'Aubiez was a pseudonym adopted by Hannong. He disappears in 1768, leaving Hannong sole director, supported by de la Borde, *valet de chambre* to Louis XV. A small quantity of porcelain was evidently made, but in 1770 Hannong was forced to relinquish the works, and he later appears as director of a Paris factory belonging to the Comte d'Artois. Vincennes passed to one, Séguin, in 1774, whose patron was the Duc de Chartres, the heraldic label of the latter being used as a mark.

Auscher's reference to the visit of King Louis-Philippe to the Sèvres factory in 1830, and the latter's recollection of assisting the Vincennes factory whilst it was in Hannong's possession, must be apocryphal, since Louis-Philippe was not born until 1773, although his father, Louis-Philippe-Joseph (known during the Revolution as *Philippe Egalité*) may well have done so.

In 1788 the director was Lemaire, later at the rue Amelot factory in Paris. Attribution of specimens to this later Vincennes factory are doubtful. Marks usually attributed to it cannot be regarded as certain, and are more likely to refer to Vaux, in the Seine-et-Oise.

The latter factory was founded about 1769, and Hannong is sometimes said to have been responsible. No definite evidence exists on this point, although the de la Borde already mentioned, in company with one, Hocquart, almost certainly participated. The mark given by Auscher of crossed *Vs*, is again very doubtful, and the *HL* sometimes awarded to Vincennes as standing for Hannong and la Borde, may equally well have meant Hocquart and la Borde. Attributions to either factory are not well supported.

A small quantity of hard porcelain was made at Orléans (see also page 101) soon after 1770, and the decoration has been said to consist of simple flower sprays. Definite identification, however, is difficult, and the mark of the heraldic label (see page 105) sometimes suggested for this factory is disputable. A very similar mark is claimed for Vincennes.

Etiolles, in the Seine-et-Oise, was established by Jean-Baptiste Monier and Etienne-Dominique Pellevé. The latter had made porcelain at the factory of Ottweiler in the Rhineland, where he had been associated with Paul-Louis Cyfflé of Lunéville (page 186), and the founding of the new factory in 1768 precedes the discovery of an effective hard porcelain formula by Millot and Macquer. The suggestion that a soft porcelain was made at Etiolles, however, is not well-founded. Specimens marked with a monogram, *MP*, and resembling the work of St. Cloud, are far more likely to have been made at the latter factory. Pellevé certainly knew how to make hard porcelain; there is no evidence that he knew how to make soft.

Hard porcelain specimens from Etiolles are variously marked. The name of *Pellevé* appears on several, in conjunction with the date, 1770. *Etiolle* appears in addition on a teapot in the Victoria and Albert Museum. The monogram, *MP*, on hard porcelain refers to Monier and Pellevé.

A factory for the manufacture of hard porcelain was established at Boissette (Seine-et-Marne) by Jacques Vermonet (father and son) in 1777, and they received a privilege enabling them to sell their wares locally. The porcelain produced was either white or with slight flower decoration. The mark was the letter 'B'.

Another factory in the Seine-et-Marne district was that of Fontainebleau which was founded in 1795 by Benjamin Jacob and Aaron Smoll. An associated factory in the same district came into the possession of Jacob and Mardochée Petit in 1830. They made decorative wares of all kinds, including a type of tea-warmer (*veilleuse*) in the form of a figure. These are called, in France, *personnages*. This factory was extremely large and productive, but only wares of commercial standard were produced, many being in the nineteenth-century revived *rococo* style.

The founding of a factory at Bordeaux in 1781 recalls the part played by the Archbishop of Bordeaux in the discovery of the clay-beds of St. Yrieix. It was located in the *château* of Bordes-en-Paludate. In 1787 the factory was taken over by Michel Vanier of Lille and Valenciennes, and Allaud,* a director at Limoges from 1788 to 1793. The influence of Paris is strong, and the mark of the crossed *Vs*, in gold or underglaze blue, resembles that of the *W* used by Wegely at Berlin in the 1750s.

It is possible to be more definite about the work of a factory at Lille, in northern France. This was started in 1783 by Leperre-Durot. He obtained a privilege for fifteen years, and like his predecessor, Dorez (page 82), he was granted a subsidy of 12,000 livres annually by the Town Council. The factory was under the patronage of the Dauphin and received permission to call itself the Manufacture Royale de Monseigneur le Dauphin.

*The Allaud family, Etienne Baignol, and one Pouyat, were all *kaolin* quarry owners at Limoges, and were associated with a number of factories here and elsewhere during the latter part of the eighteenth century.

Leperre-Durot was granted these especial favours because he fired his products with coal instead of wood, and a saucer in the Musée de Sèvres has the inscription, 'Fait à Lille en Flandre. Cuit au charbon de terre, 1785.' The use of coal for this purpose has been attributed to one Vannier or Vanier, almost certainly to be identified with the Michel Vanier mentioned as being at Bordeaux in 1787. Vanier went to Valenciennes in 1785, and the Lille factory apparently then reverted to burning wood. The use of coal for firing was important, and for this reason de Calonne, Controller-General of Finance, was interested in it. The destruction of forests and other standing timber to provide fuel for porcelain and *faïence* factories was a problem of major proportions in some areas, and in particular around Paris.

The products of Lille imitated those of Paris. The quality of the body and glaze was good, and painting was of fine quality. Gilding, too, was excellent in quality. A few figures were made. The mark is a dolphin, usually crudely drawn, in red.

Leperre-Durot sold the factory in 1790 to Gaboria, after which it declined rapidly because of competition from Tournai near by.

In 1785 the Sieur Fauquez, in company with his brother-in-law, Lamoninary, received permission to start a factory at Valenciennes, in northern France, and was given a privilege for ten years conditional upon the firing being done with coal. Michel Vanier was a director from 1785 to 1787, which makes his connection with the Vanier of Lille the more certain, since, presumably, he brought the secret of coal-firing.

In 1787, M. Commelin, the Government Inspector of Porcelain Factories, reported that the manufacture was carried on regularly, but that the workmen competed with the factory by decorating white porcelain on their own account.

F.P.—N

Production was in the manner of Lille and Paris, with some imitation of the simpler Tournai wares. Some *biscuit* porcelain figures and groups were made. One group, the *Descent from the Cross* after Rubens, sometimes claimed for Lille, was probably made here. The mark was an almost indecipherable monogram, *LFV*, in underglaze blue.

A factory is said to have existed at St. Denis-de-la-Chevasse, in the Vendée, in 1784, on the property of M. Laferté, where imitations of Sèvres *biscuit* were produced. Two attributions to this source are both doubtful.

The *faïence* factories of Marseilles, in the South, made several attempts to manufacture porcelain. In 1765 Honoré Savy, who had at one time been associated with the Veuve Perrin in making *faïence*, applied for a privilege to enable him to experiment with porcelain, which was granted. There is no record that he succeeded, but he is described as a *faïence* and porcelain manufacturer in the *Guide Marseillais* of 1793, together with Antoine Aveillard, Augustin Bonnefoy, and the Veuve Perrin. It has been suggested that Savy proposed to Sèvres that they should waive their monopoly rights in exchange for the secret of a fine green enamel which he had devised.

Jacques Morelli, a *faïence* maker, may also have experimented with porcelain, and some figures are said to exist with his signature.

We are on much firmer ground, however, in discussing Joseph-Gaspard Robert, who had made *faïence* on his own account since 1754, and added porcelain about 1773. He, too, was included in the *Guide Marseillais* as a porcelain maker.

Robert applied for a privilege to build a porcelain factory in 1759 which was not granted, despite the fact that the application was supported by the Chamber of Commerce. Subsequently he made the acquaintance of Jakob Dortu, who had worked at the Berlin royal factory, and, in 1773, the manufacture of porcelain was started. When Monsieur, the King's eldest brother (afterwards Louis XVIII), visited the factory about 1777, Robert took the opportunity to explain that his greatest difficulty was in procuring suitable raw materials, and asked for help in locating suitable deposits in the neighbourhood. At this time he was taking clay from Alençon.

Porcelain attributed to Robert is decorated very much in the manner of *faïence*. Some is painted *en camaïeu* in a warm brown. Coloured flowers—ribbands, garlands, and sprigs—together with some landscapes and figure subjects, have also been awarded to the same source. The mark is the initial R, sometimes with a dot immediately over it or to one side. The body is greyish in colour, although later specimens are much whiter. Manufacture of porcelain was probably discontinued about 1793.

Most of the factories mentioned in this chapter are small, and the wares are, as may be seen, frequently of doubtful attribution. The work of Strasbourg, and the other factories of Alsace and Lorraine, as well as that of some of the numerous small establishments working in and around Paris, is much better known, and these are discussed in the following chapters.

CHAPTER VII

The Factories of Alsace and Lorraine

STRASBOURG is the capital of the Department of the Bas-Rhin in Alsace-Lorraine, and is situated two miles from the western banks of the Rhine. It was seized by Louis XIV in 1681, passed to the Germans after the War of 1870, and was returned to France with the Provinces of Alsace and Lorraine after the First World War of 1914–18.

A factory for making pipes was established here in 1709 by Charles-François Hannong, and, in 1721, he was joined by Johann Heinrich Wachenfeld who had been at both Cassel and Ansbach, and who started a *faïence* factory in Strasbourg in 1719. Wachenfeld left in 1722, going thence to Durlach, in Germany. The Strasbourg factory was soon extremely busy, and one reason for its success can be found in the fact that the King had, in 1709, issued an edict enjoining the French nobility to give up their silver to the Mint to be melted for coinage, thus helping the *faïence* industry. Hannong found himself in a position to open another *faïence* factory at Haguenau nearby in 1724.

In 1732 he retired, and passed the ownership of the Strasbourg factory to his eldest son, Paul-Antoine Hannong, and that of Haguenau to a younger son, Balthasar, for a consideration of 4,830 livres, and a commission on future sales. Paul-Antoine reunited both factories in 1737 when Balthasar went to Durlach. The latter eventually returned as a director, but ceased at this point to have any financial interest.

Paul-Antoine was a man of varied interests, and had some skill in matters of business. His handling of the *faïence* factories showed considerable enterprise, and he was among the first to use enamel colours and gilding on tin-glazed wares. This development (soon after 1740) was accompanied by an enlargement of the premises on a fairly big scale. Somewhat naturally, therefore, when he had the opportunity of bringing Joseph Jakob Ringler, the porcelain arcanist from Vienna and Neudeck (later Nymphenburg), to Strasbourg, he did so, and, at about the same time, engaged Adam Friedrich von Löwenfinck and his brothers, Karl Heinrich and Christian Wilhelm. Von Löwenfinck was accompanied by his wife, Maria Seraphia Suzanna Magdalena von Löwenfinck, the daughter of the Court Chamberlain at Fulda, Johann Philipp Schick. Another important acquisition was the modeller, Johann Wilhelm Lanz, who first modelled in *faïence* and later in porcelain. He arrived in 1745 and followed Hannong to Frankenthal in 1754.

Paul-Antoine Hannong began to experiment with porcelain about 1745, but the first successes belong to the year 1751 when Ringler arrived. The latter's name does not appear in the factory's archives, but a letter from Joseph-Adam Hannong written later confirms his presence. The clay used probably came from Passau, in Bavaria.

Little serious trouble was experienced, and production was soon considerable in quantity, and of good quality. Conditions seemed to promise success, but, in 1753, the King issued the edict already mentioned forbidding the manufacture of porcelain elsewhere than at Vincennes.

Hannong tried various expedients to keep his factory in existence. He turned to the Maréchal de Noailles for assistance, asking him to intercede with the King, and sending him some specimens of Strasbourg porcelain. But de Noailles had small influence in comparison with that of the Marquise de Pompadour, and Paul-Antoine entered into negotiations with Boileau, trying to get permission to continue in exchange for the porcelain secret. The result I have already recorded, and, in 1754, the blow fell. Hannong was not only forbidden to make porcelain, but was given a scant three weeks to finish his half-completed work, and told that if he continued manufacture thereafter his kilns would be destroyed.

In these circumstances, he turned to the *Hofmedikus** Peter Joseph Walck as an intermediary between himself and the Elector-Palatine, Karl Theodor. Hannong wanted to take his factory to Mannheim, but Karl Theodor had plans to develop Frankenthal as an industrial centre. Hannong gave way, and, in 1755, the privilege was granted, with all the usual clauses, such as freedom from taxes, restrictions on imports, and so forth.

The equipment, clays, raw materials, moulds, and models were therefore removed across the border into the Palatinate, and Paul-Antoine's son, Charles-François-Paul, was put in control. Paul-Antoine himself returned to Strasbourg, where he continued to control the *faïence* factories.

A brief *resumé* of the connection of the Hannongs with Frankenthal is necessary in order better to follow the subsequent course of events at Strasbourg. Charles-François-Paul died in 1757, and his place was taken by another son, Joseph-Adam, who was a director until 1759, when he took over Frankenthal on his own account. Joseph-Adam wanted to marry, and his father made it a condition of his

*Court physician.

consent that the wife's dowry should be used to buy the factory. A sum was paid on account, the remainder being left to be paid by instalments.

Paul-Antoine died in 1760. A complicated will laid down how much Joseph-Adam and the third son, Pierre-Antoine, should pay for Frankenthal and Strasbourg-Haguenau respectively. The position was made more difficult by the fact that, in addition to the two sons mentioned, five daughters also survived.

When Joseph-Adam bought the Frankenthal factory from his father it was laid down that he should receive the secret formulae, but these had not been handed over at the date of his father's death, and they fell into the hands of Pierre-Antoine as part of the archives of the Strasbourg factory. The latter copied them, and despite attempts to arrange matters between his brother and himself on an equitable basis, he left for Paris to sell them to Boileau at Sèvres.

Boileau was suspicious. Pierre-Antoine did not inspire confidence, and some of the information had already come to Sèvres from his father in 1753. The remainder was useful but not essential. Boileau paid a visit to Frankenthal to assure himself that he had the right formulae, and found that they were using clay from Saxony and Bavaria (Passau). In eighteenth-century Europe transport made it impossible for a factory situated in Paris to draw on such sources, and the cost of hauling clay in sufficient quantities from either of these two places would have been prohibitive.

The rest of the family removed the *faïence* factories from the control of Pierre-Antoine, and the widow of von Löwenfinck was appointed to take charge. Joseph-Adam refused to pay any more for the Frankenthal undertaking on the ground that its value had been much diminished by his brother's action in revealing its secrets. Finally, the debts of the latter factory became so heavy that Joseph-Adam was forced to sell it to the Elector, Karl Theodor, receiving only about one-third of its value. With this money Joseph-Adam bought out his brother, and assumed charge of the Strasbourg-Haguenau undertakings in 1762.

Pierre-Antoine opened another factory at Haguenau which he gave up speedily. Alsace was now too hot to hold him. Next, we find him at Vincennes (page 174), and after many vicissitudes elsewhere mentioned in this volume, he returned to Haguenau in 1783. For two years he tried to make porcelain there. He again attempted to start a factory for the manufacture of *faïence* in 1786, and, in 1794, became a director at Sèvres.

By 1766, the force of the various edicts had been relaxed, and Joseph-Adam once more started to manufacture porcelain. Manufacture was on a considerable scale, but was not particularly important artistically. There are letters in existence in which he remarks on the dangers of aiming for perfection, and on how both his grandfather and his father had suffered financially from attempts to do so.

Joseph-Adam, however, was a poor business man, and he succeeded in loading himself with debt. His misfortunes culminated in the death of his patron, the Cardinal Constantin de Rohan, in 1779. He owed the Cardinal a great deal of money, and Louis de Rohan pursued him for payment. Hannong appealed to the King, and was allowed to restart the factory, and to pay off his debts under the supervision of his creditors. In 1781, seeing the position to be hopeless, he fled to Munich. From here he protested to the King against the injustices he had suffered, and again, in 1791, he addressed a supplication to the National Assembly. He died during the early years of the nineteenth century in poverty.

A *faïence* factory was founded at Niderviller, in Lorraine, by the Baron Jean-Louis de Beyerlé in 1744, which was situated on his estates. De Beyerlé was one of the King's Counsellors and a Director of the Mint. He was assisted by François-Antoine Anstett, a painter and chemist from Strasbourg, who became director of the *faïence* manufacture from 1759 until 1778. Anstett remained at Niderviller until about 1780, and in this year took over the Haguenau factory from Joseph-Adam Hannong. A younger brother, François-Michel, worked as a painter at Strasbourg and Niderviller. Other workmen from Strasbourg were also employed.

In 1765 experiments were made with the manufacture of hard porcelain, using clay from Germany. This was costly to procure, and de Beyerlé later obtained his supplies from St. Yrieix, where he is reputed to have bought some *kaolin* quarries. Production is said to have been started with the aid of some workmen from Meissen, but the statement lacks definite proof.

In 1780 the works passed to Adam-Philibert, Comte de Custine, whose manager was an experienced potter, Claude-François Lanfrey. De Custine was guillotined in 1793, and Lanfrey was able to buy the factory from the State. The manufacture of porcelain was apparently discontinued about the time of the Revolution, although production of *faïence-fine* was continued by Lanfrey and others well into the nineteenth century.

Of the artists who worked there, the best known is Charles-Gabriel Sauvage, called Lemire, who was at Niderviller from 1759 to 1806. He had probably been employed for a while at Lunéville before taking employment at Niderviller, and had there some contact with Paul-Louis Cyfflé, by whose work he was much influenced in his early years. His later work was in the *Louis Seize* and the classical styles, which Cyfflé did not find attractive. Lemire also founded a school of modelling and design for apprentices which, no doubt, helped to keep up the high standard of this factory's products. In 1808 he went to Paris and became a sculptor, dying in 1827 at the advanced age of eighty-six. Cyfflé did not work for Niderviller, although the factory purchased many of his moulds when he was compelled to stop work at Lunéville in 1780.

A factory at Lunéville for the manufacture of *faïence* was established in 1731. It is unnecessary for our present purpose to discuss the early years, but, about 1752, Paul-Louis Cyfflé started to model for the factory. Cyfflé had studied sculpture under Barthélemy Guibal, and was a modeller of considerable skill. He is, in fact, among the more notable of eighteenth-century personalities in this field. His first models at Lunéville were executed in a greyish-white earthenware sometimes called, erroneously, *biscuit* porcelain. Actually it was a kind of pipe-clay, and was referred to at the time as *terre de pipe*. The body is comparatively soft and friable.

After moving on to *faïence* factories at St. Clément and Bellevue near by, Cyfflé went to Ottweiler, in the Rhineland, where, for a time, he was associated with Etienne-Dominique Pellevé, later at Etiolles, in the manufacture of porcelain. Cyfflé returned to Lunéville in 1766, and started to make his characteristic figures and groups in hard porcelain of excellent quality. He received permission to continue in 1769 from Sèvres, provided he called his body *terre cuite* and not porcelain. This term means, literally, baked or fired earth, and, because of this, Cyfflé took to marking his work either *Terre de Lorraine* or, merely, *T.D.L.* A few things are marked *Cyffle a Luneville*. These marks are occasionally accompanied by a name or an initial, almost certainly that of a 'repairer'.

Somewhat naturally a large figure of Stanislas Leczinski, who held Court at Lunéville, was made in this material, and is now in the Musée de Sèvres. It is marked *Cyffle 1766*.

Cyfflé did not prosper financially, and he left Lunéville

in 1777, his stock of moulds being sold to Niderviller. His later years were spent in the ownership of a factory at Hastière-sur-Meuse in Belgium where he continued to make his characteristic figures in *biscuit* porcelain. This was destroyed in 1790 in the Brabant Revolution. He died in 1806.

*   *   *   *   *

The porcelain made by Paul Hannong at Strasbourg so much resembles the work of Frankenthal during the early period that separation is difficult. Some suggestions have been made by Heuser, Haug, and others, for differentiating between the early figures of Lanz at either place. Principally it is said that the Strasbourg bases are depicted as a grassy mound, whereas the Frankenthal specimens have slight *rococo* scrolls. An existing example found with both types of base is the early figure of a huntsman with a dead stag and a dog by his side. Lanz apparently did not use *rococo* attributes until 1755. Colouring of early Strasbourg porcelain must obviously resemble that of the *faïence*.

An impressed mark '*PH*' is similar to the painted mark on *faïence*, but this was also used at Frankenthal and is not of much assistance. Some unglazed figures were taken from Strasbourg and glazed and decorated at Frankenthal. From this it will be seen that positive identification is difficult, and in many cases impossible.

The porcelain of Joseph Hannong can be identified with more certainty. Much of it is heavy and rather coarse, the technique showing signs of imperfections perhaps understandable when we remember his remarks on this subject previously mentioned. The marks are often extremely lengthy. An '*H*', thus, is common to all of them, but there has often been added a series of workmen's marks, pattern numbers, and so forth. An example, cited by Honey, is as follows:

VG 152

.

H

VC 152

H 15^c

which is surely the most complicated mark ever recorded.

The porcelain of Joseph-Adam is in the *Louis Seize* style, and *rococo* is not to be seen. Fairly typical is a fluted tapering leg, to be found on some tureens, which is far from elegant.

Decoration includes painting in polychrome of Oriental flowers, somewhat stylized in execution and similar to those appearing on *faïence*. At the same time some unusual *chinoiseries*, which also appear on *faïence*, are to be seen. These, unlike the *chinoiseries* of the 1740s which owe at least some of their inspiration to those of Höroldt at Meissen, are much more in the manner of the engraver, Pillement. They depict Chinese fishing, catching butterflies, or something of the sort. *Genre* painting appears on some things—scenes after Teniers, Van Ostade, and others, and the Fables of La Fontaine were illustrated here and at Niderviller.

Flower painting had always been a Strasbourg speciality on *faïence*, and we find flowers of good quality on porcelain, painted with considerably more freedom than in the early period. Bird painting, too, was excellent.

Gilding, during this period, is rare. A strong violet-carmine is characteristic, and a light rose and an iron-red are also to be observed.

Joseph-Adam made a large number of figures, many of which were copied from Sèvres and Niderviller, as well as some from Frankenthal. The glaze was often poor, and the colours inferior. Valentin Gusi has been suggested as the modeller for one or two original works of merit made during this period. The letters '*VG*' appearing in some of the marks may refer to him. Some large oval medallions, with *putti* in relief, representing the *Seasons* have been attributed to Jacques Saly (see page 162).

According to Jean Hermann, a Professor of Botany at Strasbourg during the eighteenth century, Joseph-Adam introduced the use of lace-work in porcelain. Lace was dipped into porcelain slip and fired, the mesh burning away in the kiln to leave its simulacrum in porcelain. This triviality may have been devised here, or at Meissen. It reflects no credit on the factory responsible.

Some porcelain resembling that of Joseph-Adam factory, but marked *PH*, was made by Pierre-Antoine at his short-lived Haguenau factory. Since he used some models and materials belonging to his father, which were bought at a liquidation sale, confusion is understandable.

The porcelain of Niderviller in the early period shows the influence of Strasbourg, as well as some reflection of Meissen styles. Painting was perhaps in the hands of Anstett, which is sufficient to account for Strasbourg resemblances, and Mme Beyerlé is, herself, reputed to have decorated both *faïence* and porcelain. The so-called *décor bois*, a *trompe l'oeil* depiction of grained wood with an engraving pinned to it, appears in *faïence*, and probably on porcelain also, although I cannot recall having seen a specimen. The Fables of La Fontaine appear on some service-ware. Under de Custine the decorations of Sèvres were copied, and garlands of flowers were used in conjunction with good gilding.

Rococo tureens during the early period were modelled with figures or with vegetables, and perhaps owed something to Meissen. Under the direction of Lanfrey excellent figures and groups were made, both in *biscuit* and glazed and painted. Many were the work of Lemire, particularly allegorical and classical subjects, and shepherds and shepherdesses. A bacchante dancing, twenty-five inches in height, is in the Victoria and Albert Museum, and is an excellent example of his style (Plate 83). A still-existing catalogue lists a large number of figures by his hand.

The models of Cyfflé differ somewhat in style. He liked to depict figures from everyday life, such as a cobbler whistling to a bird in a cage, a sweep, or two children with a dead bird (Plate 81). Usually his touch was lighter and more humorous than that of Lemire.

The marks of Strasbourg, and those used by Cyfflé at Lunéville, have already been mentioned. A monogram '*Bl*' appears on some of the *faïence* and porcelain of de Beyerlé, although a good deal was unmarked. During the period of de Custine the mark of interlaced *C*s below a crown is similar to that used at Ludwigsburg, and the two are sometimes confused. A monogram '*CN*' has been noted on porcelain. The use of *Niderville*, impressed, or painted, has been observed on a few later examples.

CHAPTER VIII

The Later Paris Factories

MOST of the early soft porcelain factories of France were located in and around Paris. Many factories for the production of *faïence* had been established here in the seventeenth century, and imitations of Wedgwood's creamware were made in large quantities at such places as Creil and Pont-aux-Choux from about 1770 onwards.

At about the same date the first factories to make hard porcelain were founded, and the style of work is easily recognized, although it is not always very distinguished in design and decoration. Most of the more pretentious things are in the later version of the *Louis Seize* style (often termed the *style étrusque*), or in the *Empire* style. On the lesser wares, decoration is frequently of slight flower painting which is usually much more pleasant.

In the absence of marks it is difficult to differentiate between the various factories, because their work is similar, but marks were frequently added. Unmarked wares can, for the most part, be attributed to the Paris group of factories with some facility, and dating from stylistic evidence is usually easy enough within fairly close limits.

The various factories are discussed hereunder in chrono-logical order.

Fabrique de Gros Caillou, Vaugirard les Paris

Little is known of this factory or its products. The latter have not been identified. Jacques-Louis Broillet is reputed to have attempted the manufacture of porcelain as early as 1762, and he applied in this year for a mark '*LB*', in script, to be registered for hard porcelain. This was accepted. He appears to have engaged principally in the making of laboratory wares.

In 1773 Advenir Lamarr (or Advenier and Lamare) applied for permission to use the mark of the monogram, '*AD*', but little has been identified. The factory is mentioned in a decree of 1784 as *Veuve Jullien et Bugnau de Gros Caillou*, and they appear to have been successors to Advenir Lamarre.

Fabrique du Comte d'Artois

This was situated in either the Faubourg St. Denis or the Faubourg St. Lazare, and was later under the patronage of Charles-Philippe, Comte d'Artois, who was brother to Louis XVI, and afterwards became Charles X of France.

The factory was founded about 1770 by Pierre-Antoine Hannong, who registered the letter '*H*' as his mark in 1773. Barrachin was appointed director in his place about 1776, and he had the assistance of the Marquis d'Osson. Louis-Joseph Desplanches became proprietor in 1782. The mark of '*CP*' under a coronet, for the Comte d'Artois, was registered in 1779, and the factory was styled *Manufacture du Comte d'Artois* about the same time.

Desplanches used coal for firing with success, and his process was demonstrated to the directors of Sèvres, and to

Plate 81. Biscuit group, *The Dead Bird*, by Paul-Louis Cyfflé. Impressed *terre de Lorraine*. Lunéville. c. 1770. (V&AM.)

Plate 82. Cobbler whistling to a starling. Model by Cyfflé in
terre de Lorraine. Bellevue (near Toul). Early 19th century.
(V&AM.)

Plate 83. Bacchante, modelled by Lemire. *Biscuit* porcelain.
Niderviller. c. 1785. (V&AM.)

Plate 84 (a). Shepherd with a flute Modelled by Lemire. Niderviller. c. 1785. (V & AM.)

(b). Figure of a Faun, modelled by Saly. Lunéville. c. 1770. Mark: 'TDL' (Terre de Lorraine). (BM.)

Plate 85 (a). Tureen in rococo style decorated with flowers in puce monochrome. Niderviller. Mark: interlaced C's for the Comte de Custine. c. 1775. (V&AM.)

(*b*). Plate decorated with a landscape. Niderviller. Mark: 'N' in brown. 1795–1800. (V&AM.)

Plate 86 (a). Teapot painted with flowers and a shipping scene in a medallion. Mark: *Etiolle Xbre 1770 Pelleve* incised. (V&AM.)

(b). Cachepot with moulded pattern, decorated in blue underglaze. Arras. 1770–90. Mark: 'AR' in blue underglaze. (V&AM.)

Plate 87. A plate and a pair of salts, the plate with cornflower sprigs, the salts with flowers in polychrome. Lille. 1784–93. Mark: crowned dolphin (for the Dauphin) in red. (V&AM.)

Plate 88 (a). Ewer an
basin painted with
cornflower sprigs.
Paris (rue des
Amandiers Popin-
court). Factory of
J.-H.-N. Nast. c. 179
(V&AM.)

(*b*). Small spittoon
decorated in poly-
chrome. Paris (La
Courtille). Factory of
Russinger. c. 1785.
(V&AM.)

(*c*). Cup and saucer decorated with flower sprigs.
Paris (Faubourg St. Denis).
c. 1790. (V&AM.)

Plate 89 (a). Plate decorated with the head of the Emperor Vespasian. Paris. (Rue de la Roquette.) Mark: *Darte Freres a Paris.* c. 1810. (V&AM.)

(*b*). Covered milk jar formerly in the Petit Trianon Dairy at Versailles. Paris (Rue Thiroux). 1775–93. Mark: crowned 'A' (for Marie Antoinette) stencilled in red. (V&AM.)

(*c*). Cup and saucer, flowers in polychrome. Paris (Rue Thiroux). 1775–93. Mark: crowned 'A' (for Marie Antoinette) stencilled in red. (V&AM.)

Plate 90. Biscuit group allegorical of the birth of the Dauphin. Paris
(La Courtille). 1781. (V&AM.)

Plate 91. Ewer and basin in a severe classical style. Paris (Rue de Bondy). 1781–93. Mark: 'GH' in monogram under a coronet (for Guerhard and the Duc d'Angoulême) in gold in ewer and in red on the basin. (V&AM.)

(c). Group, probably modelled by Lecreux. Tournai. c. 1765. (V & A M.)

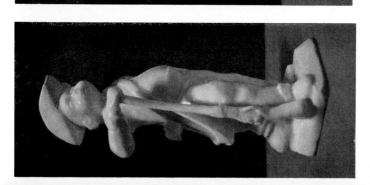

(b). A girl playing on a lute. Tournai. c. 1755. (Hastings.)

Plate 92 (a). A *putto* as a soldier. Tournai. c. 1755.

Plate 93. Pastoral group modelled round a central tree trunk,
two views of which are shown. Tournai. c. 1765. (V&AM.)

Plate 94. *Cabaret* decorated in puce monochrome and gilding. Mark: crossed swords and four crosses, in gold. Tournai. c. 1765. (V&AM.)

Plate 95. Plate decorated with birds after the *Histoire Naturelle des Oiseaux* of Buffon. 1771. Tournai. Late 18th century. (V&AM.)

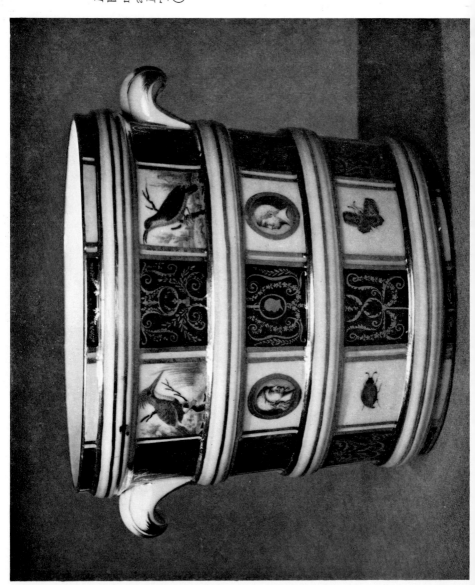

Plate 96. Cachepot decorated with birds in panels and heads in medallions, with gilding. The birds are taken from Buffon's *Histoire Naturelle des Oiseaux*. 1771. Tournai. Late 18th century. (V&AM.)

the chemist, Macquer. For this he was granted a subsidy and permitted to make the kind of wares hitherto reserved for Sèvres.

The factory's chemist, Josse, received a reward of four hundred livres for devising a blue *biscuit* body which was later used by Sèvres for work in the style of Wedgwood, an example of which appears on Plate 62a.

The edict of 1784 (page 127) was not strictly applied to a number of factories, and no doubt the use of coal for firing had much to do with the relaxation granted to the factory of the Comte d'Artois. The woods and forests around Paris had been severely depleted by porcelain manufacture in the City, and the use of coal promised a solution to the problem.

The factory applied for permission in 1785 to continue the manufacture of figures, particularly in *biscuit*, and for the right to paint in colour and to use gilding. These rights were granted conditionally in 1787. There seems little doubt that, due to the influence of its patron, a measure of co-operation with Sèvres was preserved until the Revolution. After this, the factory was in several hands, and another factory was established, probably in conjunction with it. Marc Schölcher was proprietor from about 1800 onwards. Manufacture was discontinued about 1828.

The porcelain made here was excellent in quality. The early wares of Hannong were usually vitreous and translucent, although the glaze was somewhat defective. The later work is characterisic of Paris porcelain of the period, with some more or less direct copies from Sèvres. Flower painting is in polychrome, and decoration *en grisaille* of the kind popular at Sèvres during the same period is frequent. *Biscuit* figures and groups were commonly made, the models of Sèvres and Niderviller being quite often copied. An unusually fine portrait bust of Mirabeau was made about 1790.

Fabrique du Faubourg St. Antoine

An application was made by Sieur Morelle in 1773 for permission to make porcelain here. The mark was *M.A.P.*, but no surviving specimens have so far been identified.

Fabrique de la rue de la Roquette

A factory for the manufacture of *faïence* was established here some time before mid-century, and the possibility of a factory making soft porcelain belonging to François Hébert has been mentioned in Chapter II.

Another factory was started in 1773 by Souroux who registered the letter '*S*' as his mark. It has been suggested that the *faïence* manufacturer, Ollivier, later took an interest in it. Some wares painted with flower sprigs in blue have been identified.

A factory called *Les Trois Leverettes* was founded by Vincent Dubois about 1774, or a little later. He may, in fact, have taken over the factory of Souroux. The mark is a pair of headless arrows crossed in underglaze blue, and care should be taken not to confuse it with the crossed torches of the Fabrique de la Courtille which it resembles. The seated figure of a flute player in *biscuit* is in the Musée de Sèvres.

Fabrique de la Courtille

This factory at the rue Fontaine-au-Roy was founded by Jean-Baptiste Locré de Roissy, a potter from Leipzig, in 1773. It was managed by Laurentius Russinger, the erstwhile Höchst *Modellmeister*, who arrived in 1774. The intention of Locré was to imitate German porcelain, and the factory was known as the Manufacture de Porcelaine Allemande. It was a purely commercial undertaking, without patronage, and it seems to have been very successful. Although it was not specifically authorized in 1787, no move was made to interfere with its working.

Manufacture of figures of good quality was on a considerable scale, as can be surmised from the presence of Russinger, and a few models were closely imitated from Meissen. The modeller, Christopher Mô (page 103), also worked here. An important *biscuit* group appears on Plate 90.

Ambitious vases, extremely well painted, are sometimes to be found, and an unusual marbled ground is represented in the Musée de Sèvres. Tooled and chased gilding was sometimes used.

The factory was taken over by Pouyat of Limoges about 1800, and the exact date of its closing has not been recorded. It is said to have introduced the process of casting in porcelain slip, but this claim cannot be substantiated. The mark of the Locré period was a pair of crossed torches, probably used for its resemblance to the Meissen crossed swords.

Fabrique de la rue de Reuilly, Faubourg St. Antoine

Jean-Joseph Lassia of Strasbourg, who had been associated with Pierre-Antoine Hannong in the negotiations with Boileau, applied for permission to make porcelain, registering the mark 'L'. Henri-Florentin Chanou, a former modeller at Sèvres, may have been associated with the project. The latter certainly had a factory at the near-by Barrière de Reuilly from 1779 to 1785, registering the mark 'CH'.

The history of these two factories is uncertain. It is said that the Marquis d'Aubarède was approached for capital, but was unable to get the necessary permission. Lassia appears to have discontinued porcelain manufacture in 1784, and his work (such specimens as have been identified) was of good quality. Some examples have a yellow ground, and gilding was well done. The work of Chanou at the second factory mentioned is exceedingly rare.

Fabrique de Clignancourt

This factory was founded by Pierre Deruelle in 1771, although he did not apply for permission to do so until 1775. It was under the protection of Monsieur, the King's brother, who was Louis-Stanislas-Xavier, Comte de Provence, later to become Louis XVIII. The factory passed at an unknown date into the hands of Deruelle's son-in-law, de Moitte.

Porcelain made here was of extremely good quality, rivalling that of Sèvres. It is said that an attempt was made to use the Sèvres royal monogram with an added coronet, but that 3,000 pieces were confiscated by the police in 1779, Deruelle being heavily fined for his presumption. The first mark was a windmill, alluding to the windmills of Montmartre near-by. Later, the initials 'LSX' were combined into a monogram. The letter 'D' surmounted by a coronet has been recorded, as well as an 'M' (for *Monsieur* or *Moitte*) also surmounted by a coronet.

Much of the decoration was of polychrome flower-sprays, with some landscapes. Georg Lamprecht, a Viennese painter who alternated between Vienna and Paris and spent some years at the Sèvres factory, painted landscapes in a brownish-yellow monochrome. Gilding was of good quality, and was sometimes used as the sole ornament. Figures are rare, but a *biscuit* figure of the Farnese Hercules bears the factory mark of the windmill.

Fabrique de la Reine, rue Thiroux

This factory was founded about 1778 by André-Marie Leboeuf who had the protection of Marie-Antoinette. Its products were known as the *porcelaine de la reine*. In 1779 Leboeuf was fined for copying the porcelain of Sèvres, and, because of this clash with the police, he sought the protection of the Queen. She gave permission for her monogram to be used, and some of the production was ordered for the Queen's dairies (Plate 89b).

The factory was sold to Charles Barthélemy Guy in 1797. Guy owned a decorating studio in the rue de Petit-Carrousel. The factory at the rue Thiroux was still working in the mid-nineteenth century.

Much of the decoration consisted of small sprigs of the cornflower and the daisy, and the rose was also a favourite flower. Bird-painting was of good quality and gilding was usually slight.

The rue du Petit-Carrousel existed to decorate white porcelain which was made elsewhere. Guy originally had a small factory sited on the corner of the rue d'Echelle, in the rue du Petit-Carrousel, to which the decorating studio was added. Specimens from this source are marked *'Carrousel Paris'*. An independent decorator named Perche [*fl.* 1795-1825] worked here, and also for the factory at the Faubourg St. Denis. He sometimes used the mark of a perch.

Fabrique du Duc d'Angoulême, rue de Bondy

This factory was founded by Dihl in 1780, and Guerhard was taken into partnership in 1786. The patronage of Louis-Antoine, Duc d'Angoulême, dates from 1780. The Duc d'Angoulême was the eldest son of the Comte d'Artois.

Dihl was a man of considerable attainments who had some success as a colour-chemist. He devised a number of effective ground colours, and the finer work was exceptionally well gilded. Much of the production was decorated with a slight pattern of strewn cornflowers, which became known as the 'Angoulême sprig', and was much copied elsewhere. Large naturalistic flowers were also well painted, and scattered flowers in gold were peculiar to the factory.

Some *biscuit* figures of excellent quality were produced,

and Dihl appears to have introduced the painting of portraits on porcelain. His own portrait, on a panel by Martin Drölling, is in the Musée de Sèvres. Much of the decoration was in the *Empire* style. The factory was transferred to the rue du Temple in 1796.

The earliest mark was the monogram, '*GA*', but later became '*Dihl*', '*Guerhard & Dihl*', or '*Rue de Bondy*'.

There was intense rivalry between Dihl and Alexandre Brongniart for the directorship of the Sèvres factory, which eventually passed to the latter.

Fabrique de la rue Popincourt

Lemaire, director of the second Vincennes factory, founded a factory in the rue Popincourt which was bought by Johann Nepomuc Hermann Nast in 1782. Nast was born at Radersburg, in Styria, in 1754.

In 1784 the factory was removed to the rue des Amandiers Popincourt, and the factory eventually became one of the best in Paris. Important specimens of *biscuit* porcelain by modellers such as Pajou, and *biscuit* clock-cases of excellent quality, were made. The work of Wedgwood was also imitated in the same material with a blue or lilac ground. Painting was excellent in quality, and flowers were much used, ranging from the strewn cornflowers to more elaborate flower bouquets.

The mark is usually '*Nast a Paris*', occasionally abbreviated to '*N. . . . . .*'.

Fabrique du Duc d'Orléans, rue Amelot

Louis Honoré la Marre de Villiers and Jean-Baptiste Augustin de Montarcy started a factory in 1784 in the rue des Boulets, Faubourg St. Antoine, for which they registered the monogram, '*MJ*'. In 1786 it passed to a partnership between Montarcy, Outrequin, and Toulouse, which had the protection of the duc d'Orléans, the mark being 'LP' beneath a coronet. A monogram '*OM*' may stand for Outrequin and Montarcy. The factory was then removed to the rue Amelot, at the Pont-aux-Choux. It later passed through a number of hands, including those of Lemaire and Josse.

A decoration of scattered single roses appears on some service-ware.

A factory in this neighbourhood, in the rue Saint-Pierre, was regarded as one of the most important in Paris in 1798, but little is now known of it.

The Factory of the 'Prince de Galles', rue de Crussol

The 'Prince of Wales' factory was established in 1789 by an Englishman, Christopher Potter, who applied for a monopoly of transfer printing in 1789. He is said to have been the first in Paris to decorate porcelain in this way, and, although his application was not granted, this appears to have been merely because it was then undecided whether or not to continue the practice of granting privileges of this kind. The factory was transferred to E. Blancheron in 1792, and was afterwards in several hands. Potter was also proprietor of the factory at Chantilly (page 92).

The work done here is scarce, but a few things with scattered cornflowers have been noticed. Strewn spots and stars of gold were also used, together with some painting in the fashionable *grisaille*. The first mark was '*Potter Paris*'; the later marks '*EB*' and '*PB*' are subsequent to the entry of Blancheron.

Fabrique de Petit rue Saint Gilles, Boulevard St. Antoine

This factory was founded about 1785 by François-Maurice Honoré, who later (in 1810) bought the factory of La Seynie (page 173). He was in partnership with one Dagoty, both here and in the Boulevard Poissonière. The factory had the name of the Manufacture de Mme la Duchesse d'Angoulême. Production was on a large scale, and some vases in the style of Wedgwood were made.

There were some other factories in Paris established about the turn of the century which were not of much importance. A factory, for instance, was founded in the rue de Charonne by the brothers, Darte, in 1795, which was later transferred to the rue de la Roquette and then to the rue Popincourt. Decorations include landscapes in poly-chrome, a *bleu de roi* ground, and cameo portraits of Vespa-sian and Caligula. The mark used was the name '*Darte*'.

Apart from the factories, there were also a number of decorating establishments which bought porcelain in white and painted it.

Generally, the porcelain of Paris forms a homogeneous group which is easily recognized. Much of it was decorated with strewn flower sprigs (the cornflower was particularly popular), and the more important things are usually osten-tatious, with a good deal of rather hard mercuric gilding. Most Paris wares are rather more in demand for interior decoration than for serious collections of French porcelain.

CHAPTER IX

Tournai and St. Amand-les-Eaux

THE inclusion of a Belgian factory in a book on French porcelain needs a little justification. Since the factory worked in the French tradition, and, for part of its existence, was actually situated in territory under French rule, it can conveniently be considered here, together with its related factory at St. Amand-les-Eaux which, territorially, is situated in France.

Faïence had been made at Tournai since the last years of the seventeenth century, and, in 1751, François Peterinck, a potter from Lille, took over a *faïence* factory belonging to François Carpentier. He began to make soft porcelain about the same time with the aid of Robert Dubois of Vincennes, and obtained financial help from the Municipality. In 1752 he was granted a privilege for thirty years by the Empress Maria Theresa, since Belgium was then under the Austrian Crown.

The privilege carried the usual advantages, apart from the title of Manufacture Imperiale et Royale. Peterinck paid no duties on either his raw materials or his finished products, and he was allowed to sell throughout the Austrian Empire. With this assistance he was, by 1762, employing two hundred and fifty workpeople.

The body consisted of sand, clay, and chalk, with soda from Alicante added as a flux. The process of slip casting, using plaster-of-paris moulds, was also introduced at a comparatively early date.

The earliest body was, until about 1755, greyish in colour, and the wares were inclined to warp. Early figures have sometimes sagged a little. The later body was of much better quality. Until about 1762 it was inclined to be yellowish.

The earliest decoration was in underglaze blue, and these wares found such a ready sale in northern France that factories, of which Arras is an example, were started to take advantage of the market thus created. The patterns were mostly Oriental, and derived from Chantilly and Höchst, with the 'onion' pattern (*Zwiebelmuster*) of Meissen appearing occasionally. The moulded basket-work patterns of Meissen were also used from time to time. Early polychrome wares include those decorated with flowers in the style of Meissen, and with birds. The palette was extremely limited, and the colours poor. After 1756 the range of colours increased and the quality improved. Flower painting was distinctly influenced by that appearing on Strasbourg *faïence*; occasional *chinoiseries*, and some excellent bird paintings, are also to be seen.

Decorations of a more ambitious kind in the style of Sèvres appear to have been added under the chief painter, Henri-Joseph Duvivier, who joined the factory staff in 1763. He was related to William Duvivier, originally from Liège, who had been a painter of some skill at Chelsea, and the hand of Henri-Joseph also can be identified on some rare specimens of porcelain from the English factory.

The latter is probably best known for his painting of exotic birds, which clearly resemble those of England, and another English decoration to appear about the same time was that of cut fruit, which was popular with the London decorator, James Giles, and is to be seen on some later Chelsea porcelain.

Some excellent painting was done by Duvivier and others in a purplish *rose camaïeu* of landscapes, *putti* after Boucher, and other Sèvres subjects. Coloured grounds, with such additions as the Sèvres *oeil de perdrix*, were used at the time, but since some Tournai white porcelain was decorated in the more sumptuous styles in the nineteenth century, these ought, perhaps, to be examined with more than usual care. The Sèvres practice of openwork piercing was used occasionally for important vases.

The adoption of the *Louis Seize* style dates from about 1780 when the influx of Wedgwood's creamware threatened Tournai markets. The Municipality gave additional financial support on condition that these patterns were adopted.

In 1787 Tournai produced a service for the Duc d'Orléans decorated with birds after Buffon's *Histoire Naturelle des Oiseaux* which was published in 1763. The decorator was Jean-Ghislain-Joseph Mayer, who also imitated the *décor bois* of Niderviller (plate 95). Medallions *en grisaille* belong to this period, as well as the strewn cornflowers of Paris.

A common ground colour on old Tournai porcelain of good quality is the *bleu de roi*, which is to be seen on the service made for the Duc d'Orléans in the form of broad bands. It also appears on some things of an earlier date, including jugs in contemporary *faïence* shapes with 'cut fruit' decoration.

Tournai produced figures and groups, both in *biscuit* and in glazed porcelain. The earliest are inclined to show manufacturing defects, and polychrome decoration is fairly uncommon on the latter. One of the earliest modellers was Joseph Willems, formerly of Chelsea, who died in 1763. A *Pietà* in *biscuit*, derived from Rubens, is extremely similar to another done at Chelsea by Willems about 1758. Nicholas Gauron arrived from Mennecy in 1758 and left in 1764. He appears to have been responsible for some groups of children on rock-work terraces which are similar in style to others made at Mennecy. He later went to Chelsea and Derby where somewhat similar models were done in *biscuit*, and in glazed porcelain.

Nicolas Lecreux was born in Valenciennes in 1733. Traditionally he has been awarded the *Pietà*, or *Descent from the Cross*, mentioned above, and certainly he modelled some groups of shepherds and shepherdesses. The finest model generally attributed to him is the *Jardiniers et Pêcheurs*, a group of a gardener and a fisherman with two girls. Lecreux left in 1780.

Antoine Gilles *père* was also a modeller at the factory, and has been given a figure of *St. Theresa* which was presented to Maria Theresa. His son, Jean, was a painter at Tournai. Decorative birds on high bases, somewhat in the style of Chelsea during the early 1750s, are to be seen occasionally. Tournai glazed figures in white are sometimes confused with those of Mennecy.

A few *étuis* and small boxes, mostly decorated in the *Louis Seize* style, are still in existence.

Peterinck retired in 1796 at the age of eighty, and died three years later. Peterinck's son-in-law, Jean-Maximilien-Joseph de Bettignies, took over the management, and his sons bought the factory in 1817. Until 1830 it regained much of the ground which had been lost during the French occupation of Belgium, but subsequently it was mainly occupied with service-ware. It is often said that Tournai made forgeries of Chelsea porcelain during the nineteenth century. There is no direct evidence of this, and it is probable that they came from the other factory belonging to the de Bettignies at St. Amand-les-Eaux, where many deliberate fakes and forgeries were made.

The early mark was a crudely drawn tower in blue, gold, or crimson, but the later mark, found on most porcelain from Tournai, is a pair of crossed swords (similar to those used at Meissen) with four crosses, one in each angle.

There were a number of connections between Chelsea and Tournai during the eighteenth century, the full extent of which has not yet been determined. Some white porcelain was supplied to The Hague for decoration. This usually bears the mark of the stork overglaze. When the mark is underglaze, the inference that both porcelain and decoration emanated from The Hague can safely be drawn.

The *faïence* factory of St. Amand-les-Eaux, in northern France, was established in the early part of the eighteenth century, and a soft porcelain was made here by Jean-Baptiste Fauquez in 1771. This lasted only for a few years, and the rare specimens are poor in quality. The factory subsequently passed to Jean-Maximilien-Joseph de Bettignies, who married Amélie Peterinck in 1783. His sons once more started to make soft porcelain during the early nineteenth century, and this was much used for forgeries and imitations of Sèvres, Chelsea, and other eighteenth-century soft porcelain factories. The marks were a colourable imitation of the Sèvres royal monogram. Much common ware in underglaze blue was also produced, and copies of Chantilly with coloured grounds usually come from this source.

A factory for the manufacture of soft porcelain was established at Arras, in the Pas-de-Calais, by Joseph-François Boussemaert of Lille in 1770, where Tournai service wares of the humbler kind were much copied. This closed in 1790, although the porcelain was sometimes used later for imitations of the earlier work of Sèvres (Plate 86b).

CHAPTER X

Forgeries

T O the collector of French porcelain this chapter is of considerable importance, since fakes and forgeries are much more common in this field than in any other, and some of them are particularly deceptive.

To begin with, it is desirable to define the terms used. Forgeries are copies of old porcelain made for the purpose of deception. A fake is an alteration to a genuine piece done to increase its value. A reproduction is an honest copy of earlier work which can, in some circumstances, be used for purposes of deception, but was not intended for this purpose by its maker.

One of the worst offenders was the factory at St. Amand-les-Eaux, which copied Sèvres in a kind of soft porcelain as early as 1815. Although the attentions of this factory were principally directed at Sèvres, forgeries of St. Cloud and Chantilly were also made, but are not particularly deceptive. An early nineteenth-century factory owned by Pigory at Chantilly, and another founded slightly later at the same place by Michel-Isaac Aaron, used the Chantilly mark on a hard porcelain, and the ability to discriminate between hard and soft porcelain is essential.

The prime target, however, was undoubtedly Vincennes-

Sèvres, and it is important to bring to the examination of every specimen as much knowledge and experience as possible. In all such circumstances a close acquaintance with genuine examples is the best safeguard, and study of the collections in the Victoria and Albert Museum and the Wallace Collection is recommended.

A point of considerable importance to remember is that except in the earliest work, where imperfections were sometimes allowed to pass, the work of both Vincennes and Sèvres was as near to perfection in execution as could possibly be attained, and the craftsmanship to be seen in painting, gilding, and ground-laying was always of the highest order. Imperfect pieces were either rejected, or accumulated in store for sale later, and I have elsewhere recorded a number of such sales at the end of the eighteenth century. Obvious imperfections in formation or glazing, therefore, suggest that the specimen belongs to the latter class.

The glaze of soft porcelain made at both Vincennes and Sèvres was extremely fusible, and painting and ground laying sank into it in the muffle kiln. Gilding was executed afterwards, and is always of superb quality. It was thick, and tooled and engraved with a hob-nail (*à clou*) fixed into a wooden handle. This has a different effect from the smoother and thinner gilding done with an ordinary agate burnisher. The addition of coloured grounds or painting to genuine specimens, which necessarily have to be fired on, cause any original gilding present to sink into the glaze during the process.

Fakers can clean off sparse decoration, such as floral sprays, with hydrofluoric acid, which is the only acid to attack glass and other silica products. Where colours had sunk too far into the glaze for them to be removed in this way, a grindstone was used instead, and the glaze and colour were removed. The remaining glaze could be re-melted to cover the underlying body, and the specimen redecorated with ground colours and painting of the rarer kinds. Usually some unevenness of the glaze is to be observed, which can never be seen in a genuine example.

Fakes of this kind are ingenious, but not difficult to detect as a rule. Where hydrofluoric acid has been used, and sometimes even when decoration has been ground off, inspection by transmitted light will show faint traces of the original decoration under the new painting. Refired glazes usually show some areas of black specking, particularly in the case of table-wares which have been used for greasy foods. Finally, there is to be considered the colour of the ground and the pigments used, and the style of the painting itself. The yellowish chrome green, for instance, is often used in place of the earlier copper oxide green, and since the chrome colours were not introduced until 1804 this inevit-ably condemns. The fake turquoise grounds, too, are often greenish in colour, and the *rose Pompadour* often too trans-parent, the genuine *rose* being much more opaque than most of the copies.

The connoisseur can often distinguish between the style of the Louis Quinze period and that of the early years of the nineteenth century without difficulty, but many copies were made during the mid-nineteenth century and later, and even slight experience will enable the reader readily to distinguish between genuine eighteenth-century work and the sugary sentimentality of the nineteenth century, especially with figure subjects.

Attention to such points should save the collector from all but the most accomplished piece of faking.

More difficult to detect is the fake executed on genuine white porcelain. The various sales during the Revolution, and in particular those made by Brongniart in 1815, put much of this into the hands of fakers, of which one of the most important was Perès and Ireland, a firm of Paris porcelain dealers. Much of it was decorated for them by Soiron, a painter from the factory who worked in the most sought-after styles. He did much jewelled work, which was then in greater demand than now. A cup and saucer decorated with portraits, bearing the date letter for 1761, and signed by this man, is in the Victoria and Albert Museum. Plates, particularly, with portraits of famous people, such as the King, Mme du Barry, and so forth, were never done before the Revolution, whatever the date letter may say. 'Jewelled' specimens with any date before 1780 are also fakes.

Some of this surplus white porcelain crossed to England, and was bought by a Bond Street dealer named Baldock, as well as by Mortlock of Oxford Street. Baldock employed Robins and Randall to decorate it. The latter had a decorating establishment at Spa Fields, in London, and when supplies of genuine Sèvres white ware ran short, Randall started a small factory at Madely in Shropshire to supply the deficiency, using a body somewhat similar to that of Billingsley at Nantgarw. He used turquoise grounds especially.

The porcelain of Nantgarw, the body of which is not unlike that of soft porcelain from Sèvres, was used for similar purposes occasionally, and it was then decorated in London. Most of it has an impressed mark, '*Nantgarw*', which is always plain under transmitted light.

The Sèvres factory, under the direction of M. Deck, started to produce a soft porcelain in 1887 which was made until 1900, and specimens are not uncommon, although rarely to be confused with the early things by the knowledgeable. A turquoise ground was frequently used, and is in demand for interior decoration. A certain M. Naudot of

Paris also made a soft porcelain during the latter part of the nineteenth century which was occasionally used for copies of the old wares. The firm of Edmé Samson et Cie, of Paris, have reproduced old Sèvres, as they have reproduced the work of almost every other factory of importance, but, in my experience, in a hard porcelain body. They state that copies are given the distinguishing mark of a letter '*S*'. Certainly they have used two interlaced *S*s which, at first glance, is very similar to the royal monogram. Herend of Hungary, a factory owned by Moritz Fischer, also made good copies.

In England, Minton's made some excellent reproductions during the nineteenth century which were fully marked, and are not usually dangerous. Unmarked copies, and some bearing the royal monogram, were made by John Rose of Coalport, which are not usually very deceptive, although they were so regarded when they were made. There is a story which recounts that Rose, himself, bought a vase in a London auction which he brought back as an example of how genuine Sèvres should look, only to be told by his foreman that the factory had made it a year or two before. Such copies would, however, hardly pass an expert today.

Marks should always be inspected very carefully for signs of tampering. The date letter should be compared with the paste. For instance, a hard porcelain specimen with any date before 1770 is obviously spurious. Some forgers optimistically put the date letter 'A' for 1753 on hard porcelain forgeries. The date letter should also be compared with the style and kind of decoration. A forgery may, for example, be given a date which is earlier than the first known use of a particular coloured ground. The date letter 'D' (for 1756) on a specimen of *rose Pompadour* would be conclusive evidence of fraud, since the colour was not introduced until the following year.

If a painter's sign or symbol (see list on page 223) is

present, this should be examined carefully to see whether the dates of his working agree with the date letter, and whether the decoration is likely to have been done by him. For instance, the mark of Evans on a specimen decorated with flowers or *putti* is obviously wrong, since he painted birds and landscapes. The mark of Bulidon on something decorated with bouquets which is dated before 1763 would likewise be spurious, since he did not start working until this year. Signatures in full which do not appear on the list given are always extremely suspicious.

It is obvious, therefore, that marks and symbols are often extremely revealing, and deserve very careful checking and consideration. Agreement should not, however, be regarded as necessarily proving the innocence of a specimen. A good forger will check his facts carefully, and only the less important fakes, and those done without access to the factory's lists or reprints in various books of reference, are likely to be inaccurate.

Faking was not limited to the nineteenth century. Although large sales of outmoded white-ware were made during the Revolution, and slightly later under Brongniart, there were some sales at a much earlier date. There is record of one such sale of thirty-six plates in 1753, and another much larger sale of white ware in 1756. Some of these were bought and decorated by factory artists. Catrice, an important flower painter, was arrested on a charge of this kind, and confessed to using the royal monogram on his work. Such work can, perhaps, be regarded as unofficial rather than as faking, but it does account for the occasional specimens which seem doubtful without any very obvious reason.

A *glazed* hole is to be found on some genuine specimens of Sèvres (usually plates) which was used for hanging them in the muffle kiln when the colours were fired on. If this is missing, the specimen should be considered with unusual care. If it is present, it is still no guarantee, in itself, that the decoration is genuine.

Later forgeries of Sèvres hard porcelain are not, perhaps, so frequent, because it has never been so valuable. The highest prices have always been paid for the soft porcelain, and when these are considered, it will be plain why it has always been a tempting target for the forger. The Paris factories copied Sèvres hard porcelain on a large scale during the latter part of the eighteenth century, and it has been reproduced since. Recognition is not always particularly easy.

Sèvres figures in *biscuit* made during the eighteenth century were never marked. It was probably assumed at the time that, if they were marked, other factories would glaze and paint them, and pass the resultant product off as the work of the royal factory. Those Sèvres *biscuit* figures which have a mark were made during the nineteenth century, and are reproductions. Sèvres figures which are glazed and painted are extremely rare. Less than two dozen examples are known to exist. It is, therefore, only to be expected that attempts would be made to supply the deficiency by glazing and painting *biscuit* figures. Fortunately, these attempts have nearly always been conspicuous failures, and are particularly accused by areas of black specking in the glaze, of the same kind as can be seen in the refired service-ware, and a 'burst bubble' effect in the glaze, known technically as 'spit out'. Some genuine glazed and painted figures bore the royal monogram, but this fact, by itself, is hardly of much assistance in detecting forgeries.

Unmarked *biscuit* figures from other contemporary factories are rarely very dangerous, although Sèvres models were frequently copied. The differences in the body are usually fairly obvious. *Biscuit* was, of course, strictly reserved to Sèvres, but, despite all efforts to enforce the various edicts, the government was never entirely successful.

These notes suggest that fakes and forgeries of Sèvres are particularly difficult to detect. Although this is undoubtedly true of a few, the vast number can be rejected with very little trouble, and are no more than superficial copies. The really good forgeries are extremely dangerous, and demand much knowledge and skill to detect them. Fortunately no forgeries are entirely perfect, and we have a large number of specimens which cannot be doubted, in the form of gifts made by Louis XV and Louis XVI to foreign princes, which have been in the possession of the recipient and his descendants since the eighteenth century. These can be used as a touchstone. In this way the exhibits in the great London museums have been weeded of interlopers present in collections given to them, and can therefore be studied with profit. A specimen reputed to be of soft porcelain of Sèvres coming from any but an expert and reputable source, however, needs careful study of all the factors involved—paste, glaze, decoration, marks and so forth—before it is accepted. Least dangerous are the less important wares, since forgeries are most likely to be of sumptuous painting and ground colours.

Only those among us who see a large amount of porcelain in sale-rooms, collections, and museums can even guess how much faked porcelain passes, and has passed, for Sèvres, but the quantity is fantastically high, particularly when specimens purporting to have been made before 1770 are concerned. The later wares have not attracted the attention of forgers to the same extent.

I would be doing small service to my reader if I minimized the dangers of trying to assemble a collection of specimens of soft porcelain from Sèvres, but this is not to be taken to imply that it cannot be found. It has, however, been much sought for many years, and it cannot be acquired casually. The price of undoubted specimens is high now, and it has always been high. The search for 'bargains' will have small reward.

French Porcelain Marks

The more important marks to be found on French porcelain are listed below in the order in which the factories are discussed in the text. The customary caution against reliance on marks as a means of identification applies with particular force so far as those of Sèvres are concerned. In no other case has a mark been so misused, and forgeries are innumerable. The mark is only of value, in some cases, as providing additional information about a specimen, but should not be used as the sole test of genuineness.

* A P	Mark sometimes claimed for Louis Poterat of Rouen, but perhaps that of Révérend. Sometimes regarded as a St. Cloud mark.
(mark)	St. Cloud. Incised. A very rare mark.
(sun mark)	St. Cloud. In blue.
S.ᵗ C.	St. Cloud. Incised or in blue.
t SC T	St. Cloud. The 'T' may refer to the Trou family.
CM +	Said to be the mark of the factory at the rue de la Ville-l'Evêque. The initials, presumably for Chicanneau and Moreau.
(mark)	Said to be the mark of François Hébert of the rue de la Roquette, Paris. From the neighbouring Hôtel des Arbaletriers.
Lo*	St. Cloud.
L L+	St. Cloud.
D	St. Cloud.

214

Perhaps Lille, for François & Barthélémy Dorez.

 Chantilly. In red, blue, and other colours. The most usual mark.

Chantilly. A variation of the mark above.

Chantilly. A rare mark.

D.V. Mennecy. In red, blue, and black.

DV Mennecy. Another form of the above.

D.V. Mennecy. Incised. A later mark.

DV·MŌ Mennecy. Assumed to be the mark of the modellers, Mô.

B.R. Bourg-la-Reine. Incised and painted.

D, C, o Formerly attributed to Mennecy, but now regarded as probably Crépy-en-Valois.

D.C.P As above.

SX Sceaux. An incised mark.

Sx   Sceaux. A painted version.

    Sometimes attributed to Orléans, but perhaps Chantilly.

Orléans.

   Sèvres. In blue overglaze. The royal monogram of the crossed L's. This mark was used before the introduction of the practice of adding a date letter.

Sèvres. A more elaborate monogram, probably before 1753.

Sèvres. The mark for the year 1753. The letter was altered for each successive year until 1793.

Sèvres. The mark for 1778 showing the doubling of the date letters in that year.

Sèvres. An example of the date letters being placed beside the monogram instead of inside it. 1781.

    Sèvres. The mark of the Republic—1793–1804.

Sèvres. A mark of the Republic. 1793–1804.

Sèvres. The Consular Period. 1803–1804.

Sèvres. In red. 1804–1809. The period of Napoleon I.

The date letters, and the corresponding years, are given below:

A	1753	V	1774
B	1754	X	1775
C	1755	Y	1776
D	1756	Z	1777
E	1757	AA	1778
F	1758	BB	1779
G	1759	CC	1780
H	1760	DD	1781
I	1761	EE	1782
J	1762	FF	1783
K	1763	GG	1784
L	1764	HH	1785
M	1765	II	1786
N	1766	JJ	1787
O	1767	KK	1788
P	1768	LL	1789
Q	1769	MM	1790
R	1770	NN	1791
S	1771	OO	1792
T	1772	PP	1793
U	1773		

From 1801 the following indications of the year were used:

T9	1801	8	1808
X	1802	9	1809
II	1803	10	1810
	1804	oz	1811
		dz	1812
	1805	tz	1813
ᘯ	1806	qz	1814
		qn	1815
7	1807	sz	1816

Lille. In red. The mark is intended to resemble a dolphin. Leperre-Durot's factory.

Lille.

Valenciennes. The monogram VFL—Valenciennes, Fauquez and Lamoniary.

Valenciennes. Another version of the above.

Incised. On a specimen attributed to the Comte de Lauraguais.

Limoges. Incised or in red. For the Comte d'Artois.

Limoges. Incised and in blue.

H·L· Vincennes or Vaux. Perhaps for Hannong and Laborde.

HℓK See above.

▬ Vincennes. Mark registered by Séguin in 1777. Cf. mark attributed to Orléans or Chantilly.

ﬅP Etiolles. Incised. For Monier and Pellevé.

Etiolle
Pelleve Etiolles.

Ṙ Marseilles. The mark of Robert.

Ḣ Strasbourg. The mark of Joseph Hannong. His initials were also impressed.

V.G 152
H
VC152
A 15ᶜ Strasbourg. An example of the complicated marks to be found on the wares of Joseph Hannong. Similar marks appear on *faïence* from the same factory.

ℬℓ Niderviller. In blue, black, and brown. The mark of Beyerlé.

♛
ℐ Niderviller. In blue and black. Period of Custine. This should not be confused with the mark of Ludwigsburg, which it much resembles.

ﹶ Niderviller. In blue and black.

NIDERVILLE | Niderviller. Impressed on a raised tablet.

N_1 | Niderviller. Probably a late mark.

TERRE DE LORRAINE | Lunéville. Impressed mark.

 | Lunéville. An impressed mark.

h | Paris. Faubourg St. Denis. The mark of Pierre Hannong.

CH | Paris. Barrière de Reuilly. For Chanou.

Potter Paris 86 | Paris. rue de Crussol. The mark of Christopher Potter.

EB | Paris. rue de Crussol. For E. Blancheron.

PB | Paris. rue de Crussol. Probably for Potter-Blancheron.

S | Paris. rue de la Roquette. For Souroux.

Paris. rue de la Roquette. Mark of Vincent Dubois. Compare the earlier mark of Hébert (page 214).

Paris. Clignancourt. The windmill, from those of Montmartre. In gold.

As above. In blue.

Paris. Clignancourt. The monogram of the Comte de Provence, Louis-Stanislas-Xavier, later Louis XVIII. In red.

Paris. Clignancourt. For Monsieur, the King's brother (the Comte de Provence). In red.

Paris. rue Thiroux. For Marie-Antoinette. In blue.

Paris. rue Popincourt. In red.

Paris. rue Amelot. In blue. For Louis-Philippe.

As above. Mark of Outrequin and Montarcy. In red.

As above. In blue. For Louis-Philippe.

Paris. rue de Bondy. In red.

Paris. rue de Bondy. A late mark. In red.

Paris. rue de Bondy. In red and blue.

CP

Paris. Faubourg St. Denis. For Charles-Philippe, Comte d'Artois.

As above. Perhaps an imitation Meissen mark. In blue.

Paris. Gros Caillou. In blue. For Advenir and Lamare.

Paris. La Courtille. In blue and incised. Somewhat similar marks were used at the rue de la Roquette.

Tournai. In blue, gold, and red. An early mark.

Tournai. In blue, gold, and red. The most usual mark.

St. Amand-les-Eaux. A 19th century mark.

St. Amand-les-Eaux. On *faïence* and porcelain.

Arras. In blue, purple, and red.

Marks used by Painters and Gilders at Sèvres During the Eighteenth Century

N Aloncle, François, 1758–1781, birds and animals.

Antheaume, Jean-Jacques, 1752–1758, landscapes and animals.

A or *A* Asselin. 1765–1803. Portraits, miniatures, *genre* subjects.

Aubert (*aîné*). 1754–1758. Flowers.

By Bailly (*père*). 1753–1767. Gilder.

= Bardet. 1751–1758. Flowers.

B Barré. 1773–1774, 1776–1778. Detached bouquets, flowers, ornaments.

B Barrat, 1769–1791. Garlands and bouquets, fruits.

BD Baudouin, 1750–1800. Gilder. Ornament and borders.

B Becquet. 1749–1750, 1753–1765. Flowers.

6. Bertrand. 1757–1774. Bouquets.

Bienfait, Jean-Baptiste. 1756–1762. Painter and gilder.

T Binet. 1750–1775. Flowers and bouquets.

Sc Binet, Mlle. later Mme. Chanou. To 1800. Gilder.

Boucher. 1754–1762. Flowers and gar-lands.

Bouchet, Jean. 1757–1793. Painter and gilder.

Bouillat. Either 1785–1793 or 1800 to 1811. Flowers and landscapes.

Boulanger (*père*). 1754–1785. Gilder.

Boulanger (*fils*). 1770–1781. Flowers, pastoral subjects, children.

 Boulidon. 1763–1792. Bouquets.

 Bunel (*veuve*), Marie-Barbe. 1778–1816. Flowers.

 Buteux (*aîné*), Charles. 1756–1782. Figures.

Buteux (*jeune*). 1759–1766. Flowers.

Buteux (*fils cadet*). 1773–1790. Flowers, landscapes, children.

φ | Cardin. 1749–1786. Flowers.

5 | Carrié or Carrier. 1752–1757. Flowers.

C. | Castel. 1771–1797. Landscapes and birds. ? Gilder.

✳ | Caton. 1749–1798. Pastoral subjects, portraits, children.

𝒮𝒮 | Catrice. 1757–1774. Flowers.

ch | Chabry (*fils*). 1765–1787. Miniatures and pastorals.

𝒥𝒟 | Chanou, Mme. 1779–1800. Gilder. Perhaps flowers.

△ | Chapelle, Mme. 1746–1762. ? Flowers.

c p | Chapuis (*aîné*). 1756–1793. Flowers, birds.

C j | Chapuis (*jeune*). Perhaps 1772 to 1777 or after 1800. Bouquets.

✸ | Chauveaux (*aîné*). 1753–1788. Gilder and painter.

jn | Chauveaux (*fils*). 1773–1783. Bouquets.

♪ | Chevalier. 1755–1757. Flowers and bouquets.

✻ | Choisy, Julien de. 1770–1812. Flowers and arabesques.

⊌ | Chulot. 1755–1800. Flowers, trophies, and emblems.

c.m | Commelin. 1768–1802. Flowers, bouquets, garlands.

ſ | Cornaille, Antoine-Toussaint. 1755–1800. Flowers, bouquets.

C Couturier. 1762–1785. Flowers and gilding.

Dieu. 1777–1790, 1794–1798, 1801–1811. Painter, gilder. Probably Chinese figures.

K Dodin. 1754–1802. Figures, portraits.

Drand. 1764–1775. 1780. Chinoiseries. Gilding.

Dubois, Jean. 1756–1777. Flowers.

Dusolle. 1768–1774. Bouquets.

DI   Dutanda. 1765–1802. Flowers and garlands.

Evans, Etienne. 1752–1806. Birds.

F Fallot. 1773–1790. Birds and ornaments.

Fontaine. 1752–1775, 1778–1807. Birds, ornaments, perhaps Chinese figures.

Fontelliau. 1747–1780. Flowers. Colour maker. Gilder.

Y Fouré. 1749. 1754–1762. Flowers, bouquets.

Fritsch. 1763–1764. Figures, children.

Fumez. 1777–1804. Flowers, bouquets.

Gauthier. 1787–1791. Figures, landscapes, animals.

G Genest. 1752–1789. Figures, *genre* subjects.

Génin. 1756–1757. Flowers, garlands, &c.

Gérard, Claude-Charles. 1771–1804. Pastorals, miniatures. 1805–1825. Head of painters and gilders.

Gérard, Mme. (née Vautrin). 1781–1802. Flowers.

Girard. 1762–1764. Chinese figures, arabesques.

Gomery, Edmé. 1756–1758. Birds and flowers.

Grémont (*jeune*). 1769–1775. 1778–1781. Garlands, bouquets.

Grison. 1749–1771. Gilder.

Henrion (*aîné*). 1768–1784. Flowers, garlands.

Héricourt. 1770–1773, 1776–1777. Flowers, garlands.

Hileken or Hilken. 1769–1774. Figures, pastoral subjects.

Houry. 1747–1755. Flowers.

Humy. 1791–1799. Flowers.

Joyau. 1766–1775. Bouquets.

Jubin. 1772–1775. Gilder.

La Roche. 1759–1802. Flowers, garlands, emblems.

Léandre. 1779–1785. Children, pastoral subjects.

Le Bel (*aîné*). 1766–1775. Flowers, figures.

Le Bel (*jeune*). 1773–1793. Bouquets, garlands. A similar mark was used in the nineteenth century by a painter of the same name.

Lecot. 1773–1802. Gilder. Chinese subjects.

Ledoux, Jean. 1758–1761. Birds, landscapes.

Le Guay, Etienne-Henri. 1749–1796. Gilder. (A painter and gilder, Le Grand uses an exactly similar mark).

Le Guay, Pierre-André. 1772–1818. Figures, children, Chinese subjects.

Levé, Denis. 1754–1805. Flowers, birds, emblems.

Levé, Felix. 1777–1779. Flowers, Chinese subjects.

Maqueret, Mme. 1796–1798. 1817–1820. Flowers.

Massy. 1779–1803. Flowers, garlands, birds.

Mérault or Méreaud. 1754–1791. Flowers, friezes, ornaments.

9   Mérault or Méreaud (*jeune*). 1756–1779. Bouquets, garlands.

X   Micaud, Jacques. 1757–1810. Flowers, ornaments.

m   Michel, Ambroise. 1772–1780. Detached bouquets.

M   Moiron, 1790–1791. Flowers, bouquets.

5   Mongenot. 1754–1764. Flowers.

 Morin. 1754–1787. Sea and shipping subjects, military scenes.

∧   Mutel. 1754–1759, 1765–1766, 1771–1773. Landscapes and birds.

ng   Nicquet. 1764–1792. Flowers.

≏   Noël, Guillaume. 1755–1804. Flowers and ornaments. Figures.

𝒩   Nouailhier, Mme. 1777–1795. Flowers.

👁   Pajou. 1751–1759. Figure subjects.

P   Parpette, Philippe. 1755–1757, 1773–1806. Flowers and gilding.

LP   Parpette, Mlle L. 1794–1798. 1801–1817. Flowers.

P.T.   Petit, Nicolas (*aîné*). 1756–1806. Flowers, gilder.

Pfeiffer. 1771–1800. Flowers, bouquets.

Philippine (*aîné*). 1778–1791, 1802–1825. Pastoral subjects, children.

Pierre (*aîné*). 1759–1775. Flowers, bouquets, gilding.

Pierre (*jeune*). 1763–1800. Flowers.

Pithou (*jeune*). 1760–1795. Flowers and figures.

Pouillot. 1773–1778. Flowers.

Prévost (*âiné*). 1754–1793. ?Gilding.

Raux (*âiné*) 1766–1779. Bouquets.

Rocher, Alexandre. 1758–1759. ?Figures and miniatures.

Rosset. 1753–1795. Flowers and landscapes.

Rouselle. 1758–1774. Bouquets.

Schradre. 1773–1775. 1780–1786. Birds and landscapes.

Sinsson (*père*), Jacques-Nicolas. 1773–1795. Flowers.

Sioux (*aîné*). 1752–1792. Bouquets and garlands, borders.

Sioux (*jeune*) 1752–1759. Flowers and garlands.

◊ Tabary. 1751–1755. Birds.

❋ Taillandier. 1753–1790. Flowers, bouquets and garlands.

• • • Tandart, Charles (*jeune*). 1756–1706. Flowers, garlands.

⬧ Tardi, Claude-Antoine. 1755–1759. Flowers, bouquets.

• • • • Theodore. 1765–1771. Painter and gilder.

J Thévenet (*père*). 1741–1777. Flowers, cartouches.

jt. Thévenet (*fils*). 1752–1758. Flowers, ornaments, friezes.

⅁ Vaudé or Vandé. (1753–1779) Gilder. (A similar mark was used by P.-J.-B. Vandé, 1779–1824, gilder.)

W Vavasseur (*aîné*). 1753–1770. Flowers.

▰ Vieillard. 1752–1790. Emblems, ornaments.

2000 Vincent (*aîné*). 1752–? Perhaps working till about 1806, or the mark used by a son. Gilder.

⚹ Xhrouet or Chrouet. 1750–1775. Landscapes.

♀ Yvernel. 1750–? Landscapes, birds.

Bibliography

Alfassa, P. & Guérin, J.: *Porcelaine française du XVIIe au milieu du XIXe siècle.* Paris, 1932.

Argenson, René Louis de Voyer, Marquis d': *Journal et Memoirs.* Paris, 1861–7.

Arnaud d'Agnel, G.: *La faïence et la porcelaine de Marseille.* Marseille, 1912.

Auscher, E. S.: *A History and Description of French Porcelain.* London, 1905.

Bourgeois, E.: *Le biscuit de Sèvres au XVIIIe siècle.* Paris, 1909.

Bourgeois, E. and Lechevallier-Chevignard, G.: *Le biscuit de Sèvres: Recueil de modèles de la manufacture de Sèvres.* Paris, 1913.

Brongniart, A.: *Traité des arts céramiques.* Paris, 1844.

Brongniart, A. and Riocreux, D.: *Description méthodique de la Musée Céramique de la Manufacture Royale de Porcelaine de Sèvres.* Paris, 1845.

Chavagnac, Comte X. de, and Grollier, Marquis A. de: *Histoire des manufactures françaises de porcelaine.* Paris, 1906.

Chavagnac, Comte X. de: *Catalogue des porcelaines tendres françaises.* Sale catalogue. Hôtel Drouot. Paris, 1911.

Duvaux, Lazare: *Livre-journal de, marchand bijoutier, 1748–1758.* Paris, 1873.

Hannover, E.: *Pottery and Porcelain, Vol. III.* London, 1925.

Haug, H.: *Les faïences et porcelaines de Strasbourg.* Strasbourg, 1922.

Honey, W. B.: *Dictionary of European Ceramic Art.* London, 1952.

Honey, W. B.: *French Porcelain of the 18th century.* London, 1950.

Labadie, E.: *Les porcelaines bordelaises.* Bordeaux, 1913.

Lane, Arthur: *French faïence*. London, 1948.
Lechevallier-Chevignard, G.: *La manufacture de porcelaine de Sèvres*. Paris, 1908.
Lejéal, A.: *Récherches historiques sur les manufactures de faïence et de porcelaine de Valenciennes*. Valenciennes, 1768.
Lister, Dr. Martin: *A Journey to Paris in the year 1698*. London, 1698.
Papillon, G.: *Musée céramique de Sèvres*. Paris, 1921.
Peyre, R.: *La céramique française*. Paris, 1910.
Soil de Moriamé, E. J.: *Les porcelaines de Tournay*. Tournay. 1910. (A later edition by L. Delplace de Formanoir was published in 1937).
Strange, T. A.: *An Historical Guide to French Interiors . . . during the last half of the 17th century, the whole of the 18th century, and the early part of the 19th*. London, 1950.
Verlet, Pierre; Grandjean, Serge; and Brunet, Marcelle: *Sèvres*. Paris, 1954.

INDEX

234